THE
BUDDHA-DHAMMA

THE BUDDHA-DHAMMA OR THE LIFE AND TEACHINGS OF THE BUDDHA

NARADA THERA

WITH A FOREWORD BY
DR. CASSIUS A. PEREIRA

GYAN

Published by

Gyan Publishing House
5, Ansari Road
Daryaganj, New Delhi-110002
Phone: 011-47034999, 9811692060
E-mail: books@gyanbooks.com

Distribution Network
gyanbooks.com
India, USA, Canada, UK, Australia, France

ISBN : 978-81-212-4500-5 (HB)
First Published, Kendy, 1942

2nd Impression 2020

Printed at: Gyan Press, Delhi.

The Buddha-Dhamma or the Life and Teachings of the Buddha
Author: Narada Thera

Vajirarāma Publication Series — No. 6

"THE GIFT OF TRUTH EXCELS ALL OTHER GIFTS."

The Buddha-Dhamma

or

The Life and Teachings of the Buddha

BY

NĀRADA THERA

VAJIRĀRĀMA

BAMBALAPITIYA

WITH A FOREWORD BY

DR. CASSIUS A. PEREIRA

PUBLISHED BY

THE CHILDREN OF THE

LATE DR. & MRS. C. P. DE FONSEKA

PALM GROVE

PANADURA

2486

1942

CONTENTS

Dr. C. P. de Fonseka

Born
23rd March 1856
Died
20th September 1913

Mrs. Leonora de Fonseka Sri Chandrasekera

Born
14th October 1867
Died
5th March 1935

Idan vo ñatīnan hotu!
Sukhitā hontu te sadā!

PREFACE

This book is the outcome of a series of articles written by me at different periods to various journals.

The first few chapters deal with the "Life of the Buddha" in His own words. The commentarial explanations are given in foot-notes.

Very often the lives of great spiritual teachers are either exaggerated by over-zealous followers or distorted by prejudiced writers. Here one will find the simple but the noble life of the greatest religious Teacher, free from such exaggeration and distortion.

The remaining few chapters deal with the Dhamma—the Teachings of the Buddha.

I have tried my best to present the fundamental teachings of Buddhism in the simplest language possible, so that the book may also serve as a Buddhist text book for children.

This elementary book on Buddhism is not intended to satisfy critical scholars. Nor have I written it as a scholar but as a humble student who is expected not only to study the Dhamma intelligently, but also to practise sincerely and diligently what little he has learnt from books and saintly teachers.

In preparing this volume I have made use of several works written by Buddhists and non-Buddhists. At times I may have merely echoed their authentic views and even used their appropriate wording. Wherever possible I have acknowledged the source.

I express my deep indebtedness to my venerable teacher, Pélêne Siri Vajirañāna Mahā Nāyaka Thera, for his interesting sermons and scholarly writings which helped me to acquire a good knowledge of the Dhamma.

My thanks are due to Bhikkhu Piyadassi, Bhikkhu Metteyya, and Dr. Cassius A. Pereira, in particular, for writing an interesting foreword which will, no doubt, tend to embellish this humble attempt of mine.

I have also to thank the generous publishers, the devoted children of the late Dr. and Mrs. C. P. de Fonseka of Palm Grove, Panadura, for inviting me to compile this book so that they may transfer the merit acquired thereby to their beloved parents.

Nārada.

Vajirarāma,
Bambalapitiya, 2486
30th April, 1942

FOREWORD

A THEORY, with which I entirely disagree, starting in the West among Christian research scholars, claims that, for a proper understanding of Christianity, it is essential first to know the background of religious thought at the time of Jesus' appearance, and also the basic doctrines of Judaism on which, it is claimed, Jesus built up the structure of his teaching.

This line of thought, a most unhappy misapplication of alleged laws behind that blessed word "evolution," has induced some prominent students of Buddhism,—mostly Western pundits, though a few aping Easterns follow,—to dogmatize about their ideas of the "origin" of the Eternal Law which the Buddhas see and reveal. And this is done forsooth in the name of "science."

These good people argue foolishly for two reasons. They are constitutionally incapable of accepting all the data offered. And, secondly, they are constitutionally incapable of fully appreciating the few data they accept.

By "constitutionally" one means inherently, through a lack of development of that delicate intuition or insight which is the "religious sense" of those who have pursued truth unflinchingly for many births.

The study of a pot, its date make and material, and the soil or manure it holds, would doubtless be extremely interesting to a devotee of exact science or a natural science. But such study will in no way help us to unravel the origins of an *imported* plant that is set in the soil of that pot. And when the plant blooms, and its fruit appear, these blooms and fruit arc the blooms and fruit of the plant, not of the pot, or even of the manure, though these were necessary details for the plant to fulfil its cycle. The plant itself must be studied. The pot and its manure are mere incidents.

Every being, every flux of mind and matter that we style an "individual," is "imported." No being at birth belongs, or is indigenous to the soil where he happens to take birth. Each flux of mind and matter is unique and a Bodhisatta, in his final birth, is unique in a unique way, for his is that rarest resolution of all beings, to suffer all, to sacrifice all, to fulfil every perfection, so that, on some distant day, he may achieve his unique goal,—the goal of winning, not only for himself, but for all beings, deliverance from the heavy painful shackles of Death, which we misname "life." He is the Amatassa Dātā,-the Giver of the Deathless, the seer, Knowledge-incarnate, Truth-incarnate, Holiness-incarnate, Dhammassāmi,—the Lord of the Eternal Law.

Of His "origin" the Buddha Himself speaks. It started with an inflexible aspiring resolve, in a distant aeon. He tells us of the gradual perfection, through countless births, of the flux that made that aspiration. He tells us how he sacrificed, unflinching and glad, property, limb, and life, to win that perfection. How, at last, utterly perfect in all but the Final Achievement of the Deathless, He sojourned in Tusita's happy Deva realm, awaiting the favourable time for His final birth and His last fight for Deliverance. He tells us how He, at last, saw the time was ripe. Leaving Tusita, He entered Māyā Devī's womb, and was in due time reborn as Siddhattha, the Heir of the Sākya Throne. He tells us how He renounced all that earthly rule offered, to continue His search. How, with Ālāra and Uddaka, he won the highest flights of mental concentration only to realize that this was but a blind alley, not the goal. He tells us how he then sought alone, suffering, fasting, fainting with exhaustion, but ever resolute. He tells us how, finally, under the

Bodhi Tree, at Uruvela, He won Full Enlightenment, became a Sammā Sambuddha, Teacher of Gods and men, and Embodiment of Truth,—Tathāgata. How, thus victorious, was one of the glorious line of the Sambuddhas, men who, on their own, win through to the Hypercosmic, and having won, are able to reveal the Path to the Deathless to all who would listen with confidence, learn, and tread the Path so revealed.

And of this Buddha and His Teaching, all sorts of non-Buddhist philosophasters now prate how the Dhammassāmi was something called a "Hindu,"—and His Teaching "a natural growth" from that complex of amazing conflict, hair-splitting, crudity, high philosophy and elemental worship known today as "Hinduism." They would imprison the stars in a bucket of their muddy waters.

Here, in this book, the Thera Nārada offers, to a student or sincere seeker, the true and plain account of the Master and the Law. It is not claimed that this book is a literary gem. If that were all, it would not have taken birth. It is not intended to ornament somebody's bookshelves. Nor is it intended to be controversial or to supply quotations for debate, though it does offer much ammunition to those who, in these restless days of war and uncertainty argue about it and about, when the foundations of pure, noble and selfless living are shaken to their utmost depths.

This book sees the light when men's hearts are torn with doubt, when the gods of the theistic faiths have gone asleep, and abandoned men to exploit to the full their hard-won fruit of research and science in a mad orgy of warring nations lusting for world-dominion.

Here, the Prince of Peace pitying, speaks again to tell us that the only dominion worth striving for, the only dominion that satisfies and is worth while, is the dominion over self and all these selfish thirsts that, once unleashed, result in just such heart-rending suffering as the world sees today with its tanks and flame-throwers, its war planes and bombs.

The lust for power, the aggression of superior noxiousness that saw birth in Christian Europe, has now extended to apt Far-eastern pupils of those western teachers of war-craft and power-lust; and we of a race that once saw Arahants passing overhead by their power of purity and *iddhi*,—and worshipped as we watched,—are now told to crawl into trenches and lie "on our stomachs" when in this same Buddhist Lankā, the sirens wail their warning, and not Holy Arahants, but foul war-planes traverse these same sky-paths. Now, when "men tormented by terror" (*manussā bhaya tajjitā*) seek mountain and forest for Refuge, the good Thera Narada offers this labour of love to the public, warning us that not near mountains not near forests is true refuge. Safe Refuge, now as ever, is only with the Triple Gem of our Holy Heritage.

Relying on such a Refuge, we Singhalas of the Lion Race, and all our brothers of whatever race or birth, have no need to fear any enemy stink–beetle of the skies or his foul droppings, nor need we hide in holes on our bellies. For with such a Refuge we remain victors even in death. Nor need we perish if we use the Buddha's Triple shield and with confidence repeat His words of Pirit (protection). To all who fear, now or hereafter, I say,—memorize the Mora-paritta, repeat the appropriate verse, at sunrise and sunset,—and fear not. Practise Mettā, and fear not. Practise any of the Brahma Vihāra, and fear not. Remember of what you are the treasurers, and fear not. Turn to the Buddha merely with trust and love, and fear not.

CASSIUS A. PEREIRA

Nugegoda,

15th March, 1942.

THE BUDDHA-DHAMMA

Namo Tassa Bhagavato Arahato Sammā-Sambuddhassa!

CHAPTER I.

THE BUDDHA

ABOUT 623 B. C. there was born in the district of Nepal an Indian Sākyan Prince by name Siddhattha Gotama. At the age of sixteen he married his cousin, the beautiful Princess Yasodharā.

For nearly thirteen years, since his happy marriage, he led a luxurious life, blissfully ignorant of the vicissitudes of life outside the palace gates.

With the march of time truth gradually dawned upon him. In his 29th year, which witnessed the turning point of his career, his son Rāhula was born unto him. He regarded his offspring as a bondage, for he realised that all without exception were subject to birth, decay, and death, and that all worldly pleasures were only a prelude to pain. Comprehending thus the universality of sorrow, he decided to find out a panacea for this universal sickness of humanity.

Accordingly he renounced his royal pleasures, donned the simple garb of an ascetic, and wandered as a Seeker of Truth. He approached many a distinguished teacher of his day, but nobody was competent enough to give him what he earnestly sought.

All the so-called philosophers were groping in the dark. It was a matter of blind leading the blind, as they were all enmeshed in ignorance and were caught in the whirlpool of life and death.

As it was the belief in the ancient days that no salvation could be gained unless one leads a life of strict asceticism, he strenuously practised all forms of severe austerities. "Adding vigil after vigil and penance after penance" he made a superhuman effort for six long years.

Eventually his delicate body was reduced to almost a skeleton. The more he tormented his body the farther his goal receded from him.

His strenuous and unsuccessful endeavours taught him an important lesson—that is the utter futility of self-mortification.

Benefiting by this invaluable experience of his, he finally decided to follow an independent course avoiding the two extremes of self-mortification and self-indulgence. The former weakens one's intellect; the latter retards one's moral progress. The new path which he discovered was entirely his own. It was the middle path, *Majjhima Paṭipadā*, which subsequently became one of the salient characteristics of his teaching.

One happy morning as he was seated under the Bodhi tree at Gayā, unaided and unguided by any supernatural agency, but solely relying on his efforts and wisdom, he understood things as they truly are and attained enlightenment (Buddhahood).

Having attained Buddhahood, that supreme state of perfection, He devoted the remainder of His precious life to serve humanity both by example and precept, dominated by no personal motive whatsoever.

After a very successful ministry of 45 years the Buddha, as every other human being, succumbed to the inexorable law of transiency and finally passed away into Nibbāna.

The Buddha was, therefore, a human being. As a man He was born, as a man He lived, and as a man His life came to an end. Though a human being He became an extraordinary man—*acchariya manussa*. The Buddha laid stress on this important point and left no room whatsoever for anyone to fall into the error of thinking that He was an immortal divine being. There is no deification in the case of the Buddha.

Neither does the Buddha claim to be an incarnation of Vishnu, as the Hindus are inclined to believe, nor does He call Himself a saviour who saves others by his personal salvation. The Buddha exhorts His disciples to depend on themselves for their salvation, for both defilement and purity depend on oneself. In the Dhammapada the Buddha says—"You yourselves should make the exertion. The *Tathāgatas* are only teachers."

The Buddhas point out the path, and it is left for us to follow that path to save ourselves.

"To depend on others for salvation is negative, but to depend on oneself is positive." Dependence on others means a surrender of one's effort.

In exhorting His disciples to be self-dependent the Buddha says in the Pari-Nibbāna Sutta—"Be ye islands unto yourselves, be ye a refuge unto yourselves, seek no refuge in others."

Furthermore, the Buddha does not claim the monopoly of Buddhahood which, as a matter of fact, is not the prerogative of any specially graced chosen person. He reached the highest possible state of perfection any person could aspire to, and without the closed fist of a teacher. He revealed the only straight path that leads thereto. According to the Teachings of the Buddha anybody may aspire to that supreme state of perfection if he makes the necessary exertion. The Buddha does not condemn men by calling them sinners, but, on the contrary, He says that they are pure in heart at birth. In His opinion the world is not wicked but is dominated by ignorance. Instead of disheartening His followers and reserving that exalted state only to Himself, He encourages and induces them to emulate Him.

As a man He attained Buddhahood and proclaimed to the world the latent possibilities and the creative power of man. Instead of placing an unseen, almighty God over man and making him subservient to him, He raised the worth of mankind. It was He who taught that man can gain his salvation by his own exertion without depending on a God, or mediating priests, or offering sacrifices or prayers. It was He who taught the ego-centric world the noble ideal of selfless service. It was He who revolted against the degrading caste system and taught equality of mankind. He opened the gates of success and prosperity to all deserving ones in every walk of life despite the natural barriers of birth. He gave complete freedom of thought and made us open our eyes to see things as they truly are. He comforted the bereaved by His consoling words. He ministered to the sick that were deserted. He helped the poor that were neglected. He ennobled the lives of sinners, purified the corrupted lives of criminals. He encouraged the feeble, united the divided, enlightened the ignorant, clarified the mystic, guided the benighted, elevated the base, dignified the noble. Both rich and poor, saints and sinners loved Him alike. Despotic and righteous kings, glorious and obscure princes and nobles, generous and stingy millionaires, haughty and humble scholars, destitute paupers, downtrodden scavengers, wicked murderers, despised courtesans—all benefited by His words of wisdom and compassion.

His noble example was a source of inspiration to all. His message of peace was welcomed by all with indescribable joy and was of eternal benefit to everyone that came in contact with it.

Wherever His Teaching penetrated, it left an indelible impression upon the character of the peoples. The cultural advancement of all the Buddhist nations was mainly due to His sublime teaching. Though nearly 2,500 years have elapsed since the passing away of the great Teacher, yet His noble personality still influences all those who come to know Him, and His Sublime Teaching still exists in its pristine purity.

Of the Buddha a St. Hillaire might say-"The perfect model of all the virtues He preaches. His life has not a stain upon it." A Fausboll would say- "The more I know Him, the more I love Him." A humble follower of His would say-"The more I know Him, the more I love Him; the more I love Him the more I know Him."

The Buddha was a unique Being. He was a profound thinker, a persuasive speaker, an energetic worker, a successful reformer a compassionate and tolerant teacher, an efficient administrator, and, above all, the Holiest of Holies.

During His early period of renunciation He sought the advice of the then distinguished religious teachers, but He could not obtain what He sought from outside sources. Circumstances compelled Him to think for Himself and seek within. He sought, He thought, He reflected; ultimately He found His quest of life. Having discovered the truth, He opened the gates of Immortality to all who wished to hear Him and seek their Deliverance from this ever-recurring cycle of birth and death.

As He knew everything that ought to be known and as He obtained the key to all knowledge He is called *Sabbaññu*—Omniscient. This knowledge He acquired by His own efforts as the result of a countless series of a births.

What He taught was merely an infinitesimal part of what He knew. He taught only that which is necessary for our salvation.

Daily He preached His Doctrine to both the Sangha and the laity. In the forenoon He goes in search of individuals who need His advice. Immediately after His noon meal He exhorts and instructs

His monk disciples. In the evening for about an hour He preaches to the lay-folk who flock to hear Him. During the first watch of the night He again preaches to His monk disciples. Throughout the middle watch He receives the Devas and other invisible beings and explains the Doctrine to them.

Practising what He preached, resting only for one hour at night, wandering from place to place for eight months during the year, permeating the whole world with thoughts of loving-kindness for nearly two hours daily, He worked incessantly for the good and happiness of all even upto His last moment.

The Order of monks and nuns He established to represent His Teaching, the efficient way He maintained the discipline of his numerous followers, testify to His unsurpassing administrative ability. He anticipated even the present Parliamentary system. Says Lord Zetland—"And it may come as a surprise to many to learn that in the Assemblies of the Buddhists in India two thousand years and more ago are to be found the rudiments of our own Parliamentary practice of the present day."

Very effectively and very wisely He endeavoured to eradicate some social evils that prevailed during His day. He vehemently protested against the degrading caste system that debarred the progress of mankind. It was He who attempted to abolish slavery for the first time in the history of the world. It was also He who raised the status of women and emancipated them from some fetters that prevented their moral progress.

The most notable characteristic of the Buddha was His absolute purity and perfect holiness. He was so pure and so holy that He should be called the "Holiest of Holies." He was absolutely pure in thought, word, and deed. On no occasion did the Buddha manifest any human weakness. Everybody that came in contact with Him acknowledged His indubitable greatness and was deeply influenced by His magnetic personality.

His will, wisdom, compassion, service, renunciation, holiness, personal life, noble methods that were employed to propagate the Dhamma, His final success —all these factors have compelled mankind to hail the Buddha as the greatest religious Teacher that ever lived on earth.

The Teaching founded by the Buddha is termed the *Dhamma*, and is popularly known as Buddhism.

CHAPTER II

THE LIFE OF THE BUDDHA
(IN HIS OWN WORDS)

(From Anguttara Nikāya, Part 1, Eka-Puggala Vagga, XIII, P. 22)[1]

A Unique Being, O disciples, arises in this world for the benefit of the many, for the happiness of the many, out of compassion for the world, for the good, benefit, and happiness of gods and men.

Who is this Unique Being? It is the Tathāgata[2], the Exalted, Fully Enlightened One.

The arising of a Unique Being, O disciples, is rare in this world. Who is this Unique Being? It is the Tathāgata, the Exalted, Fully Enlightened One.

A Unique Being, O disciples, an extraordinary Man, is born in this world. Who is this Unique Being? It is the Tathāgata, the Exalted, Fully Enlightened One.

The Unique Being, O disciples, who arises in this world, is unequalled, unparallelled, peerless, matchless, unrivalled, incomparable, comparable to the Incomparables, and pre-eminent amongst men.

Who is this Unique Being? It is the Tathāgata, the Exalted, Fully Enlightened One.

---

1 All references are to the Pali text of the Buddhist Scriptures edited by the Pali Text Society of London.

2 Tathāgata—lit. Thus who hath come—Thus who hath gone The Buddha uses this term when referring to Himself.

With the arising of this Unique Being, O disciples, there come into existence a great eye, a great light, a great radiance[1], six supreme blessings[2], there come the intuition of the four kinds of analytical knowledge[3], the realisation of various elements, the comprehension of elements in diverse ways, the acquisition of wisdom, Deliverance, Fruits, and the realisation of Fruits of a Stream-Winner[4], Once-Returner[5], Never-Returner[6], and a Perfect Saint[7].

Who is this Unique Being? It is the Tathāgata, the Exalted, Fully Enlightened One.

---

1 All these three terms refer to wisdom

2 *Anuttariyo* The six supreme Blessings are:
- i The Blessing of Sight *(Dassana A.)*
- ii The Blessing of Hearing *(Savaṇa A.)*
- iii The Blessing of Acquisition, such as Confidence. *(Lābha A.)*
- iv The Blessing of Discipline *(Sikkhā A.)*
- v The Blessing of Ministration. *(Pāricariyā A.)*
- vi The Blessing of Contemplation. *(Anussati A.)*

3 *Paṭisambhidā.* The four kinds of analytical knowledge are:
- i Meaning *(Attha.)*
- ii Text *(Dhamma.)*
- iii Etymology *(Nirutti.)*
- iv Understanding *(Paṭibhāna.)*

4 *Sotāpatti* —The first stage of Saintship on the Path of Holiness At this stage Nibbāna is realised for the first time. A stream-winner is re-born seven times at the most, and is not subject to any state of misery.

5 The second stage: *Sakadāgāmi.* A Once-Returner is re-born in this world of human beings only once.

6 The third stage: *Anāgāmi.* One who attains this stage in this world is, after death, born in the "Pure Abodes" *(Suddhāvāsa)*, a camping place, so to say, of Anāgāmins and Arahants.

7 The fourth stage: *Arahant.* He who attains this last and final stage is not reborn anymore. He attains Parinibbāna.

The Buddha and His immediate disciples

(From Buddhavaṁsa, XXVI, p 65.)

I am the Buddha of to-day, Gotama[1] of Sakya growth. Striving in my striving, I have attained the Supreme Enlightenment.

My city is called Kapilavatthu[2], my father King Suddhodana[3], my mother who bore me the Queen Māyā.

For nine and twenty years I dwelt at home. I had three peerless mansions, Rāma, Surāma and Subhata.

There were forty thousand women, beautifully adorned, Bhaddakaccānā, the woman[4], Rāhula, the son.

---

1 *Gotama* is the family name, and *Sakya* is the name of the clan to which the Buddha belonged.

Tradition holds that the sons of Okkaka of the Mahasammata line, were exiled through the plotting of their step-mother. These princes in the course of their wanderings arrived at the foothills of the Himalayas. Here they met the sage Kapila, on whose advice, and after whom, they founded the city of Kapilavatthu, the site of Kapila. King Okkāka, hearing of the enterprise of the princes, exclaimed—Sākya (capable) indeed are the noble princes. Hence the clan and kingdom they originated was known by the name Sākya.

See "The Life of the Buddha" by E. J. Thomas, page 6.

2 See above.

The Sākya kingdom was situated south of Nepal and extended over much of modern Oudh. The site of Kapilavatthu has been identified with Bhuila (Bhulya) in the Basti district, three miles from the Bengal and N. W. Railway station of Babuan.

3 See the genealogical table—pp. 15, 16.

4 The Princess Yasodharā whom Prince Siddhattha married. Their son was Rāhula.

Seeing the four signs[1], I set out on horse-back, and for six long years I led a life of painful striving.

At Benares, in Isipatana, I established the Law of Righteousness[2]. I am Gotama, the Enlightened One, the Refuge of all beings.

The two Bhikkhus[3], Kolita and Upatissa[4], are my chief disciples. Ānanda[5] is my attendant ever near me.

---

1 Four Sights seen in the city were:

- i A man broken down by age.
- ii A sick man.
- iii A decaying corpse.
- iv A dignified hermit.

2 The *Dhammacakka Sutta* is the first sermon delivered by the Buddha to His five Disciples who attended on Him during His Struggle for Enlightenment. This Discourse starts with the two extremes which should be avoided by an ascetic. and deals mainly with the Middle Path and the Four Noble Truths.

3 Bhikkhu, which means a mendicant, is the technical term used by the Buddha for those who accepted Him as their guide and furthermore put on the yellow robe of the monk and enrolled themselves as His disciples. The Bhikkhus, it should be understood, are not "priests" who act as mediators between God and men. They lead the Holy Life and teach others both by example and precept. They are not bound by any vows, but they have to observe the rules that pertain to the Order as long as they remain in the robe.

4 Generally known as *Moggallāna* and *Sāriputta*. The former, the second disciple, is distinguished for psychic powers, whilst the latter, the first disciple, is distinguished for wisdom, and is also the general of the Dhamma.

5 Ānanda is the Treasurer of the Dhamma See the genealogical table.

The Bhikkhunis Khemā and Uppalavannā[1], are my chief female disciples. Citta and Hatthālavaka are my chief attendant laymen[2].

Nandā's mother and Uttarā are my chief attendant laywomen. At the foot of the *Assattha* tree[3] I attained to supreme Enlightenment.

* * * *

The Buddha's Birth-Place and Ancestry

(From Sutta Nipāta, Mahāvagga, Pabbajjā Sutta
p. 73, vs. 422—4)

Just straight, O king, upon the Himālayas, there is, in the district of Kosala of ancient families, a country endowed with wealth and energy.

I am sprung from that family which, by clan, belongs to the Solar Dynasty[4], by birth to the Sakyas. I crave not for pleasures of the senses.

---

1 The nuns who were accepted by the Buddha into His Order of disciples

2 Attendant laymen and laywomen, *Upāsakas* and *Upāsikās*, accepted the Lord as their Guide without however becoming Bhikkhus and Bhikkhunis The term Upāsaka means one who associates with the Triple Gem.

3 The famous Pipal tree, still existing at Buddha Gayā in northern India, better known as the Bodhi Tree, the Tree of Wisdom.

4 The solar race, i e , "the royal dynasty of Rāmacandra, king of Ayodhya, hero of the Rāmāyana, who was descended from Ikshvāku, son of Vaivasata Manu, son of the sun. Many Rajput tribes still claim to belong to this race; it is one of the two great lines of kings, the other being called —lunar." Monier Williams.

"Although the Sakyas belong to the race of the Sun, this is said to mean, not that they trace their descent from this primitive ancestor, as in the Puranas, but that two of their predecessors were born from eggs, which were formed from coagulated blood and semen of their father Gautama and hatched by the sun. From one of the eggs came the famous Ikshvaku, who in the Puranas is the immediate son of Manu, son of the Sun." Dr. Thomas

Realising the evil of pleasures of the senses, and seeing renunciation as safe, I proceeded to seek the Highest, for in that my mind rejoices.

* * * *

His luxurious life as Prince

(From the Anguttara Nikāya—Part I, p. 145)

I was delicate excessively delicate. In my father's dwelling three lotus-ponds were made purposely for me. Blue lotuses bloomed in one, red in another, and white in another. I used no sandal-wood that was not of Kāsi. My turban, tunic, dress, and cloak were all from Kāsi. Night and day a white parasol was held over me so that I might not be touched by heat or cold, dust, grass or dew.

There were three palaces for me—one for the cold season, one for the hot season, and one for the rainy season. During the four rainy months, I lived in the palace for the rainy season, entertained by female ministrels, without coming down from the palace. Just as in the houses of others food from the husks of rice together with sour gruel is given to the slaves and workmen, even so in my father's dwelling food with rice and meat was given to the slaves and workmen.

Prince Siddhattha's Genealogical Table

FATHER'S SIDE:

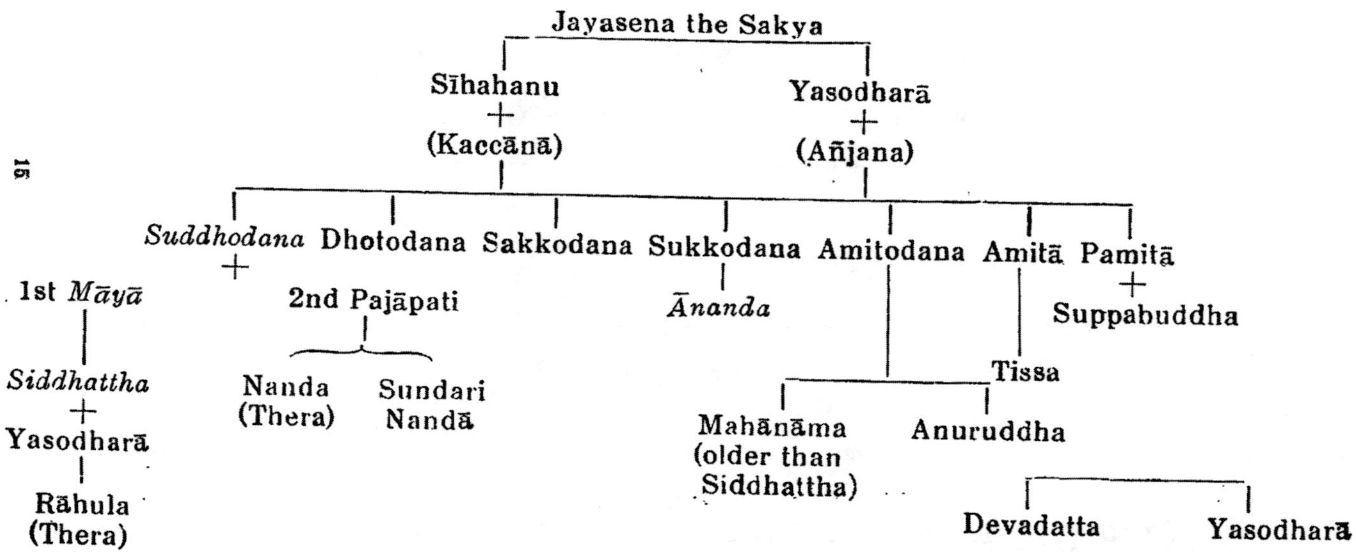

Prince Siddhattha's Genealogical Table (Contd.)

MOTHER'S SIDE:

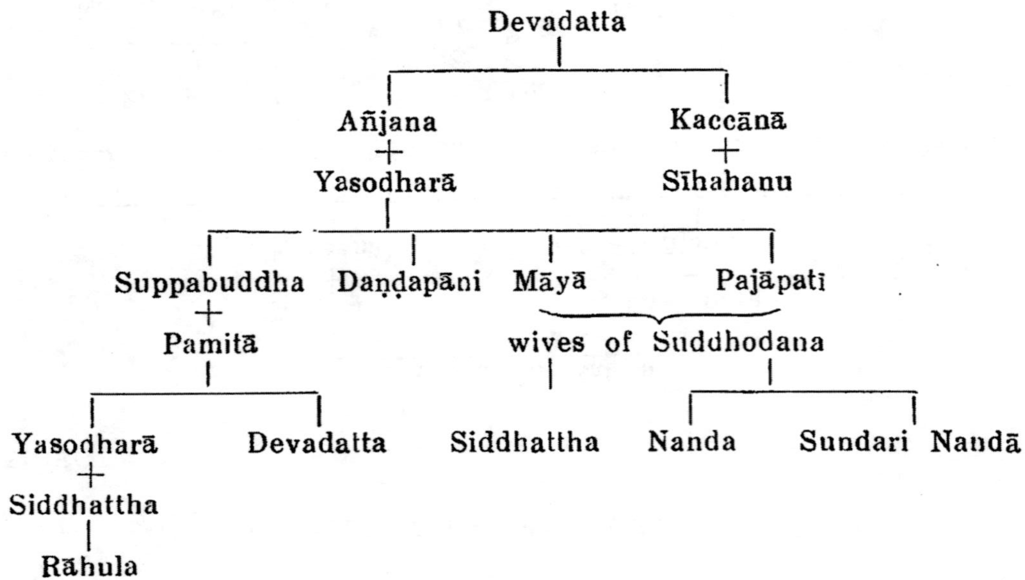

CHAPTER III

THE LIFE OF THE BUDDHA

(Continued)

The Dawn of Truth

(From the Anguttara Nikāya part 1, 145.)

THEN I, O disciples, endowed with such majesty and such delicacy, thought thus:—"An uninstructed worldling, being himself subject to old age, not being freed from old age, on seeing an old person, is troubled, ashamed, and disgusted, overlooking himself. I too am subject to old age, have not escaped old age and should I, who am subject to old age, not freed from old age, on seeing an old person, be troubled, ashamed, and disgusted?"—This would not be fitting to me. As I thus reflected on it, that elation in youth completely disappeared.

"An uninstructed worldling, being himself subject to sickness, not being freed from sickness, on seeing a sick man, is troubled, ashamed, and disgusted overlooking himself. I too am subject to sickness, have not escaped sickness, and should I, who am subject to sickness, not freed from sickness, on seeing a sick person, be troubled, ashamed, and disgusted?"—This would not be fitting to me. As I thus reflected on it, that elation in health completely disappeared.

"An uninstructed worldling, being himself subject to death, not being freed from death, on seeing a dead person, is troubled, ashamed, and disgusted, overlooking himself. I too am subject to death, have not escaped death and should I, who am subject to death, not freed from death, on seeing a dead person, be troubled, ashamed, and disgusted?" This would not be fitting to me. As I thus reflected on it, that elation in life completely disappeared.

* * * *

His Renunciation and Preliminary Efforts

(From Majjhima Nikāya, 1 Ariya-Pariyesana Sutta No 26 p 163)

Now I, O disciples, before my Enlightenment, being not yet fully enlightened, but as a Bodhisatta[1], myself still subject to birth, decay, disease, death, sorrow, and impurities, sought after that which is subject to birth, decay, disease, death, sorrow, and impurities.

Then there came to me the thought—Why do I, being subject to birth, decay, disease, death, sorrow, and impurities, thus search after things of like nature? How if I, who am subject to things of such nature, realise their disadvantages and seek after the unattained, unsurpassed, perfect security, which is Nibbāna!

Then, disciples, after some time while I was still young, a black haired stripling, endowed with happy youth, in the prime of manhood, against the wishes of my father and mother who lamented with tearful eyes, I had my head and beard shaved, and, wearing yellow garments, went forth from home to the homeless state.

Thus as a wanderer, a seeker after what is good, searching for the unsurpassed, peaceful state, most

---

1 Literally, "a wisdom-being," one whose destiny is to attain to complete Enlightenment or Buddhahood.

excellent, I approached Ālāra Kālāma, and said: "I desire, friend Kalama, to lead the Holy Life in this Dispensation of yours."

Thereupon, O disciples, Ālāra Kālāma told me: "You may stay with me, O venerable One. Of such sort is this teaching that an intelligent man before long may realise by his own intuitive wisdom his master's doctrine, and abide in the attainment thereof."

And before long, O disciples, very speedily I learnt his doctrine, and by mere lip-recital and oral repetition, I said I knew and was firm; I acknowledged that I understood and perceived (the doctrine).

Then there came to me the thought: "When Ālāra Kālāma declared: 'Having myself realised by intuitive knowledge the doctrine, I abide in the attainment thereof,' it could not have been a mere profession of faith; surely Alārā Kālāma lives having understood and perceived this doctrine."

So I went to Ālāra Kālāma and said to him; "How far, friend Kālāma, does this doctrine extend which you yourself have by intuitive wisdom realised and attained?"

Upon this Alāra Kālāma made known to me '*The Realm of Nothingness*' [1].

Then, O disciples, it occurred to me: "Not only in Ālāra Kālāma are to be found faith, energy, recollectedness, concentration, and wisdom. I too possess faith, energy, recollectedness, concentration, and wisdom. How now if I strive to realise that doctrine whereof Alāra Kālāma says that he

---

1 The Realm of Nothingness—*Ākiñcaññāyatana,* is the third Arūpa Jhāna (Ecstasy)—an advanced stage in Concentration.

himself has realised by his wisdom and abides in the attainment thereof!"

And so, O disciples, before long, very speedily I realised by my intuitive wisdom that doctrine and lived, having attained to that state.

Then I went to Ālāra Kālāma and said to him: "Is this the full extent, friend Kālāma, of this doctrine of which you say that you yourself have realised by your wisdom and abide in the attainment thereof?"

"Thus far, friend, this doctrine extends of which I say that I myself have realised and abide in the attainment thereof."

"But I also, friend, have realised thus far in this doctrine, and abide in the attainment thereof."

"Happy, friend, are we; yea, extremely happy, in that we look upon such a venerable fellow-ascetic as you! That same doctrine which I myself have realised by my wisdom and proclaim having attained thereunto, have you yourself realised by your wisdom and abide in the attainment thereof; and that doctrine you yourself have realised by your wisdom and abide in the attainment thereof, that have I myself realised by my wisdom and proclaim having attained thereunto. Thus the doctrine which I know, that also do you know; and the doctrine which you know, that I know also. As I am, so are you; as you are, so am I. Come, friend, let both of us lead the company of ascetics."

Thus did Ālāra Kālāma, the teacher, take me, the pupil, and placed me on a perfect level with himself and did me great honour. But I thought: "This teaching does not lead me to disgust, detachment, cessation, tranquillity, intuition, enlightenment and Nibbāna, but only to the attainment of "*The Realm of Nothingness.*" And so, disciples, dissatisfied with this doctrine, I took my departure content therewith no longer.

Then, O disciples, as a seeker after what is good, searching for the unsurpassed, peaceful state, most excellent, I went to Uddaka Rāmaputta and said: "I wish, O friend, to lead the Holy Life in this Dispensation."

Whereupon, O disciples, Uddaka Rāmaputta replied: "You may stay with me, O venerable One. Of such sort is this teaching that before long an intelligent man may realise by his own wisdom his master's teaching, and abide in the attainment thereof."

And I, O disciples, before long speedily learnt his doctrine, and by mere lip-recital and oral repetition I said I knew and was firm; I acknowledged that I understood and perceived the doctrine.

Then it occurred to me: "When Rāma declared: 'Having myself realised by my wisdom the doctrine, I abide in the attainment thereof,' it could not have been a mere profession of faith; surely Rāma lives, having understood and perceived the doctrine!"

So I went to Uddaka Rāmaputta and said to him: "How far does this doctrine extend of which Rāma says that he himself has by wisdom realised and attained?"

Thereupon Uddaka Rāmaputta revealed to me '*The Realm-Of-Neither-Perception-Nor-Non-Perception*' [1]

Then, O disciples, I thought: "Not only in Rāma are to be found faith, energy, recollectedness, concentration, and wisdom. I too possess faith, energy, recollectedness, concentration, and wisdom. How now if I also strive to realise that doctrine whereof Rāma says that he himself has realised by his wisdom and abide in the attainment thereof!"

And so, O disciples, before long very speedily I realised by my wisdom that doctrine and lived having attained to that state. Then I went to Uddaka Rāmaputta and asked him: "Is this the full extent, friend Rāma, of the doctrine whereof you say that you yourself have realised by your wisdom and abide in the attainment thereof?"

"Thus far, friend, this doctrine extends of which I say that I myself have realised by my wisdom and abide in the attainment thereof."

"But I also, friend, have realised thus far in this doctrine and abide in the attainment thereof."

"Happy, friend, are we; yea extremely happy, in that we see such a venerable fellow-ascetic as you! That same doctrine which Rāma has by his wisdom realised and proclaimed having attained thereunto, have you yourself realised by your wisdom and abide in the attainment thereof, and the doctrine you yourself have realised by your wisdom and abide in the attainment thereof, that has Rāma himself realised by his own wisdom and proclaimed having attained there-

1 The Realm of Neither-Perception nor Non-Perception. *N'eva saññā n'asaññāyatana*—is the fourth Arūpa Jhāna, the highest stage in worldly concentration. The ancient sages could not proceed beyond this state.

unto. The doctrine which Rāma knew you know; the doctrine which you know Rāma knew. As was Rama, so are you; as you are, so was Rama. Come, friend, henceforth you shall lead this company of ascetics."

Thus, O disciples, did Uddaka Ramaputta set me his equal fellow disciple in the position of the teacher and did me great honour.

But I thought: "This doctrine does not lead me to disgust, detachment, cessation, tranquillity, intuition, enlightenment, and Nibbana, but only to the attainment of *'The-Realm-of-Neither-Perception-nor-Non-Perception.'*"

And so, O disciples, dissatisfied with this doctrine also, I departed thence content therewith no longer.

* * * *

The Buddha's Struggle for Enlightenment

(From Majjhima Nikāva, Vol. 1, Ariya-Pariyesana Sutta No. 26, p. 166)

And I, as a seeker after good, seeking for the incomparable state of peace supreme, wandering in the district of Magadha, arrived in due course at Uruvela, the market town of Senani. There I espied a lovely spot of ground, a charming forest grove, a flowing river with pleasant sandy fords, and hard by was a village where I could beg my food. Then I thought thus:

"Lovely, indeed, O venerable One, is this spot of ground; charming is the forest grove, pleasant is the flowing river with sandy fords, and hard by is the village where I could beg my food. Suitable indeed is this place for spiritual exertion for those noble scions who desire to strive." And I sat down there thinking that it was a suitable place for such exertion.

* * * *

(From Majjhima Nikāya, Vol I, Mahā Saccaka Sutta, No 36, p.242)

Then the following thought occurred to me:—"How if I were to clench my teeth, press my tongue against palate, and with (moral) thoughts hold down, subdue and destroy my (immoral) thoughts!"

So I clenched my teeth, pressed my tongue against my palate and strove to hold down, subdue, destroy my (immoral) thoughts with (moral) thoughts. As I struggled thus, perspiration streamed forth from my armpits.

Like unto a strong man who might seize a weaker man by head or shoulders and hold him down, force him down, and bring into subjection, even so did I struggle.

Strenuous and indomitable was my energy. My mindfulness was established and unperturbed. My body, however, was fatigued and was not calmed as a result of that painful endeavour—being overpowered by exertion. Even though such painful sensations arose in me, they did not at all affect my mind.

Then I thought thus:—"How if I were to cultivate the non-breathing ecstasy!"

Accordingly, I checked inhalation and exhalation from my mouth and nostrils. As I checked inhalation and exhalation from mouth and nostrils, the air issuing from my ears created an exceedingly great noise. Just as a blacksmith's bellows being blown make an exceedingly great noise, even so was the noise created by the air issuing from my ears when I stopped breathing.

Nevertheless, my energy was strenuous and indomitable. Established and unperturbed was my mindfulness. Yet my body was fatigued and was not calmed as a result of that painful endeavour—being over-powered by exertion. Even though such painful sensations arose in me, they did not at all affect my mind.

Then I thought to myself: "How if I were to cultivate that non-breathing exercise!"

Accordingly, I checked inhalation and exhalation from mouth, nostrils, and ears. And, as I stopped breathing from mouth, nostrils, and ears, the (imprisoned) airs beat upon my skull with great violence. Just as if a strong man were to bore one's skull with a sharp drill, even so did the airs beat my skull with great violence as I stopped breathing. Even though such painful sensations arose in me, they did not at all affect my mind.

Then I thought to myself:—"How if I were to cultivate that non-breathing ecstasy again!"

Accordingly, I checked inhalation and exhalation from mouth, nostrils, and ears. And, as I stopped breathing thus, terrible pains arose in my head. As would be the pains if a strong man were to bind one's head tightly with a hard leathern thong, even so were the terrible pains that arose in my head.

Nevertheless, my energy was strenuous and indomitable. Established and unperturbed was my mindfulness. Yet my body was fatigued and was not calmed as a result of that painful endeavour—being overpowered by exertion. Even though such painful sensations arose in me, they did not at all affect my mind.

Then I thought to myself:—"How if I were to cultivate that non-breathing ecstasy again!"

Accordingly, I stopped breathing from mouth, nostrils, and ears. As I checked breathing thus, plentiful airs pierced my belly. Just as if a skilful butcher or butcher's apprentice were to rip up the belly with a sharp butcher's knife, even so plentiful airs pierced my belly.

Nevertheless, my energy was strenuous and indomitable. Established and unperturbed was my mindfulness. Yet my body was fatigued and was not calmed as a result of that painful endeavour—being overpowered by exertion. Even though such painful sensations arose in me, they did not at all affect my mind.

Again I thought to myself: "How if I were to cultivate that non-breathing ecstasy again!"

Accordingly, I checked inhalation and exhalation from mouth, nostrils, and ears. As I suppressed my breathing thus, a tremendous burning pervaded my body. Just as if two strong men were each to seize a weaker man by his arms and scorch and thoroughly burn him in a pit of glowing charcoal, even so did a severe burning pervade my body.

Nevertheless, my energy was strenuous and indomitable. Established and unperturbed was my mindfulness. Despite which my body was fatigued and was not calmed as a result of that painful endeavour,—being overpowered by exertion. Yet though such painful sensations arose in me they did not at all affect my mind.

Thereupon, the deities who saw me thus said: "The ascetic Gotama is dead;" some said: "The ascetic Gotama is not dead yet, but is dying." Whilst some others said: "The ascetic Gotama is neither dead nor is dying, but an Arahant is the ascetic Gotama. Such is the way in which an Arahant abides!"

* * * *

CHAPTER IV

THE LIFE OF THE BUDDHA

(Continued)

Change of method: Abstinence from food

THEN I thought to myself:—"How if I were to practise complete abstinence from food!"

Then, deities approached me and said:—"Do not, good sir, practise total abstinence from food. If you do practise it, we will pour celestial essence through your body's pores; with that you will be sustained."

And I thought:—"If I claim to be practising complete starvation, and if these deities pour celestial essence through my body's pores and I am sustained thereby, it would be a fraud on my part." So, I refused them, saying: "There is no need."

Then the following thought occurred to me:— "How if I take food little by little, and a small quantity of the juice of green gram, or vetch or lentils or peas."

As I took such a small quantity of solid and liquid food, my body became extremely emaciated. Just as are the joints of knot-grasses or bulrushes, even so were the major and minor parts of my body owing to lack of food. Just as is the camel's hoof, even so were my hips for want of food. Just as is a string of beads, even so did my backbone stand out and bent in, for lack of food. Just as the rafters of a dilapidated hall fall this way and that, even so appeared my ribs through lack of sustenance. Just as in a deep wall may be seen stars sunk deep in the water, even so did my eye-balls appear deep sunk in their sockets, being devoid of food. Just as a bitter pumpkin when cut whilst raw will by wind and sun get shrivelled and withered, even so did the skin of my head get shrivelled and withered, due to lack of sustenance.

And I, intending to touch my belly's skin, would instead seize my backbone. When I intended to touch my backbone, I would instead seize my belly's skin. So was I that, owing to lack of sufficient food, my belly's skin clung to the backbone, and I, on going to pass excreta or urine, would in that very spot stumble and fall down, for want of food. And I stroke my limbs in order to revive my body. Lo, as I did so, the rotten roots of my body's hairs fell from my body owing to lack of sustenance. The people who saw me said:—"The ascetic Gotama is black." Some said: "The ascetic Gotama is not black but blue." Some others said: "The ascetic Gotama is neither black nor blue but tawny."

To such an extent was the pure clear colour of my skin impaired owing to lack of food.

Then the following thought occurred to me: "Whatsoever ascetics or brahmins of the past have experienced acute, painful, sharp and piercing sensations, they must have experienced them to such a high pitch, and not beyond. Whatsoever ascetics and brahmins of the future will experience acute, painful, sharp and piercing sensations, they, too, will experience them to such a high pitch, and not beyond. Whatsoever ascetics and brahmins of to-day experience acute, painful, sharp and piercing sensations, they, too, experience them to such a high pitch, and not beyond. Yet by all these bitter difficult austerities I shall not attain to excellence, worthy of supreme knowledge and insight, transcending that of human states. Might there be another path for Enlightenment!"

* * * *

The Temptation of Mara, the Evil one

(Sutta Nipāta—Padhāna Sutta p. 74)

To me who was intent on the Highest[1] and who was by the Nerañjarā river, striving and contemplating in order to attain to that state of Perfect Security, came Namuci[2] uttering kind words thus:

You are lean and deformed. Near to you is death.

Thousand steps (you are nearer) to death; to life (there remains) one. Live, O good sir; life is better. Living you could perform merit.

By leading a life of celibacy and making fire sacrifices, much merit could be acquired. What will you do with this striving?

Hard is the path of striving, difficult and not easily attained.

Māra reciting these verses stood in the presence of the Buddha.

---

1 *Padhāna*—i.e. Nibbāna.

2 A name for Māra.

To Māra who spoke thus, the Buddha addressed as follows:

O Evil One, the kinsman of the heedless! You have come here for your own sake.

Even an iota of merit is of no use to me. To them who are in need of merit it behoves you, Māra, to speak thus.

Confidence, self-control[1], energy, and wisdom do I possess. From me who am thus intent, why do you question about life?

Even the streams of rivers will this wind dry up. Why should the blood of me who am thus striving not dry up?

When blood dries up the bile and phlegm also dry up. When my flesh wastes away more and more does my mind get clarified. Still more do my mindfulness, wisdom, and concentration become firm.

Whilst I lived thus, experiencing the utmost pain, my mind did not long for lusts. Behold the purity of a being!

Sense-desires (*Kāma*) are your first army. The second is called aversion (*Arati*). The third is hunger and thirst (*Khuppipāsā*). The fourth is called craving (*Tanhā*). The fifth is sloth and torpor (*Thīna-Middha*). The sixth is called fear (*Bhaya*). The seventh is doubt (*Vicikicchā*), and the eighth is detraction and obstinacy (*Makkha-Thamba*).

The ninth is gain (*Lābha*), praise (*Siloka*), honour (*Sakkāra*), and that fame (*Yasa*), falsely obtained.

---

1 "*Tapo*"—Pali Text Society reading "*Tato.*"

The tenth is the exalting of oneself and the despising of others.

This, Namuci, is your army, the opposing host of the Evil One. That army the coward does not overcome, but he who overcomes obtains happiness.

This grass I carry about[1]. Shame be to my life here! Better to me is death in battle (with passions) than that I should live defeated.

Plunged in this battle some ascetics and Brahmins show themselves not. They knew not the way in which the virtuous go.

Seeing the army on all sides with Māra arrayed with elephant, I go forward to battle. Let not Māra drive me from the post.

That army of yours, which the world together with gods conquers not, (destroying) by my wisdom, I go as an unbaked bowl with a stone.

Controlling my thoughts and with mindfulness well-established, I shall wander from country to country, training many a disciple.

Diligent, intent, and practising my teaching, they, disregarding you, will go where having gone they do not grieve.

(Māra says:) For seven years I followed the Blessed One step by step but no loophole in the mindful All-Enlightened One could I find.

---

1 Warriors wear *Muñja* grass on their heads or on their banners to indicate that they will not retreat from the battlefield.

As a crow that went after a yellow-coloured stone thinking here I shall experience something soft or there will be something enjoyable,—

But not finding any enjoyment therein the crow departed thence. Like a crow attacking a rock I leave in disgust, O Gotama.

The lute of Māra who was overcome with grief fell from beneath his arm. Thereupon the displeased Yakkha disappeared there and then.

* * * *

The Middle Path

(Mahā Saccaka Sutta, Majjhima Nikāya—No. 36)

Then it occurred to me:—I recalled how when my father the Sakya was engaged in ploughing, I sat in the cool shade of the rose-apple tree, having attained to the First Ecstasy[1], which is born of seclusion, associated with joy and happiness, remote from lust and immoral states, and accompanied by reflection and investigation. Could this be the path to Enlightenment!

Thereupon, there came to me the conciousness, followed by memory:—"Yes, this is the path to Enlightenment!"

And I thought:—"Am I afraid of that happiness which is exempt from lust and immoral states?" Then it occurred to me: "Nay, I am not afraid of that

1 The young prince developed this first Jhāna by concentrating on "inhalation and exhalation"—"*Ānāpāna Sati.*" Neither the text nor the commentary supports the view that the prince rose up into the air.

state of happiness." But I thought that with such an utterly exhausted body it was not possible to attain to that happiness. Suppose I take some coarse food such as boiled and forced rice!

So I partook of such coarse food.

At that time five disciples were attending on me, thinking that whatever truth ascetic Gotama would comprehend, that would he impart to them. But when I began to partake of coarse food such as boiled and forced rice, the five disciples got disgusted and left me, saying that the ascetic Gotama had become luxurious, had ceased from striving, and has turned to a life of comfort.

The Discovery of Truth

And I, having partaken of coarse food, revived strength, and lived abiding in that joy and bliss of the First Ecstasy (Jhāna), born of seclusion, accompanied by reflection and investigation, remote from lust and immoral states. Even though such pleasurable sensations arose in me, they did not at all affect my mind. Stilling reflection and investigation, having tranquillity within, mind predominating, reflection and investigation having ceased, in the joy and happiness born of concentration, I lived abiding in the Second Ecstasy. Even though such pleasurable sensations arose in me, they did not at all affect my mind. Separated from joy I lived with equanimity. Mindful and completely conscious, I experienced in the body that happiness of which the Ariyas say: "Endowed with equanimity and mindfulness, he abides in bliss." Thus I lived, abiding in the Third Ecstasy. Even though such pleasurable sensations arose in me, they did not at all affect my mind. Abandoning pleasure and pain, with the disappearance of former joy and grief,—painless and pleasureless, perfect in equanimity and mindfulness—I lived abiding in the Fourth Esctasy. Even though such pleasurable sensations arose in me, they did not at all affect my mind.

Thus with thoughts tranquillised, purified, cleansed, free from lust and impurity, pliable, alert, steady, and unshakable, I directed my mind to the knowledge as regards the "*Reminiscence of Previous Births*" (*Pubbe-Nivāsānussati Ñāṇa*). I recalled my varied lot in former existences, as follows: first one life, then two lives, then three, four, five, ten, twenty, up to fifty lives; then a hundred, a thousand, a hundred thousand; then the dissolution of many world cycles, then the evolution of many world cycles, then both the dissolution and evolution of many world cycles. In that place I was of such a name, such a family, such a caste, such a dietary, such the pleasure and pain I experienced, such my life's end. Vanishing from there, I came into existence elsewhere. Then, such was my name, such my family, such my caste, such my dietary, such pleasure and pain did I experience, such that life's end. Thence departing, I came into existence here. Thus I recalled the mode and details of my varied lot in my former existences. This, indeed, was the First Knowledge that I realised, in the first watch of the night. Ignorance was dispelled, and knowledge arose; darkness vanished, and light arose—as it would be to a person who is strenuous, energetic and resolute. Even though such pleasurable sensations arose in me, they did not at all affect my mind.

Thus with thoughts tranquillised, purified, cleansed, free from lust and impurity, pliable, alert, steady, and unshakable, I directed my mind to the "*Perception of the Disappearing and Reappearing of Beings*," (*Cutūpapāto ñāna*). With clairvoyant vision, purified and supernormal, I perceived beings disappearing from one state of existence and reappearing in another; I beheld the base and the noble, the beautiful and the ugly, the happy and the miserable, and beings passing according to their deeds. I knew that these good individuals, by evil deeds, words, and thoughts, by reviling the Noble Ones, by being misbelievers, and by conforming themselves to the actions of the misbelievers, after the dissolution of their bodies and after death, had been born in sorrowful, miserable, and woeful states. I knew that these good individuals, by good deeds, words, and thoughts, by not reviling the Noble Ones, by being right believers, and by conforming themselves to the actions of the right believers, after the dissolution of their bodies and after death, had been born in happy celestial worlds. Thus with clairvoyant vision I beheld the disappearing and the reappearing of beings.

This, indeed, was the Second Knowledge that I realised, in the middle watch of the night. Ignorance was dispelled, and knowledge arose; darkness vanished, and light arose—as it would be to a person who is strenuous, energetic, and resolute. Even though such pleasurable sensations arose in me, they did not at all affect my mind.

Thus with thoughts tranquillised, purified, cleansed, free from lust and impurity, pliable, alert, steady, and unshakable, I directed my mind to the

"*Comprehension of the Cessation of the Corruptions*" (*āsavakkhaya Ñāṇa*). I realised in accordance with fact: "This is Sorrow," "This, the Arising of Sorrow," "This, the Cessation of Sorrow," "This, the Path leading to the Cessation of Sorrow." Likewise, in accordance with fact, I realised: "These are the Corruptions,[1]........."This, the Arising of the Corruptions,"......... "This, the Ceasing of the Corruptions," .... "This, the Path leading to the Cessation of the Corruptions." Thus cognising, thus perceiving, my mind was delivered from the Corruption of Sensual Craving; from the Corruption of Craving for Existence; from the Corruption of Ignorance. Being delivered, I knew, "Delivered am I," and I realised, "Rebirth is ended; fulfilled the Holy Life; done what was to be done; there is none other beyond this life."

This is the Third Knowledge that I realised, in the last watch of the night. Ignorance was dispelled, and wisdom arose; darkness vanished, and light arose—as would be to a person who is strenuous, energetic, and resolute.

Even though such pleasurable sensations arose in me, they did not at all affect my mind.

---

1 *Āsavas* (Defilements)—are those which flow right up to the top-most plane of existence, with respect to spheres, or right up to the *Gotrabhu*, with respect to mind-flux. There are four *Āsavas*, viz: Sense-desires *(Kāma)*, Becoming *(Bhava)*, False Views *(Diṭṭhi)*, and Ignorance *(Avijjā)*.

Here *Bhava Āsava* means the desire to be born in the realms of form and formless realms *(Rūpa* and *Arūpa* Bhava).

One of the First Utterances of the Buddha

(Dhammapada, VV. 153, 154.)

Thro' many a birth in Sansāra wandered I,
Seeking, but not finding, the builder of this house.
Sorrowful is repeated birth.
O house-builder[1]! you are seen. You shall build no house[2] again,
All your rafters[3] are broken, your ridge-pole[4] is shattered.
To dissolution (Nibbāna) goes my mind.
The End of Craving have I attained.

"Thro' many a birth in existence wandered I,
Vainly seeking an architect. A torment is repeated birth.
Architect I see thee. Never a house shalt thou build again.
All demolished are thy timbers, thy keystone shattered.
Mind attains the unconditioned.
Achieved is the Cessation of Thirst."[5]

---

1 I.e. craving *(Tanhā)*.
2 Body.
3 Passions.
4 Ignorance.
5 Dr. Cassius A. Pereira.

CHAPTER V

THE LIFE OF THE BUDDHA

(Continued)

Soon After the Enlightenment

(Reflection on the Paṭicca-Samuppāda
Udāna Bodhivagga, p.1)

ON one occasion the Blessed One, soon after the Enlightenment, was dwelling at Uruvelā, on the banks of the Nerañjarā river, at the foot of the Bodhi Tree. At that time the Blessed One was sitting in one posture for seven days experiencing the Bliss of Emancipation.

Thereupon the Blessed One, after those seven days have elapsed, emerged from that state of concentration, and in the first watch of the night thoroughly reflected on the "Dependent Arising" in direct order thus: When this (cause) exists this (effect) is, with the arising of this (cause) this (effect) arises, as for example:—

Dependent on Ignorance (*avijjā*) arise Volitional Activities (*Saṅkhārā*), dependent on Volitional Activities arises (Rebirth) Consciousness (*Viññāna*), dependent on (Rebirth) Consciousness arise Mind and Matter (*Nāma Rūpa*), dependent on Mind and Matter arise the six Spheres of Sense (*Salāyatana*), dependent on the six Spheres of Sense arises Contact (*Phassa*), dependent on Contact arises Craving (*Tanhā*), dependent on Craving arises Attachment (*Upādāna*), dependent on Attachment arise Actions (*Kamma*), dependent on Actions arises Rebirth (*Jāti*), dependent on Rebirth arise Decay, Death, Sorrow, Lamentation, Pain, Grief and Despair.

Thus does this whole mass of suffering originate.

Thereupon the Blessed One knowing this meaning uttered, at that time, this pæan of joy:—

When indeed the Truths become manifest unto the strenuous meditative Brahman, then do all his doubts vanish away, since he knows the Truth together with its cause.

* * * *

On one occasion the Blessed One, soon after the Enlightenment, was dwelling at Uruvelā, on the banks of the Nerañjarā river, at the foot of the Bodhi tree. At that time the Blessed One was sitting in one posture for seven days experiencing the Bliss of Emancipation.

Thereupon the Blessed One, after those seven days have elapsed, emerged from that state of concentration, and in the middle watch of the night thoroughly reflected on the "Dependent Arising" in reverse order thus:—When this (cause) does not exist this (effect) is not; with the cessation of this (cause) this (effect) ceases, as for example:—

With the cessation of Ignorance, Volitional Activities cease; with the cessation of Volitional Activities, Rebirth Consciousness ceases; with the cessation of (Rebirth) Consciousness, Mind and Matter cease; with the cessation of Mind and Matter, the Six Spheres of Sense cease; with the cessation of the Six Spheres of of Sense, Contact ceases; with the cessation of Contact, Craving ceases; with the cessation of Craving, Attachment ceases; with the cessation of Attachment, Actions cease; with the cessation of Actions, Rebirth ceases; with the cessation of Rebirth, Decay, Death, Sorrow, Lamentation, Pain, Grief, and Despair cease.

Thus does this whole mass of suffering cease.

Thereupon the Blessed One knowing this meaning uttered, at that time, this pæan of joy:—

When indeed the Truths become manifest unto the strenuous and meditative Brāhmaṇa[1], then all his doubts vanish away since he has understood the destruction of the causes.

*   *   *   *

In the third watch of the night the Blessed One reflected on the Dependent Arising in direct and reverse order thus: When this exists this is, with the arising of this (cause) this (effect) arises; when this (cause) does not exist this (effect) is not, with the cessation of this (cause) this (effect) ceases, as for example:—

Dependent on Ignorance arise Volitional Activities .... Thus does this whole mass of suffering arise.

With the cessation of Ignorance cease Volitional Activities......... Thus does this whole mass of suffering cease.

---

1 Brahmin is a racial term which means "one who studies the the Vedas." Sometimes the Buddha uses this term in the sense of "one who has discarded evil"—a Saint. In this book "*Brāhmaṇa*" is used to denote a Saint; and "Brahmin," to denote a member of that particular caste.

Thereupon the Blessed One knowing this meaning uttered, at that time, this pæan of joy:

When indeed the Truths become manifest to the strenuous meditative Brāhmaṇa, then he stands routing the hosts of the Evil One even as the sun illumines the sky.

* * * *

The Question of a Brahmin

On one occasion the Blessed One, soon after the Enlightenment, was dwelling at Uruvelā on the banks of the Nerañjarā River, at the foot of the *Ajapāla* Banyan tree. At that time the Blessed One sat in one posture for seven days enjoying the Bliss of Emancipation. Then the Blessed One, after these seven days have elapsed, emerged from that state of concentration.

Thereupon a certain conceited (*Huhunkajātika*) Brahmin came to where the Blessed One was, and, drawing near, exchanged friendly greetings with Him and, after the customary salutation, remained standing aside. Thus standing the Brahmin spoke to the Blessed One as follows:—"In what respect, O venerable Gotama, does one become a Brahmin and what are the conditions that make a Brahmin?"

Then the Blessed One, knowing this meaning, uttered in this connection this pæan of joy:

That Brahmin who has discarded evil, without conceit (Huhunka), free from defilements[1], self-controlled, versed in knowledge, who has led the Holy Life—rightly he would call himself a Brāhmaṇa. For him there is no elation anywhere in this world.

---

1 See *Āsavas*, p. 37.

The Serpent-King Protects the Buddha from the Rain

Thereupon the Blessed One, at the end of those seven days, emerged from that state of concentration and went from the *Ajapāla* Banyan tree to the *Mucalinda* tree. Having reached it He sat in one posture for seven days, enjoying the Bliss of Emancipation.

At that time there arose an unexpected great shower. Rain clouds and gloomy weather with cold winds prevailed for seven days.

Thereupon Mucalinda the serpent-king came out of his abode and coiling round the body of the Blessed One seven times, remained keeping his large hood over the head of the Blessed One so that the Blessed One may not be touched by cold, heat, gadflies, gnats, wind, sun, or reptiles.

At the close of the seven days Mucalinda the serpent-king seeing the clear, cloudless sky, uncoiled the body of the Blessed One, and leaving his own form took the guise of a young man, and stood in front of the Blessed One, saluting Him with joined hands.

And the Blessed One perceiving this uttered on that occasion this pæan of joy:—

Happy is seclusion to him who is contented, to him who has heard the Truth, and to him who sees. Happy is goodwill in this world, and so is restraint towards all beings. Happy in this world is passionless, the passing beyond sense-desires. The suppression of the "I" conceit is indeed the highest happiness.

The Dhamma as the Teacher

(Anguttara Nikāya—Catukka Nipāta)

On one occasion soon after my Enlightenment, I was dwelling at the foot of the Ajapāla Banyan Tree by the bank of the Nerañjarā river. As I was engaged in solitary meditation the following thought arose in my mind:—Painful indeed is to live without someone to pay reverence and show deference. How if I should live near an ascetic or Brahmin respecting and reverencing him?

Then it occurred to me:—Should I live near another ascetic or Brahmin, respecting and reverencing him, to perfect the mass of *morality* which has not been perfected? But I do not see in this world together with gods, Māras, and Brahmas, amongst beings together with ascetics, Brahmins, gods and men, another ascetic or Brahmin who is superior to me in morality and whom I could associate, respecting and reverencing.

Should I live near another ascetic or Brahmin, respecting and reverencing, in order to perfect the mass of *concentration* which has not been perfected? But I do not see in this world any ascetic or Brahmin who is superior to me in concentration whom I should associate, respecting and reverencing.

Should I live near another ascetic or Brahmin, respecting and reverencing, in order to perfect the mass of *wisdom* which has not been perfected? But I do not see in this world any ascetic or Brahmin who is superior to me in wisdom whom I should associate, respecting and reverencing.

Should I live near another ascetic or Brahmin, respecting and reverencing, in order to perfect the mass of *emancipation* which has not been perfected? But I do not see in this world any ascetic or Brahmin who is superior to me in emancipation whom I should associate, respecting and reverencing.

Then it occurred to me:—How if I should live respecting and reverencing this very Dhamma which I myself have realised?

Thereupon the Brahmā *Sahampatī* understanding with his own mind my thought, and just as a strong man would stretch his bent arm or bend his stretched arm, even so did he disappear from the Brahma realm and appeared before me. And covering one shoulder with his upper robe and placing his right knee on the ground, he saluted me with clasped hands and said thus:—"It is so, O Blessed One! It is so, O Accomplished One! O Lord, the exalted, supremely Enlightened Ones who were in the past did live respecting and reverencing this very Dhamma. The exalted, supremely Enlightened Ones who will be in the future, will also live respecting and reverencing this very Dhamma. O Lord, may the Blessed One, the exalted, supremely Enlightened One of the present age also live respecting and reverencing this very Dhamma!"

This the Brahmā Sahampatī said and, uttering which, furthermore he spoke as follows:—

Those Enlightened Ones of the past, those of the future, and those of the present age, who dispel the grief of many—all of them lived, will live, and live, respecting the noble Dhamma. This is the nature of the Buddhas.

Therefore he who desires his welfare and expects his greatness should certainly respect the noble Dhamma, remembering the message of the Buddhas.

This the Brahmā Sahampatī said, and, uttering which, he respectfully saluted me and, passing round me to the right, disappeared straightway.

And I knowing the wish of the Brahma did live respecting and reverencing this very Dhamma which I realised and which is suitable to me.

As the Sangha is also endowed with greatness there is also my reverence towards the Sangha[1].

---

1 This discourse was delivered by the Teacher while residing in Jetavana, Sāvatthi, long after the establishment of the Order of the Sangha. He showed His reverence towards the Sangha by asking the Queen Mahā Pajāpati Gotamī to offer to the Sangha the robe especially made for Him.

CHAPTER VI

THE LIFE OF THE BUDDHA

(Continued)

The First Two Converts

(Vinaya–Mahāvagga p. 3)

THEN the Blessed One, at the close of seven days, emerged from that state of concentration, and went from the foot of the *Mucalinda* tree to the *Rājāyatana* tree. Having drawn near, the Blessed One sat at the foot of the Rājāyatana tree in one posture for seven days enjoying the Bliss of Emancipation.

At that time two merchants, *Tapassu* and *Bhallika*, from Ukla, were travelling on their way to that place. Then a *devatā*, who was a blood relative of those two merchants, spoke to them as follows: "The Blessed One, good sirs, is dwelling at the foot of the Rājāyatana tree, soon after His Enlightenment. Go and serve the Blessed One with flour and honey-comb. It will conduce to your well-being and happiness for a long time."

Thereupon the two merchants, Tapassu and Bhallika, took with them flour and honey-comb and went where the Blessed One was, and, drawing near, respectfully saluted Him and stood at one side. Thus standing they addressed the Blessed one as follows:

"O Lord, may the Blessed One accept this flour and honey-comb so that it may long be to our well-being and happiness!"[1]

---

1 The Buddha fasted for seven weeks after His Enlightenment. It was on the fiftieth day that these two merchants offered this Dāna to the Buddha.

Then it occurred to the Blessed One:—"The Tathāgatas do not accept (food) with their hands. How shall I accept this flour and honey-comb?"

Forthwith the four Great Kings[1] understood the thoughts of the Blessed One with their own minds and from the four directions offered Him four bowls made of stone, saying: "O Lord, may the Blessed One accept herewith this flour and honey-comb!"

The Blessed One accepted the new bowls made of stone, and receiving the flour and honey-comb He ate.

Then the two merchants, Tapassu and Bhallika, seeing that the Blessed One has removed his hands from the bowl, prostrated themselves before the feet of the Blessed one and said: "We, O Lord, seek refuge in the Blessed One and in the Dhamma. May the Blessed One treat us as lay disciples who have sought refuge from today till death!"

These were the first disciples in the world who took the twofold formula.[2]

* * * *

The Invitation to Teach the Dhamma

Then the Blessed One, at the end of seven days, emerged from that state of concentration, and went from the foot of *Rājāyatana* to the *Ajapāla* Banyan tree, and drawing near dwelt at the foot of that tree. And as He was engaged in solitary meditation the following thought occurred to Him:—This Dhamma

1 The Guardian Deities of the four Quarters.

2 Viz:—the Buddha and the Dhamma,—*Buddhaṅ saraṇaṅ gacchāmi—Dhammaṅ saraṇaṅ gachchāmi*. The Sangha or the Order was not in existence then.

which I have realised is indeed profound, difficult to perceive, difficult to understand, tranquil, exalted, not within the sphere of logic, subtle, and to be understood by the wise. These beings are attached to desires, cling to desires, and delight in desires. To those who are attached to desires, cling to desires, and delight in desires, this causally connected "Dependent Arising" is a matter which is difficult to perceive. And this Nibbāna, the quietude of all activities, the renunciation of all passions, the destruction of craving, the dispassion and the cessation, is also a matter which is not easily perceptible. If I too were to preach this Dhamma, the others would not understand me. That will be wearisome to me, that will be tiresome to me.

Then these wonderful verses unheard before occurred to the Blessed One:—

With difficulty have I realised (the Dhamma). No need to proclaim it now. This Dhamma is not easily understood by those who are overcome by lust and hatred. The lust-ridden, shrouded by the mass of darkness, do not see this Dhamma, which goes against the stream, which is abstruse, profound, difficult to perceive, and subtle.

As the Blessed One reflected thus His mind turned to inaction and not to the preaching of the Dhamma.

Thereupon Brahmā Sahampatī understanding with his mind the thoughts of the Blessed One thought thus:

Verily this world will perish, verily this world will perish entirely, since the mind of the Tathāgata, the exalted, the Buddha Supreme, is turned to inaction and not to the preaching of the Dhamma.

Then the Brahmā Sahampatī, just as a strong person would stretch his bent arm or would bend his stretched arm, even so did he vanish from the Brahma realm and appeared before the Blessed One. Covering one shoulder with his upper robe and placing his right knee on the ground, he saluted the Blessed One with clasped hands and said as follows:—"O Lord, may the Blessed One expound the Dhamma! May the Accomplished One expound the Dhamma! There are beings with little dust in their eyes, who, not hearing the Dhamma, will fall away. There will be those who will understand the Dhamma."

This the Brahmā Sahampati said, and, uttering which, furthermore said :—

"In ancient times there arose in Magadha a Dhamma, impure, thought out by the corrupted. Open this Door to the Deathless. May they hear the Dhamma, understood by the stainless! Just as one standing on the summit of a rocky mountain would behold the people around, even so may the All-seeing, Wise One ascend this palace of Dhamma! May the Sorrowless One look down upon the people who are plunged in grief and are overcome by birth and decay!

"Rise, O Hero, the victor in battle, the caravan-leader, the debt-free One, and wander in the world! May the Blessed One preach the Dhamma! There will be those who will understand the Dhamma."

When he said so the Blessed One spoke to the Brahmā Sahampatī thus:—The following thought, O Brahma, occurred to me. This Dhamma which I have realised is not easily understood by those who are overcome by lust and hatred. The lust-ridden, shrouded by the mass of darkness, do not see this Dhamma, which goes against the stream, which is abstruse, profound, difficult to perceive, and subtle.

As I reflected thus, O Brahma, my mind turned to inaction and not to expound the Dhamma.

For the second time the Brahmā Sahampati made the same request, and the Blessed One made the same reply.

For the third time the Brahmā Sahampatī made the same request.

Thereupon the Blessed One, knowing the request of the Brahma, out of pity for beings, surveyed the world with His Buddha vision.

As the Blessed One surveyed the world with His Buddha vision, He saw beings with little and much dust in their eyes, with keen and dull intellect, with good and bad characteristics, who are easy and difficult to be taught, and few others who live perceiving the dangers of evil and of a future life.

As in the case of a blue, red or white lotus pond, some lotuses are born in the water, grow in the water, immersed in the water, and thrive plunged in the water; some are born in the water, grow in the water, and remain on the surface of the water; some others are born in the water, grow in the water, and remain emerging out of the water, unstained by the water.

Even so as the Blessed One surveyed the world with His Buddha vision He saw beings with little and much dust in their eyes, with keen and dull intellect, with good and bad characteristics, who are easy and difficult to be taught, and few others who live perceiving the dangers of evil and of a future life. And He addressed the Brahmā Sahampatī in a verse thus:—

"Opened to them are the Doors to the Deathless.[1] Let those who have ears send forth faith. Being aware of the weariness, O Brahma, I did not preach amongst men this glorious and excellent Dhamma."

Then Brahmā Sahampatī thinking—I made myself the occasion for the Blessed One to expound the Dhamma—respectfully saluted the Blessed One and, passing round Him to the right, straightway disappeared.

* * * *

On the Way to Benares to Preach the Dhamma

(Mahāvagga—p. 7.—Majjhima Nikāya No. 26)

Then the following thought occurred to the Blessed One:—To whom shall I preach the Dhamma first? Who will understand the Dhamma quickly?

And the Blessed One thought thus: This Ālāra Kālāma,[2] is learned, clever, wise, and has for long been with little dust in his eyes. How if I were to preach the Dhamma to him first? He will understand this Dhamma quickly.

Then a deity appeared before the Blessed One and said:—"Lord! Ālāra Kālāma died a week ago."

---

1 Note the positive term *Amata* (Immortality) which is applied to Nibbāna.

2 The first religious teacher who taught the Bodhisatta the *Jhanas* extending to "The Realm of Nothingness." See p 19.

To the Blessed One also the intelligence arose that Ālāra Kālāma died a week ago.

And the Blessed One thought:—Very learned indeed is Ālāra Kālāma. If he had heard the Dhamma, he would have quickly understood the Dhamma.

Again the Blessed One reflected: To whom shall I preach the Dhamma first? Who will understand the Dhamma quickly?

And He thought:—Uddaka Rāmaputta[1] is indeed learned, clever, wise, and has for long been with little dust in his eyes. How if I were to preach the Dhamma to him first! He will quickly understand the Dhamma.

Then a deity appeared before Him and said:—"Lord! Uddaka Rāmaputta died the evening before."

To the Blessed One also the knowledge arose that Uddaka Rāmaputta died the evening before.

And the Blessed One thought: Very learned indeed is Uddaka Rāmaputta. If he had heard the Dhamma, he would have understood the Dhamma quickly.

Again the Blessed One reflected: To whom shall I first preach this Dhamma? Who will understand the Dhamma quickly?

And He thought:—Those Five Bhikkhus were very helpful to me. They ministered to me when I was striving after the Highest. How if I were to

1 The second religious teacher who taught the Bodhisatta the highest state of mundane spiritual development—"The Realm of Neither Perception nor Non-Perception." See p. 21.

preach the Dhamma to them first! Where do they reside at present?

Then with Divine Eye, clear and superhuman, He perceived that they were in the Deer Park at Isipatana in Benares. So the Blessed one stayed at Uruvelā as long as He wished and set out for Benares.

Between Gayā and the Bodhi[1], Upaka, a wandering ascetic, saw the Blessed One travelling on the high way and said:—"Extremely clear are your senses, friend? Pure and clean is your complexion. On account of whom have you renounced, friend? Who is your teacher? Whose doctrine do you profess?"

When he said thus the Blessed One spoke to him in verse:—

All have I overcome, all do I know.
From all am I detached, all have I renounced.
Wholly absorbed am I in the destruction of craving (Arahantship).
Having comprehended all by myself whom shall I call my teacher?

No teacher[2] have I. An equal to me there is not.
In the world together with gods there is no rival to me.

Indeed, an Arahant am I in this world.
An unsurpassed teacher am I.
Alone am I the All-enlightened.
Cool and appeased am I.

To establish the wheel of Dhamma I go to the city of Kāsi.
In this blind world I shall beat the drum of Deathlessness.

---

1 The Tree of Enlightenment.

2 The Buddha made such a statement because He attained Enlightenment by Himself without the aid of a teacher. He had teachers before His Enlightenment. But nobody taught Him the way to attain Buddhahood.

Then, friend, you do admit that you are an Arahant, a limitless Conqueror.

"Like me are conquerors who have attained to the destruction of defilements.[1] All the evil conditions have I conquered. Hence, Upaka, I am called a conqueror."

When I spoke thus, Upaka, the wandering ascetic, said:—"It may be so, friend." Nodding his head, he turned into a side road and departed.

And I wandering from place to place, arrived in due course at the Deer Park in Isipatana, near Benares, where the five Bhikkhus were.

They saw me coming from afar, and seeing me they decided amongst themselves:—Friends, this ascetic Gotama is coming. He is luxurious. He has given up striving and has turned into a life of abundance. He should not be greeted and waited upon. His bowl and robe should not be taken. Nevertheless a seat should be prepared. If he wishes, let him sit down.

However, as I continued to draw near, the five Bhikkhus were not able to abide by their decision. One came forward and took my bowl and robe, another prepared a seat, and yet another kept water for my feet. Nevertheless they addressed me by name and the title 'friend' (Āvuso)[2].

At this I told the five Bhikkhus: "Do not, O Bhikkhus, address the Tathāgata[3] by name or by the title 'friend.' An Exalted One, O Bhikkhus,

---

1 I.e. Arahantship.

2 *Āvuso*—a term by which the seniors address the juniors.

3 See p. 9, note 2.

is the Tathāgata, a Fully Enlightened One is He. Give ear, O Bhikkhus, the Immortal has been attained. I shall instruct and teach the Dhamma. If you act according to my instructions, you will before long realise, by your own intuitive wisdom, and live, attaining in this life itself, that supreme consummation of the Holy Life, for the sake of which sons of noble families rightly leave the household for the homeless."

When I spoke thus the five Bhikkhus addressed me as follows:—"By that demeanour of yours, friend Gotama, by that discipline, by these painful austerities, you did not attain to any super-human specific knowledge and insight worthy of an Arya. How will you, when now you have become luxurious, have given up striving, and have turned into a life of abundance, gain any such superhuman specific knowledge and insight worthy of an Arya ?"

Thereupon I replied to the five Bhikkhus:—"The Tathāgata, O Bhikkhus, is not luxurious, has not given up striving, and has not turned into a life of abundance. An Exalted One, O Bhikkhus, is the Tathāgata, a Fully Enlightened One is he. Give ear, O Bhikkhus! Immortality has been attained. I shall instruct and teach the Dhamma. If you act according to my instructions, you will before long realise, by your own intuitive wisdom, and live attaining in this life itself, that supreme consummation of the Holy Life, for the sake of which sons of noble families rightly leave the household for the homeless."

For the second time the Bhikkhus repeated the same words.

For the second time the Blessed One replied in the same way.

For the third time the Bhikkhus repeated the same words.

Thereupon the Blessed One replied:—"Do you know, O Bhikkhus, that I ever spoke to you thus before?"

"Nay, indeed, Lord!"

"The Tathāgata, O Bhikkhus, is not luxurious, has not given up striving, and has not turned into a life of abundance. An Exalted One, O Bhikkhus, is the Tathāgata; a Fully Enlightened One is He. Give ear, O Bhikkhus! Immortality has been attained. I shall instruct and teach the Dhamma. If you act according to my instructions, you will before long realise, by your own intuitive wisdom, and live attaining in this life itself, that supreme consummation of the Holy Life, for the sake of which sons of noble families rightly leave the household for the homeless."

The Blessed One was then able to *convince the five Bhikkhus.*

Two of the Bhikkhus I instruct, whilst three went out for alms. With what the three Bhikkhus bring from their alms round we six maintain ourselves. Three of the Bhikkhus I instruct, whilst two Bhikkhus go out for alms. With what the two Bhikkhus bring from their alms round we six maintain ourselves.

And those five Bhikkhus, thus admonished and instructed by me, being themselves subject to birth, decay, death, sorrow, and passions, realised the wretchedness (of life) and seeking out the birthless, decayless, diseaseless, deathless, sorrowless, passionless, incomparable Supreme Peace, Nibbāna, attained that incomparable Security, Nibbāna, which is free from birth, decay, disease, death, sorrow, and passions. The knowledge and insight arose in them that their Deliverance was unshakable, that it was their last birth, and that there would be no existence again.[1]

---

1 The five Bhikkhus who thus attained Arahantship and became His first disciples were—*Kondañña, Bhaddiya, Vappa, Mahānāma,* and *Assaji.*

When the Bodhisatta was only five days old King Suddhodana, in accordance with the ancient custom, summoned eight learned Brahmins to name the infant Prince and predict his future. They named him *Siddhattha* (Wish-fulfilled).

The senior seven of them foretold that the prince would either become a Universal Monarch or a Supreme Buddha. *Kondañña,* the youngest and the cleverest, boldly declared that the Prince would definitely become a Buddha.

These aged Brahmins had four sons, named *Bhaddiya, Vappa, Mahānāma,* and *Assaji. Kondañña,* accompanied by them, retired to the forest as ascetics in anticipation of the renunciation of Prince Siddhattha.

These five monks dwelt at *Uruvelā* and attended on the Bodhisatta when he was endeavouring to attain Buddhahood.

For six years the Bodhisatta made a superhuman struggle to achieve his noble goal, but the more he tormented his body farther the goal receded from him. He realised the utter futility of self-mortification. He was completely exhausted for want of substantial food. He was reduced to almost a skeleton. Consequently he gave up his useless penances and severe austerities and began to nourish his body sparingly to regain his lost strength.

Disappointed at this unexpected change of method his favourite followers deserted him and went to Isipatana. Soon after their departure the Bodhisatta attained Buddhahood. Seven weeks after His Enlightenment the Buddha went to Isipatana and expounded the *"Dhammacakka Sutta"* to those five monks. Hearing which *Kondañña,* the eldest, attained *Sotāpatti,* the first stage of Sainthood. The other four attained *Sotāpatti* later. It was after hearing the *"Anattalakkhana Sutta"* that they all attained Arahantship—the final stage of Sainthood.

Kondañña became the first Arahant, and the chief, in seniority, of the Sangha. It was Assaji, one of the five, who "converted" the great *Sāriputta* that became the first chief disciple of the Buddha.

CHAPTER VII

THE LIFE OF THE BUDDHA

(Continued)

The First Discourse of the Buddha

DHAMMACAKKAPPAVATTANA SUTTA[1]

(Mahāvagga — p. 10. Sanyutta V. p. 420)

THUS HAVE I HEARD:—

ON one occasion the Blessed One was residing at the Deer Park[2], in Isipatana, near Benares. Thereupon the Blessed One addressed the five Bhikkhus[3] as follows:—

---

1. "Dhammacakka" is frequently rendered by "The Wheel of Truth", "The Wheel of Righteousness", "The Kingdom of Righteousness", etc According to the commentators "*Dhamma*" here means wisdom or knowledge, and "*cakka*" means establishment. *Dhammacakka*, therefore, means "The Establishment of Wisdom".

   In this discourse the Buddha expounds the Middle Path which He Himself discovered and which became one of the salient features of His teaching. He opens the discourse by advising the monks to avoid the two extremes of sensual indulgence and self-mortification. The former retards one's spiritual progress, the latter weakens one's intellect.

   This Dhammacakka Sutta is one of the most favourite sermons of the devotees. It is committed to memory and repeated daily by many a follower. King Asoka also advises both monk and laic to meditate constantly on this sermon of the Buddha.
2. Modern Sarnath where, in a former existence the Master sacrificed His life to save a helpless doe and her unborn little one. The locality takes its modern name from the Bodhisatta who in that ancient birth was SĀRANGA NĀTHA, Protector of the Deer.
3. *Pañcavaggiye Bhikkhū*. See p.58, note 1.

There are two extremes, O Bhikkhus, which should be avoided by a recluse.

This continual attachment to **sensual enjoyment**[1] (*Kāmasukhallikānuyoga*) which is base, vulgar, worldly, ignoble, and profitless; and this addiction to **self-mortification**[2] (*Attakilamathānuyoga*) which is painful, ignoble, and profitless.

Avoiding these two extremes[3], O Bhikkhus, the Tathāgata has discovered the **Middle Path** (*Majjhimā Paṭipadā*) which yields sight, knowledge, which tends to Peace (*Vupasamāya*), Higher Wisdom (*Abhiññāya*), Enlightenment (*Sambodhāya*), and Nibbāna.

What, O Bhikkhus, is that Middle Path the Tathāgata has discovered which yields sight and knowledge, which tends to Peace, Higher Wisdom, Enlightenment, and Nibbāna?

It is this **Noble Eightfold Path**—namely, Right Understanding (*Sammā-Diṭṭhi*), Right Thoughts (*Sammā-Sankappa*), Right Speech (*Sammā-Vācā*), Right Action (*Sammā-Kammanta*), Right Livelihood (*Sammā-Ājīva*), Right Endeavour (*Sammā-Vāyāma*), Right Mindfulness (*Sammā-Sati*), and Right Concentration (*Samma Samadhi*). This, O Bhikkhus, is the Middle Path which the Tathāgata has found out.

---

1. This first extreme is the view of materialists. Cārvāka who flourished in the time of the Buddha held this view.
2. The five monks along with the ascetics of old adhered to this belief.
3. The Buddha was conversant with both views and was able to speak of their profitlessness from personal experience He criticised those views and suggested the most practicable, rational, and beneficial path which alone leads to perfect purity and perfect Deliverance.

1. Now, this, O Bhikkhus, is the **Noble Truth of Suffering**:—

Birth is suffering, decay is suffering, disease is suffering, death is suffering, to be united with the unloved is suffering, to be separated from the loved is suffering, not to receive what one craves for is suffering, in brief the five Aggregates of Attachment[1] are suffering.

2. Now this, O Bhikkhus, is the **Noble Truth of the Cause of Suffering**[2]:—

It is the craving which produces rebirth, accompanied by passionate clinging, welcoming this and that (life). It is the craving for sensual pleasures, (*Kāmataṇhā*) craving for becoming (*Bhavataṇha*)[3] and craving far annihilation (*Vibhavataṇha*).[4]

3. Now, this, O Bhikkhus, is the **Noble Truth of the Cessation of Suffering**:—It is the complete separation from, and destruction, of this very craving, its forsaking, renunciation, liberation and detachment[5].

---

1. *Pañcakkhandha*—According to Buddhism this so-called being is composed of five groups, viz: *Rūpa*, matter, *Vedanā*, sensations, *Saññā*, perceptions, *Sankhārā*, volitional activities, and *Viññāṇa*, consciousness.

   These are the five psycho-physical component parts that constitute an individual. Matter is composed of forces and qualities. Mind too is composed of mental properties, *Cetasikas*. They are fifty-two in number. Of them *Vedanā* and *Saññā* are usually treated as two distinct groups. The remaining fifty are collectively called *Sankhāra*.

2. "Christianity can never explain suffering.—Rev. J. Estlin Carpenter, D.D. in Buddhism and Christianity.

3. *Bhava Taṇhā* is craving connected with the view of Eternalism *(Sassata Diṭṭhi)*.

4. *Vibhava Taṇhā* is craving connected with the view of Nihilism *(Uccheda Diṭṭhi)*.

5. I.e., Nibbāna

4. Now, this, O Bhikkhus, is the **Noble Truth of the Path leading to the Cessation of Suffering:—**

It is this Noble Eightfold Path—namely, Right Understanding, Right Thoughts, Right Speech, Right Action, Right Livelihood, Right Endeavour, Right Mindfulness, and Right Concentration.

* * * *

1. i. **"This is the Noble Truth of Suffering."**

Thus, O Bhikkhus, with respect to things unheard before, there arose in me the eye, the knowledge, the wisdom, the insight, and the light.

ii. **"This Noble Truth of Suffering should be comprehended."** *(Pariññeyya).*

Thus, O Bhikkhus, with respect to things unheard before, there arose in me the eye, the knowledge, the wisdom, the insight, and the light.

iii. **"This Noble Truth of Suffering has been comprehended."** (*Pariññāta*)

Thus, O Bhikkhus, with respect to things unheard before, there arose in me the eye, the knowledge, the wisdom, the insight, and the light.

2. i. **"This is the Noble Truth of the Cause of Suffering."**

Thus, O Bhikkhus, with respect to things unheard before, there arose in me the eye, the knowledge, the wisdom, the insight, and the light.

ii. **"This Noble Truth of the Cause of Suffering should be eradicated (*Pahātabba*)."**

Thus, O Bhikkhus, with respect to things unheard before, there arose in me the eye, the knowledge, the wisdom, the insight, and the light.

iii. **This Noble Truth of the Cause of Suffering has been eradicated** *(Pahīna).*"

Thus, O Bhikkhus, with respect to things unheard before, there arose in me the eye, the knowledge, the wisdom, the insight, and the light.

3. i. "**This is the Noble Truth of the Cessation of Suffering.**"

Thus, O Bhikkhus, with respect to things unheard before, there arose in me the eye, the knowledge, the wisdom, the insight, and the light.

ii. "**This Noble Truth of the Cessation of Suffering should be realised** (*Sacchikātabba*)."

Thus, O Bhikkhus, with respect to things unheard before, there arose in me the eye, the knowledge, the wisdom, the insight, and the light.

iii. **This Noble Truth of the Cessation of Suffering has been realised** (*Sacchikata*)."

Thus, O Bhikkhus, with respect to things unheard before, there arose in me the eye, the knowledge, the wisdom, the insight, and the light.

4. i. "**This is the Noble Truth of the Path leading to the Cessation of Suffering.**"

Thus, O Bhikkhus, with respect to things unheard before, there arose in me the eye, the knowledge, the wisdom, the insight, and the light.

ii. **"This Noble Truth of the Path leading to the Cessation of Suffering should be developed** (*Bhavetabba*)."

Thus, O Bhikkhus, with respect to things unheard before, there arose in me the eye, the knowledge, the wisdom, the insight, and the light.

iii. **"This Noble Truth of the Path leading to the Cessation of Suffering has been developed** (*Bhavita*)."

Thus, O Bhikkhus, with respect to things unheard before, there arose in me the eye, the knowledge, the wisdom, the insight, and the light.

As long as, O Bhikkhus, the absolute true intuitive knowledge regarding these Four Noble Truths under their three aspects[1] and twelve modes[2] was not perfectly clear to me, so long I did not acknowledge, in this world together with gods, Māras and Brahmas, amongst the hosts of ascetics and priests, gods and men, that I had gained the incomparable, Supreme Enlightenment. When, O Bhikkhus, the absolute true intuitive knowledge regarding these Four Noble Truths under their three aspects and twelve modes became perfectly clear to me, then only did I acknowledge in this world together with gods, Māras, and Brahmas, amongst the hosts of ascetics and priests, gods and men, that I had gained the incomparable Supreme Enlightenment.

---

1. The three aspects are—the knowledge of the Truths *(Sacca Ñaṇa)*, the knowledge as regards the function of Truth *(Kicca Ñaṇa)*, and the knowledge that the function has been accomplished *(Kata Ñāṇa)*
2. Each Truth consists of the above three aspects. Thus four Truths consist of twelve modes.

And there arose in me the knowledge and insight: "Unshakable is the deliverance of my mind, this is my last birth, and now there is no existence again!"

This the Blessed One said, and the delighted Bhikkhus applauded the words of the Blessed One.

When this doctrine was being expounded there arose in the venerable Kondañña the dustless, stainless Eye of Truth[1]. Whatsoever has arisen all that must inevitably perish.

When the Buddha expounded this "Dhamacakka", the earth-bound deities exclaimed:—"This excellent Dhammacakka, which could not be expounded by any ascetic, priest, god, Māra, or Brahma in this world, was expounded by the Blessed One at the Deer Park, in Isipatana, near Benares."

Hearing which the devas *Cātummahārājika*, *Tāvatiṃsa*, *Yāma*, *Tuista*, *Nimmāṇarati*, *Paranimmitavasavatti*, and the Brahmas of *Brahma Pārisajja*, *Brahma Purohita*, *Mahā Brahma*, *Parittābha*, *Appamāṇābha*, *Ābhassara*, *Parittasubha*, *Appamāṇa-Subha*, *Subhakiṇha*, *Vehapphala*, *Aviha*, *Attappa*, *Sudassa*, *Sudassī*, and *Akaniṭṭha* also made the same cry.

Thus at that very moment. at that very instant, this cry extended as far as the Brahma realm. These ten thousand world systems quaked, trembled, and violently shook.

A great brilliant aura, surpassing the effulgence of the gods, appeared in the world.

---

1. He attained the first stage of Sainthood *(Sotāpatti)*. The other Bhikkhus attained *Sotāpatti* later.

Then the Blessed One said, "Friends, Kondañña has indeed understood. Friends, Kondañña has indeed understood."

Therefore the venerable Kondañña was named *Aññāta Kondañña*.

* * * *

The Second Discourse

(Anattalakkhaṇa Sutta)
(Mahāvagga p. 13. Sanyutta Nikāya III; 66).

On one occasion the Blessed One was dwelling at the Deer Park, in Isipatana, near Benares. Then the Blessed One addressed the Band of five Bhikkhus, saying, "O Bhikkhus!"

"Lord!" they replied.

Thereupon the Blessed One spoke as follows:

"The body *(Rūpa)*, O Bhikkhus, is soulless (*Anatta*). If, O Bhikkhus, there were in this a soul,[1] then this body would not be subject to ill. "Let this body be thus, let this body be not thus,"—such possibilities would also exist. But, O Bhikkhus, inasmuch as this body is soulless, it is subject to ill, and no possibility exists for (ordering)—"Let this be so, let this not be so."

In like manner sensations (*Vedanā*), perceptions (*Saññā*), volitional activities (*Sankhāra*) and consciousness *(Viññāṇa)*,[2] are soulless[3].

1. A permanent unchanging "entity" or "ego" created by a God or emanating from a *Paramātma*.
2. The so-called being is composed of these five Groups. Outside them there is *no* being. If one removes the Groups, nothing remains. A *Saul* abides neither in any one Group nor in all of them nor outside them.
3. The Buddha makes the same statement as above in connection with each of the remaining four component parts of the so-called being.

"What think ye, O Bhikkhus, Is this body permanent or impermanent?"

"Impermanent (*Anicca*), Lord."

"Is that which is impermanent, happy or painful?"

"It is painful (*Dukkha*), Lord."

"Is it justifiable, then, to think of that which is impermanent, painful, and transitory:—'This is mine; this am I; this is my soul?'"

"Certainly not, Lord!"

[1]Similarly, O Bhikkhus, sensations, perceptions, volitional activities, and consciousness are impermanent and painful. "Is it justifiable to think of these which are impermanent, painful and transitory.—This is mine; this am I; this is my soul?[2]"

"Certainly not, Lord!"

"Then, O Bhikkhus, all body, whether past, present or future, personal or extraneous, coarse or subtle, low or high, far or near, should be understood by right knowledge in its real nature—This is not mine; this am I not; this is not my soul.

"All sensations, perceptions, volitional activities, and consciousness, whether past, present or future, personal or extraneous, coarse or subtle, low or high, far or near, should be understood by right knowledge in their real nature as:—These are not mine; these am I not; these are not my soul.

---

1. The Buddha raises similar queries with regard to each of the other constituents of being. The translation is abridged here.

2. With Craving (*Taṇhā*) one thinks—"This is mine! With Pride (*Māna*) one thinks—"This am I," with Error (*Diṭṭhi*) one thinks "This is my soul." These are the three false notions or *maññanās*.

"The learned Ariyan disciple who sees thus, O Bhikkhus, gets a disgust for body, for sensations, for perceptions, for volitional activities, for consciousness, gets detached from the abhorrent thing, and is emancipated through detachment. Then dawns on him the knowledge—'Emancipated am I.' He understands that rebirth is ended, lived is the Holy life, done what should be done, there is none other beyond this."

This the Blessed One said, and the delighted Bhikkhus applauded the words of the Blessed One.

When this doctrine was being expounded the minds of the group of five Bhikkhus were freed of defilements, without any attachment[1].

1 That is—they all became Arahants.

CHAPTER VIII

THE LIFE OF THE BUDDHA

(Concluded)

The Sending of the Missionaries

(Mahāvagga p. 20)

AT that time there were sixty-one Arahants[1] in the world.

Then the Blessed One addressed the Bhikkhus and said:—

"Freed am I, O Bhikkhus, from all bonds whether divine or human. You, too, O Bhikkhus, are freed from all bonds whether divine or human.

"Go forth, O Bhikkhus, for the good of the many, for the happiness of the many, out of compassion for the world, for the good, benefit, and happiness of gods and men. Let not two go by one way. Preach, O Bhikkhus, the Dhamma, excellent in the beginning, excellent in the middle, excellent in the end, both in the spirit and in the letter. Proclaim the Holy Life, altogether perfect and pure.

---

1. They were—the Buddha, the Band of Five Bhikkhus, Yasa, and his forty-four friends.

It is related that Yasa, a millionaire's son, realising the vanities of worldly life, stole away from home at night and meeting the Buddha attained Arahantship. His friends hearing this good news saw the Buddha, and attaining Arahantship, entered the Order. The venerable Yasa's parents were the first lay disciples to take the Three Refuges.

"There are beings with little dust in their eyes, who not hearing the Dhamma will fall away. There will be those who understand the Dhamma.

"I, too, O Bhikkhus, will go to Uruvelā, to Senānigāma, in order to preach the Dhamma."

* * * *

The Passing away of the Buddha

(Digha Nikāya, Vol. II, Parinibbāna Sutta, No. 16, p. 120)

Then the Blessed One addressed the disciples and said:—"Behold, O disciples! Now I speak to you. Transient are all component things. Strive on with diligence. In no long time the Final Release of the Accomplished One will take place. After the lapse of three months from now, the Accomplished One will attain Parinibbāna." Thus the Blessed One said; after which the Auspicious One, the Teacher, furthermore addressed the disciples as follows:—

"Ripe is my age; short is my life. Leaving you I shall go. I have made myself my Refuge. Be diligent, O disciples, mindful and virtuous. With thoughts collected guard your minds. He who lives strenuously in this Dispensation will escape the cycle of rebirth and put an end to suffering."

* * * *

His Last Meal

(From Digha Nikāya, Vol. II,
Parinibbāna Sutta, No. 16, p. 126)

Now at that time the Blessed One was staying at Pāvā in the mango grove of Cunda, the smith.

Then Cunda, the smith, heard that the Blessed One had arrived at Pāvā and was staying in his mango grove. So Cunda went to where the Blessed One was, and approaching Him, respectfully saluted Him and sat at one side. As he sat thus, the Blessed One instructed, incited, inspired and gladdened him with a religious discourse.

Then Cunda who was thus instructed, inspired and gladdened by the Blessed One spoke to the Buddha as follows:—

"Lord, let the Blessed One accept my alms for tomorrow together with the company of disciples."

The Blessed One assented by His silence.

Thereupon Cunda, the smith, knowing that the Blessed One had accepted his invitation, rose from his seat, respectfully saluted the Blessed One, passed round Him to the right, and departed. And Cunda, after that night was over, made ready in his house choice food both hard and soft, together with a large quantity of *Sūkaramaddava*[1], and intimated the time to the Blessed One, saying:—"It is time, O Lord! Alms is ready."

Then the Blessed One dressed Himself, in the forenoon, and taking bowl and robe went, together with the company of disciples, to the abode of Cunda, the smith, and sat on the prepared seat. Seated thus, the Blessed One addressed Cunda as follows:—"O Cunda, serve me with that *Sūkaramaddava* which you have prepared; but serve the company of disciples with other food—both hard and soft."

---

1. *Sūkaramaddava*—According to the commentary it is tender boar's flesh. Some say it is a kind of mushroom. See "Questions of Milinda" Vol. 1 p. 244 and "Dialogues of the Buddha" part 2, p. 137, N. 1.

"So be it, Lord!" said Cunda in response to the words of the Blessed One, and did accordingly.

Thereupon the Blessed One said to Cunda:— "Whatsoever, Cunda, remains of the *Sūkaramaddava*, bury that in a hole in the ground; for, Cunda, I perceive not in this world of gods, Māras, and Brahmas, and amongst other beings, together with ascetics and priests, and gods and men, anyone who could eat this food and well digest it, save the Accomplished One."

"So be it Lord!" responded Cunda, and buried the remainder of that *Sūkaramaddava* in a hole in the ground, and approaching the Blessed One, respectfully saluted Him, and sat at one side. As he was seated thus, the Blessed One instructed, incited, inspired and gladdened him with a religious discourse and departed.

Then arose in the Blessed One, who partook of the meal of Cunda, the smith, a grievous sickness, a dysentery, and severe pains, resembling those of death. But the Blessed One, conscious and reflective, bore them up unwaveringly.

Thereupon the Blessed One addressed Ānanda and said:—"Come, Ānanda, let us go to Kusināra."

"So be it Lord!" replied Ānanda.

* * * *

His Last Convert

(From Dīgha Nikāya, Vol. II; Parinibbāna Sutta; No. 16, p. 148)

At that time a wandering ascetic named Subhadda[1] was living at Kusinārā. He heard the news that the Ascetic Gotama would attain Pari-Nibbāna in the last watch of that night. And he thought:— "I have heard grown-up and elderly teachers and their teachers, the wandering ascetics, say that seldom and very seldom, indeed, do Exalted, Fully Enlightened Arahants arise in this world. To-night in the last watch the Ascetic Gotama will attain Pari-Nibbāna. A doubt has arisen in me, and I have confidence in the Ascetic Gotama. Capable, indeed, is the Ascetic Gotama to teach the doctrine so that I may dispel my doubts."

Thereupon Subhadda, the wandering ascetic, went to Upavattana Sāla Grove of the Mallas where the venerable Ānanda was, and approaching him spoke as follows:— "I have heard grown-up and elderly teachers and their teachers, the wandering ascetics, say that seldom, and very seldom, indeed, do Exalted, Fully Enlightened Arahants arise in this world. To-night in the last watch the Ascetic Gotama will attain Pari-Nibbāna. A doubt has arisen in me, and I have confidence in the Ascetic Gotama. Capable, indeed, is

1. This Subhadda, the wandering ascetic, should be distinguished from Subhadda who entered the Order in his old age. It was the latter who remarked that the death of the Buddha was no occasion for sorrow as the Bhikkhus were free to do whatever they liked, without being bound by the injunctions of the Master. This remark of Subhadda prompted the Venerable Kassapa to take immediate steps to hold a convocation of the Dhamma and Vinaya.

the Ascetic Gotama to teach the doctrine so that I may dispel my doubts. Shall I, O Ānanda, obtain a glimpse of the Ascetic Gotama?"

When he spoke thus, the venerable Ānanda said:—"Enough, friend Subhaddha, do not worry the Accomplished One. The Blessed One is wearied."

For the second and third time Subhadda made his request, and for the second and third time Ānanda replied in the same manner.

The Blessed One heard the conversation between the venerable Ānanda and the wandering ascetic, and addressing Ānanda said:

"Nay, Ānanda, do not prevent Subhadda. Let Subhadha, O Ananda, behold the Accomplished One. Whatsoever Subhadda will ask of me, all that will be with the desire for knowledge, and not to annoy me. And whatever I shall say in answer he will readily understand."

Thereupon the venerable Ananda told Subhadda the wandering ascetic:—"Go, friend Subhadda, the Blessed One gives you leave."

And Subhadda, the wandering ascetic, went to where the Blessed One was, and approaching Him, rejoiced with Him, and exchanging friendly greetings sat on one side. Seated thus, Subhadda, the wandering ascetic, spoke to the Buddha as follows:—

"There are these ascetics and priests, O Gotama, who are leaders of companies and congregations, who are heads of sects, and are well-known, renowned religious teachers,[1] esteemed as good men

1. They flourished in the time of the Buddha.

by the multitude, as for instance—Pūraṇa Kassapa, Makkhali Gosāla, Ajita Kesakambali, Pakudha Kaccayana, Sañjaya Belaṭṭhiputta, Nigaṇtha Nātaputta,—have they all, as they themselves claim, thoroughly understood or not, or have some of them understood, and some not?"

"Let it be, O Subhadda! Trouble not yourself as to whether all or some have realised or not. I shall teach the doctrine to you. Listen and bear it well in mind. I shall speak."

"So be it, Lord!" replied Subhadda.

The Blessed One spoke as follows:—

"In whatever Dispensation there exists not the Noble Eightfold Path, neither is the first Samaṇa[1], nor the second[2], nor the third[3], nor the fourth[4], is to be found therein. In whatever Dispensation, O Subhadda, there exists the Noble Eightfold Path, there are also to be found the first Samaṇa, the second Samaṇa, the third Samaṇa, and the fourth Samana. In this Dispensation, O Subhadda, there exists the Noble Eightfold Path. Here, indeed, are found the first Samana, the second Samana, the third Samana, and the fourth Samana. The other foreign Schools are empty of Samanas. If, O Subhadda, the disciples lived rightly, the world would not be void of Arahants."

---

1. The first Samaṇa is the *Sotapanna,* literary "The Stream-Winner."
2. The Second Samaṇa is the *Sakadagāmi,* literary "Once-Returner."
3. The Third Samaṇa is the *Anāgāmi,* literary "Never-Returner."
4. The Fourth Samaṇa is the *Arahant,* literary "The Worthy One," who is the Perfect Saint.
   See ch. II, p. 10.

"My age was twenty-nine when I went forth as a seeker after what is good. Now one and fifty years are gone since I was ordained, O Subhadda. Outside this fold there is not a single ascetic who acts even partly in accordance with this realisable doctrine."

Thereupon Subhadda spoke to the Buddha as follows:—

"Excellent, Lord, excellent! It is as if, O Lord, a man were to set upright that which was overturned, or were to reveal that which was hidden, or were to point the way to one who has gone astray, or were to hold a lamp amidst the darkness, so that whoever has eyes may see; even so has the doctrine been expounded in various ways by the Blessed One.

And I, O Lord, seek refuge in the Buddha, the Doctrine, and the Order. May I receive the Lesser and the Higher Ordination in the presence of the Blessed One!"

"Whosoever, Subhadda, being already committed to the other doctrines, desires the Lesser[1] and Higher Ordination[2] in this Dispensation, remains on probation[3]

---

1. *Pabbajjā*—Renunciation. The ordination as a novice is here meant. This is done by donning the yellow robe after having shaved hair and beard and taking the Three Refuges and the Ten Precepts. The novice is called a "*Sāmaṇera.*" He has cut himself off from the world and its ways. Henceforth, by him even his parents are addressed "lay-disciples."
2. *Upasampadā*—This refers to the Higher Ordination, which is bestowed only after the completion of the 20th year of life. He who receives it is a full member of the Order, and is called a *Bhikkhu*. He is bound to observe the *Patimokkha Precepts,* the commission of any of the major offences of which, involves "defeat" and expulsion from the Bhikkhu Order. If willing, he could remain as a Sāmaṇera.
3. A probation is not demanded of the Buddhist aspirant to ordination.

for four months. At the end of four months, the disciples approving, he is ordained and raised to the status of a Bhikkhu. Nevertheless, on understanding I make individual exceptions."

"If, Lord, those already committed to other doctrines, who desire the Lesser and Higher Ordination in this Dispensation remain on probation for four months, and after the lapse of that period, the disciples approving, are received into the Order, I will remain on probation for four months, and at the end of that period, the disciples approving, let me be received into the Order and raised to the status of a Bhikkhu."

Thereupon the Blessed One addressed Ananda and said:—"Then, Ananda, you may ordain Subhadda."

"So be it, Lord!" replied Ananda.

And Subhadda, the wandering ascetic, spoke to the venerable Ananda as follows:—"It is a gain to you, O venerable Ananda! It is indeed a great gain to you, for you have been anointed by the anointment of discipleship in the presence of the Blessed One Himself."

Subhadda, the wandering ascetic, received in the presence of the Blessed One the Lesser and the Higher Ordination.

And in no long time after his Higher Ordination, the venerable Subhadda, living alone, remote from men, strenuous, energetic, and resolute, realised, in this life itself, by his own intuitive wisdom, the consummation of that incomparable life of Holiness, and lived abiding (in that state), for the sake of which sons of noble families rightly leave the householder's life for the homeless life. He perceived that rebirth was ended, completed was the Holy Life, that after this life there was none other.

And the venerable Subhadda became one of the Arahants. He was the last personal convert of the Blessed One.

* * * *

The Last Scene

(Digha Nikāya, Vol. II, Parinibbāna Sutta, No. 16, p. 154)

Then the Blessed One addressed Ananda and said:—

"It may be, Ananda, that you will say thus:— 'Without the Teacher is the Sublime Teaching! There is no Teacher for us.' Nay, Ananda, you should not think thus. Whatever Doctrine and Discipline taught and promulgated by me, Ananda, they will be your Teacher when I am gone."

* * * *

Then the Blessed One addressed the disciples and said:—"If, O disciples, there be a doubt or perplexity in any disciple with regard to the Buddha, Doctrine, Order, and the Practice, question me, and repent not afterwards thinking—We were face to face with the Teacher, yet we were not able to question the Blessed One in His presence."

When He spoke thus, those disciples were silent.

For the second and third time the Blessed One addressed the Disciples in the same way. And for the second and third time the disciples were silent.

Then the Blessed One addressed the disciples and said:—"Perhaps it may be out of respect for the Teacher that you do not question me. Let a friend, O disciples, intimate it to another!"

Still the disciples were silent.

Thereupon the venerable Ananda spoke to the Buddha as follows:—"Wonderful, Lord! Marvellous, Lord! Thus am I pleased with this company of disciples. There is not a single disciple who entertains a doubt or perplexity with regard to the Buddha, the Doctrine, the Order, and the Practice."

"You speak out of faith, Ananda. With regard to this matter there is knowledge in the Accomplished One, that in this company of disciples there is not a single disciple who entertains a doubt or perplexity with regard to the Buddha, the Doctrine, the Order, and the Practice. Of these five hundred disciples, Ananda, he, who is the last, is a Stream-Winner, not subject to fall, but certain and destined for enlightenment[1]."

Then the Blessed One addressed the disciples and said:—"Behold, O disciples, I exhort you. **Subject to change are all component things. Strive on with diligence.**"

These were the last words of the Accomplished One.

* * * *

From Height to Height of Final Liberation

(What follows in the Parinibbāna Sutta is in the words of the disciples who arranged the Lord's Teaching for succeeding generations.)

---

1. The reference was to the venerable Ānanda who, encouraged by those words, attained Arahantship later.

Thereupon the Blessed One attained to the First Ecstasy. Emerging from which He attained in order to the Second, Third, and Fourth Ecstasies. Emerging from the Fourth Ecstasy He attained to "*The Realm of Infinity of Space (Ākāsānañcāyatana).*" Emerging from the Fourth Ecstasy He attained to "*The Realm of Infinity of Consciousness (Viññānañcāyatana).*" Emerging from which He attained to "*The Realm of Nothingness.*" Emerging from which He attained to "*The Realm of neither Perception nor Non-Perception.*" Emerging from which He attained to "*The Cessation of Perceptions and Sensations. (Saññāvedayitanirodha).*"

Thereupon the venerable Ananda addressed the venerable Anuruddha and said: "O, Lord Anuruddha, the Blessed One has passed away."

"Nay, Brother Ananda, the Blessed One has not passed away but has attained to "*The Cessation of Perceptions and Sensations.*"

Then the Blessed One emerged from "*The Cessation of Perceptions and Sensations*" and attained to "*The Realm of neither Perception nor Non-Perception.*" Emerging from which He attained to "*The Realm of Nothingness.*" Emerging from which He attained to "*The Realm of Infinity of Consciousness.*" Emerging from which He attained to "*The Realm of the Infinity of Space.*" Emerging from which He attained to the Fourth Ecstasy. Emerging from which He attained to the Third Ecstasy. Emerging from which He attained to the Second Ecstasy. Emerging from which He attained to the First Ecstasy. Emerging from which He attained to the Second Ecstasy. Emerging from which He attained to the Third Ecstasy. Emerging from which He attained to the Fourth Ecstasy. Emerging from which and, immediately after, the Blessed One finally passed away.

CHAPTER IX

THE DHAMMA

WHAT IS BUDDHISM?

Is it a Philosophy, or a Religion, or an Ethical System?

The Dhamma

THE all-merciful Buddha has passed away, but the sublime Dhamma which He unreservedly bequeathed to humanity still exists in its pristine purity.

Although the Master has left no written records of His Teachings, His distinguished disciples preserved them by commilting to memory and transmitting them orally from generation to generation.

Immediately after the final passing away of the Buddha 500 distinguished Arahants held a convocation to rehearse the Doctrine taught by the Buddha. Venerable Ānanda Thera, the favourite attendant of the Buddha, who had the special privilege of hearing all the discourses, recited the Dhamma, whilst the venerable Upāli recited the Vinaya.

The **Tipitaka** was compiled and arranged in its present form by those Arahants of old.

During the reign of the pious Sinhala King **Vattagamani Abhaya,** about 80 B. C., the Tipitaka was first, for the first time in the history of Buddhism, commited to writing on ola leaves in Ceylon.

This voluminous Tipitaka which contains the essence of the Buddha's teaching is estimated to be about eleven times the size of the Bible. A striking contrast between the Tipitaka and the Bible is that the former is not a gradual development like the latter.

As the word itself implies the Tipitaka consists of three Baskets. They are the Basket of Discipline **(Vinaya Pitaka)**, the Basket of Discourses **(Sutta Pitaka)**, and the Basket of Ultimate Doctrine **(Abhidhamma Pitaka)**.

The **Vinaya Pitaka** mainly deals with the rules and regulations of the Order of monks (Bhikkhus) and nuns (Bhikkhunis). It describes in detail the gradual development of the **Sasana** (Dispensation). It also gives an account of the life and ministry of the Buddha. Indirectly it reveals some useful information about ancient history, Indian customs, arts, sciences, etc.

For nearly twenty-years, since His Enlightenment, no rules were laid down for the control of the Sangha. Later, as occasion arose, the Buddha promulgated rules for the future discipline of the Sangha.

This Pitaka consists of the five following books:—

1. **Parajika Pali** } **Vibhanga** (Major Offences)
2. **Pacittiya Pali** } **Vibhanga** (Minor Offences)
3. **Mahavagga Pali** } **Khandaka** (Greater Section)
2. **Cullavagga Pali** } **Khandaka** (Smaller Section)
5. **Parivara Pali** (Epitome of the Vinaya)

The **Sutta Pitaka** consists chiefly of discourses delivered by the Buddha Himself on various occasions. There are also a few discourses delivered by some of His distinguished disciples, such as the venerable

Sāriputta, Ānanda, Moggallāna, etc. included in it. It is like a book of prescriptions, as the sermons embodied therein were expounded to suit the different occasions and the temperament of various persons. There may be seemingly contradictory statements, but they should not be misconstrued as they were opportunely uttered by the Buddha to suit a particular purpose; for instance, to the self-same question He would maintain silence (when the inquirer is merely foolishly inquisitive, or give a detailed reply when He knew the inquirer to be an earnest seeker.

This Pitaka is divided into five Nikāyas or Collections, viz:—

1. **Digha Nikaya** (Collection of Long Discourses)
2. **Majjhima Nikaya** (Collection of Middle-length Discourses)
3. **Sanyutta Nikaya** (Collection of Kindred Sayings)
4. **Anguttara Nikaya** (Collection of Discourses arranged in accordance with number)
5. **Khuddaka Nikaya** (Smaller Collection)

The fifth is subdivided into fifteen books:—

1. **Khuddaka Patha** (Shorter Texts)
2. **Dhammapada** (The Way of Truth)
3. **Udana** (Heartfelt Sayings or Pæons of Joy)
4. **Iti Vuttaka** ("Thus said" Discourses)
5. **Sutta Nipata** (Collected Discourses)
6. **Vimana Vatthu** (Stories of Celestial Mansions)
7. **Peta Vatthu** (Stories of Petas)
8. **Theragatha** (Psalms of the Brethren)
9. **Therigatha** (Psalms of the Sisters)

10. **Jataka** (Birth Stories)
11. **Niddesa** (Expositions)
12. **Patisambhida** (Analytical Knowledge)
13. **Apadana** (Lives of Saints)
14. **Buddhavamsa** (The History of the Buddha)
15. **Cariya Pitaka** (Modes of Conduct)

The **Abhidhamma** is, to a deep thinker, the most important and the most interesting, as it contains the profound philosophy of the Buddha's teaching in contrast to the illuminating and simpler discourses in the Sutta Pitaka.

In the Sutta Piṭaka one often finds references to individual, being, etc., but in the Abhidhamma, instead of such conventional terms, we meet with ultimate terms, such as aggregates, mind, matter, etc.

In the Sutta is found the *Vohāra Desanā* (Conventional teaching), whilst in the Abhidhamma is found the *Paramattha Desanā* (Ultimate teaching).

In the Abhidhamma everything is analysed and explained in detail, and as such it is called *analytical doctrine* (Vibhajja Vāda).

Four ultimate things (Paramatthas) are enumerated in the Abhidhamma. They are *Citta*, (Consciousness), *Cetasika* (Mental concomitants), *Rūpa* (Matter), and *Nibbāna*.

The so-called being is microscopically analysed and its component parts are minutely described. Finally the ultimate goal and the method to achieve it are explained with all necessary details.

The main object of the Abhidhamma is to understand things as they truly are (*Yathābhūtañāṇadassana*). One who knows the Abhidhamma is not a surface seer but a seer of reality.

It is generally admitted by most exponents of the Dhamma that a knowledge of the Abhidhamma is essential to comprehend the Teachings of the Buddha.

The Abhidhamma Pitaka is composed of the following works:—

1. **Dhamma-Sangani** (Enumeration of Phenomena)
2. **Vihbanga** (The Book of the Treatises)
3. **Katha Vatthu** (Points of Controversy)
4. **Puggala Pannatti** (Discription of Individuals)
5. **Dhatu Katha** (Discussion with reference to Elements)
6. **Yamaka** (The Book of the Pairs)
7. **Patthana** (The Book of Relations)

* * * *

According to another classification, mentioned by the Buddha Himself, the whole Teaching is ninefold, namely— 1. *Sutta*, 2. *Geyya*, 3. *Veyyākaraṇa*, 4. *Gāthā*, 5. *Udāna*, 6. *Itivuttaka*, 7. *Jātaka*, 8. *Abbhutadhamma*, 9. *Vedalla*.

1. *Sutta*—These are the short, medium, and long discourses expounded by the Buddha on various occasions, such as Mangala Sutta (Discourse on Blessings), Ratana Sutta (The Jewel Discourse), Metta Sutta (Discourse on Goodwill), etc.

   According to the Commentary the whole Vinaya Pitaka is also included in this division.

2. *Geyya*—These are discourses mixed with Gāthās or verses, such as the Sagāthāvagga of the Sanyutta Nikāya.

3. *Veyyākarana*—Lit. exposition. The whole Abhidhamma Piṭaka, discourses without verses, and everything that is not included in the remaining eight divisions belong to this class.

4. *Gāthā*—These include verses found in the Dhammapada (Way of Truth), Theragāthā (Psalms of the Brethren), Therīgātha (Psalms of the Sisters), and those isolated verses which are not classed amongst the Suttas.

5. *Udāna*—These are the "pæons of joy" found in the Udāna, one of the divisions of the Khuddaka Nikāya.

6. *Itivuttaka*—These are the 112 discourses which commence with the phrase—"This the Blessed One hath said." Itivuttaka is one of the fifteen books that comprise the Khuddaka Nikāya.

7. *Jātaka*—These are the 547 birth-stories related by the Buddha in connection with various incidents.

8. *Abbhutadhamma*—These are the few discourses that deal with wonderful and marvellous things, as for example the Acchariya-Abbhutadhamma Sutta of the Majjhima Nikāya (No. 123).

9. *Vedalla*—These are the pleasurable discourses, such as Culla Vedalla, Maha Vedalla (M. N. Nos. 43, 44), Sạmmā Diṭṭhi Sutta, (M.N. No. 9), etc. In these are found some answers given to questions which were put with a certain amount of joy.

The sublime Dhamma enshrined in these sacred Texts deals with truths and facts, and is not concerned with theories and philosophies which may be accepted as profound truth today only to be thrown overboard tomorrow. The Buddha has presented us with no new astounding philosophical theories, nor did He venture to create any new material science. He explained to us what is within and without, so far as it concerns our emancipation, and ultimately expounded a Path of Deliverance which is unique.

It should be understood that the Buddha did not teach all that He knew.

On one occasion whilst the Buddha was passing through a forest He took a handful of leaves and said: "O Bhikkhus, what I have taught you is comparable to the amount of leaves in my hand, what I have not taught you is comparable to the amount of leaves in the forest"

He taught us only that which is absolutely essential for our emancipation. Incidentally He has, however, forestalled many a modern scientist and philosopher.

Schopenhauer in his "World as Will and Idea" has presented the Truth of Suffering and its cause in a Western garb. Spinoza whilst admitting the existence of a permanent reality asserts that all existence is transitory. In his opinion sorrow is conquered "by finding an object of knowledge which is not transient, not ephemeral, but is immutable permanent, everlasting." Berkeley proved that the so-called indivisible atom was a metaphysical fiction. Hume analysed the mind and came to the conclusion that consciousness consists of fleeting mental states. Bergson advocated the doctrine of change. Professor James refers to a stream of consciousness.

The Buddha expounded these doctrines of transiency (Anicca), Sorrow (Dukkha), and soul-lessness (Anatta) some 2500 years ago whilst He was sojourning in the valley of the Ganges.

As Dr. Dahlke says, "Buddhism, alone among all world religions, stands in not *a priori* contradiction to scientific thought." Buddhism no doubt accords with science, but both should be treated as parallel teachings, since one deals mainly with the material realm whilst the other confines itself to the mental and moral realm. The subject-matter of both are different.

The moral truth He taught is not merely to be preserved in books, nor is it a subject to be studied from a historical or literary point of view. On the contrary, it is to be studied and practised in the course of one's daily life, for without actual practice one cannot appreciate the truth. The Dhamma is to be studied, more to be practised, and above all to be realised The realisation of Nibbāna is its ultimate goal. As such the Dhamma is compared to a raft which is meant for the sole purpose of escaping from the ocean of life.

Buddhism, therefore, cannot strictly be called a philosophy because it is not merely "the love of, inducing the search after, wisdom."[1] Nor is Buddhism

---

1. Webster's Dictionary.

" a hypothetical interpretation of the unknown (as in metaphysics), or of the inexactly known (as in ethics or political philosophy)."[1] If by philosophy is meant "an inquiry not so much after certain particular facts as after the fundamental character of this world in which we find ourselves, and of the kind of life which in such a world it behoves us to live,"[2] Buddhism may approximate a philosophy;[3] but it is something very much more.

The Dhamma, which comprises the Nibbāna, the four Paths, and the four Fruits, collectively called the Nava Lokuttara (nine supramundane states), does not, it should be understood, lie within the domain of logical reasoning (*atakkāvacara*), because those stages of sainthood and the ultimate goal of the Holy Life are to be realised by direct insight into the Supramundane, whereas mundane logic naturally is confined to the mundane. The Tipitaka Dhamma, however, is perfectly logical.

* * * *

Is Buddhism a Religion?

Buddhism is not a religion[4] in the sense in which that word is commonly understood, for it is not "a system of faith and worship."

---

1. William Durant—"The Story of Philosophy", p. 2
2. Webb—"History of Philosophy", p. 7
3. A philosophy in the sense of an epistomological system which furnishes a complete reply to the question of the *what*, of the what is life?—this is not. "Buddhism" by *Dr. Paul Dhalke*—p. 25.
4. " What is meant by Religion? The word, as is well known, is not found in languages not related to our own, and its derivation is uncertain. Cicero, in one passage, derived it from *re* and *lego*, and held that its real meaning was the repetition of prayers and incantations. Another interpretation derives the word from *re* and *ligo*, and makes its original sense that of attachment, of a continual binding (that is, no doubt, to the gods) A third derivation connects the word with *lex*, and explains it as a law-abiding, scrupulously conscientious, frame of mind."—*Prof. Rhys Davids*—"Buddhism," p. 1.

Buddhism does not demand blind faith from its adherents. Here mere belief is dethroned and is substituted by "confidence based on knowledge," which, in Pāli, is known as Saddhā. A Buddhist will entertain occasional doubts until he attains the first stage of sainthood (Sotāpanna) when he completely discards all doubts pertaining to the Buddha, Dhamma, and the Sangha. One becomes a genuine sharer of the Ariyan knowledge[1] revealed by the Buddha only after attaining this stage.

The confidence of a follower of the Buddha is like that of a sick person in a noted physician, or a student in his teacher. A Buddhist seeks refuge in the Buddha because it is He who discovered the Path of Deliverance.

We are sick men suffering from an acute but curable disease. Then an experienced physician comes, diagnoses the case, and prescribes an effective remedy. However efficient the physician may be, we cannot be cured unless we take the remedy ourselves. The Buddha is the kind physician who discovered this panacea for the ills of life and gave it free to all.

It is the Buddha who shows us the Path of Deliverance. It is He who holds the Light of Truth to us benighted travellers. We grope in the dark, not finding a way of escape. Then, to our indescribable joy, a kind person comes with a light in hand and holds it aloft so that we may see. Instead of admiring the bright light and keeping on constantly thanking Him for His kindness, we must seek our escape with its aid.

1. The puthujjana upāsaka (ordinary adherent) may be *genuine* enough, as a *follower;* but he is not a *sharer by realization* of the Buddha-Dhamma.

A Buddhist does not seek refuge in the Buddha with the hope that he will be "saved" by His personal salvation. The Buddha gives no such guarantee. It is not within the power of a Buddha to wash away the impurities of others. One can neither purify nor defile another. The Buddha, as Teacher of devas and men, is instrumental, but we ourselves are directly responsible for our purification or defilement.

The Dhammapada says:—

By oneself alone is evil done, by oneself is one defiled.
By oneself is evil avoided, by oneself alone is one purified.
Purity and impurity depend on oneself.
No one can purify another.

However fervently we may pray to the Buddha, He has no power to take us to Nibbāna by His personal effort. He cannot wash away our impurities by His purification.

Although a Buddhist seeks refuge in the Buddha, he does not thereby become His slave, for no one, according to the Buddha, is a slave of another. A Buddhist does not make any self-surrender.

Neither does a Buddhist sacrifice his freedom of thought by becoming a follower of the Buddha. He can exercise his own freewill and develop his knowledge even to the extent of becoming a Buddha himself.

The starting point of Buddhism is right understanding (Sammādiṭṭhi). The Buddha advises the seekers of truth not to accept anything merely on the authority of another but to exercise their own reasoning and judge for themselves whether anything is right or wrong.

On one occasion the Kālāmas of Kessaputta approached the Buddha and said that many ascetics and Brahmins, who come to preach to them, used to exalt their own doctrines and denounce the doctrines of others, and that they were at a loss to understand which of those worthies were speaking the truth and which were speaking falsehood.

"Yes, O Kālāmas, it is right for you to doubt, it is right for you to waver. In a doubtful matter wavering has arisen."

Thus remarked the Buddha, and gave them the following advice which applies with equal force to the modern rationalists as it did to those sceptic Brahmins of yore.

"Come, O Kālāmas! Do not accept anything on (mere) hearsay (i.e., *thinking that thus have we heard it from a long time*). Do not accept anything by mere tradition (i.e., *thinking that it has thus been handed down through many generations*). Do not accept anything on account of rumours (i. e., *by believing what others say without any investigation*). Do not accept anything just because it accords with your scriptures. Do not accept anything by mere supposition Do not accept anything by mere inference. Do not accept anything by merely considering the reasons. Do not accept anything merely because it agrees with your preconceived notions. Do not accept anything merely because it seems acceptable (i e., *thinking that as the speaker seems to be a good person his word should be accepted)*. Do not accept anything thinking that the ascetic is respected by us *(and therefore it is right to accept his word).*[1]

"But, Kālāmas, when you know for yourselves—These things are immoral; these things are blameworthy; these things are censured by the wise; these things, when performed and undertaken, conduce to ruin and sorrow—then indeed do you reject them, Kālāmas.

"When, Kālāmas, you know for yourselves—These things are moral; these things are blameless; these things are praised by the wise; these things, when performed and undertaken, conduce to well-being and happiness—then do you live acting accordingly."

These words of the Buddha, uttered some 2500 years ago, still retain their original force and freshness.

Now, though it be admitted that there is no *blind faith* in Buddhism, one might argue whether there is no worshipping of images etc. amongst Buddhists.

Buddhists do not worship an image expecting any worldly favours, but pay their homage to what it represents. A Buddhist goes before an image and offers flowers and incense not to the image but to the Buddha. As a mark of gratitude he does so, and reflects on the virtues of the Buddha and meditates on

1. The bracketed explanatory parts of the above translation are supplied by the writer following the interpretations of the commentary and the sub-commentary.
The Pali Text of this important passage is as follows:—
Etha tumhe Kālāma. Mā aussavena, mā paramparāya, mā itikirāya. mā piṭakasampādānena, mā takkahetu, mā nayahetu, mā ākāraparivitakkena, mā diṭṭhinijjhānakkhantiya ma bhabbarūpataya, ma samaṇo no garū'ti. Ang. N. Vol. 1, p. 189.)

the transiency of the fading flowers. An understanding Buddhist designedly makes himself feel that he is in the presence of the living Buddha, and thereby gains inspiration from His noble personality, and breathes deep of His boundless compassion. He tries to follow His noble example.

The Bo-tree is also a symbol of Enlightenment.[1]

These external objects of homage are not absolutely necessary, they are useful as they tend to concentrate one's attention. An intellectual could dispense with them as he could easily focus his attention and visualise the Buddha.

For our own good, and out of gratitute, we pay such external homage, but what the Buddha expects from His disciples is not so much obeisance as the actual observance of His Teaching.

On one occasion, as the Buddha was about to pass away, many disciples came to pay their respects to Him. One Bhikkhu, however, remained in his cell, engaged in meditation. This matter was brought to the notice of the Buddha. He was summoned, and on being questioned as to his conduct, he replied: "Lord, I know that You will pass away three months hence, and I thought that the best way to honour the Teacher is by trying to attain Arahantship even before Your decease.

"Excellent, excellent," the Buddha said and remarked:

> **"He who loves me should emulate this Bhikkhu. He honours me best who practises my teaching best."**

---

1. *Nam'atthu Bodhiya*—Homage be to Enlightenment.

Further, it must be mentioned that there are no prayers in Buddhism. However much we may pray to the Buddha we cannot be saved. The Buddha does not grant any worldly favours to those who pray to Him. Instead of prayers there are meditations intended to purify the mind. The Buddha not only speaks of the futility of prayers but also disparages a slavish mentality. A Buddhist should not pray to be saved, but should rely on himself and win his freedom. Hence the Buddha's advice—"Be ye islands unto yourselves, be ye a refuge unto yourselves, seek not for refuge in others."

"Prayer takes the character of private communications, selfish bargaining with God. It seeks for objects of earthly ambitions and inflames the sense of self. Meditation on the other hand is self-change."[1]

In Buddhism there is no one almighty creator God whom Buddhists should obey and fear. There are no dogmas that we must believe. There are no creeds that we must accept on faith. There are no priests to act as mediators. There are no special rites and ceremonies to become a Buddhist, no prayers and sacrifices to be offered, no penance and repentance to be made to gain one's salvation.

Buddhism cannot, therefore, be strictly called a religion, because it is neither "a system of faith and worship," nor "the outward act or form by which men indicate their recognition of the existence of a god or

---

1. Sir S. Radhakrishna.

Comp. "Prayer is an activity in which I frankly confess I am not adept." Canon B. H. Streeter in "Modern Churchman" Sept. 1924, p.347.

"I do not understand how men continue to pray, unless they are convinced that there is a listening ear."—Rev. C. Beard in "Reformation" p.419.

gods having power over their own destiny, to whom obedience, service, and honour are due."[1]

If by religion is meant "a teaching which takes a view of life that is more than superficial, a teaching which looks *into* life and not merely at it, a teaching which furnishes men with a guide to conduct that is in accord with this its 'in-look', a teaching which enables those who give it heed to face life with fortitude and death with serenity,"[2] or even a teaching (*Āgama*) that distinguishes between right and wrong, then it is certainly a *religion of religions*.[3]

* * * *

Is Buddhism an Ethical System?

Buddhism, no doubt, contains an excellent moral code, which is adaptable to all climes and ages, but it is much more than an ordinary moral teaching.

Morality, or Sila, is only the A. B. C. of Buddhism, and is the first stage on the Path of Purity. Conduct, though essential, does not alone lead to one's emancipation. It should be coupled with wisdom or knowledge (*Paññā*). Wisdom and conduct are like the pair of wings of a bird. One of the appellatives of the Buddha is *Vijjā-caraṇa-sampanna*, "endowed with

1. Webster's Dictionary.
2. Mr. J. F. McKechnie (Ex-Bhikkhu Silacara). See Ceylon Daily News—Vesak Number, May, 1939.
3. Dr. Dahlke, in arguing what Buddhism is, says—"With this, sentence of condemnation is passed upon Buddhism as a religion. Religion in the ordinary sense, as that which points beyond this life to one essentially different, it cannot be."
"Buddhism and its Place in the Mental Life of Mankind," p. 27.

wisdom and conduct." Wisdom is like the eyes, conduct is like the feet.

In Buddhism there are deeds which are ethically good, deeds which are ethically bad, deeds which are neither good nor bad, and deeds which tend to the ceasing of all deeds. Good deeds are essential for one's emancipation, but when once the ultimate goal of the Holy Life is attained, one transcends both good and evil. Says the Buddha—

> "*Righteous things* (*Dhamma*) *you have to give up, how much more the unrighteous things* (*Adhamma*).
> —(Majjhima Nikāya – No. 22).

The deed which is connected with attachment (Lobha), ill-will (Dosa), and delusion (Moha) is evil. That deed which is connected with non-attachment, goodwill, and wisdom is good.

The deeds of an Arahant, a perfect Saint, are neither good nor bad because he has gone beyond both good and bad. This does not mean that he is passive. He *is* active, but his activity is selfless and is directed to keep others to tread the Path he has trod himself. His deeds, ordinarily accepted as "good", lack creative power as regards himself. Purest gold cannot be further purified. He accumulates no fresh Kammic activities. Understanding things as they truly are, he has finally shattered his cosmic chain of cause and effect.

The four stages of Sainthood, which, strictly speaking, are the four classes of supramundane Path consciousness, namely, *Sotāpanna*, (Stream-winner), *Sakadāgāmi*, (Once-returner), *Anāgāmi*, (Never-returner), and *Arahatta* (Worthy)—though wholesome, lead to the graduated cessation of the individual flux of becoming, and therewith, to the cessation of good and evil deeds. In these types of supramundane consciousness the "wisdom" factor is predominant, whilst in mundane types of consciousness volition or Cètanā, which produces Kammic results, is predominant.

Now, how should a deed be assessed, as to its being good or bad? Is it by the motive or by the result?

Intention is the chief factor in assessing morality. In some cases both motive and result have to be taken into account in judging a deed. Sometimes the motive is good, but the result bad; at times the reverse is the case.

A person may strike a burglar with the object of over-powering him. Accidentally, as the result of the blow, the burglar may meet with his death. Yet the striker is not responsible for that death, as he had no intention to murder.

One may dissect an animal with the best of motives. The inevitable result would be the death of the poor animal.

With the alleged motive of maintaining peace and order, one nation may war with another nation, but the results may be disastrous.

In that well-known story[1] Nanda Bhikkhu, the Buddha's step-brother, meditated with the object of obtaining celestial nymphs,—a craving to be strictly shunned by those who pursue the Holy Life. But eventually, his mind being led along proper channels under the guidance of the Buddha, he attained Arahantship.

His initial motive was bad, but the ultimate result was good.

This should not be misunderstood to mean that the end always justifies the means.

What then is the *criterion* of morality according to Buddhism?

The reply is found in the admonition given by the Buddha Himself to young Sāmanera Rāhula.

The Buddha says:—

---

1. Prince Nanda was ordained on his wedding day. As it was not an ordination done purely of his own accord, he could not concentrate his energies on spiritual development. He had no interest in the Holy Life, for he was constantly thinking of his *fiancee*. The Buddha reading his thoughts devised a means to set him on the right path. With the object of showing him celestial nymphs the Buddha took him to heaven by means of His psychic powers. On the way Nanda Thera was shown a singed she-monkey clinging to a burnt up stump in a scorched forest Reaching heaven Nanda Thera beheld the celestial nymphs and was so fascinated by their beauty that he compared his charming *fiancee* to the old she-monkey he saw on the way.

   "Would you like to have them Nanda?" the Buddha questioned him.

   "Yes, lord!" he childishly replied.

   "Well, then, I guarantee that you will possess them if you persevere as I bid you."

   But the Teacher informed the monks that Nanda Thera was living the Holy Life in the hope of winning heavenly nymphs, and they, in turn tormented Nanda Thera by calling him "hireling." Thereupon he became ashamed of the meanness of his motive, and by striving diligently, attained the supreme goal.

   See Dhammapadaṭṭhakathā.

"Is there a deed, Rahula, thou dost wish to do? then bethink thee thus:—

Is this deed conducive to mine harm, or to others' harm, or to that of both? then is this a bad deed entailing suffering. Such a deed must thou surely not do.

"*Is there a deed, Rāhula, thou dost wish to do? then bethink thee thus:—Is this deed not conducive to mine harm, nor to others' harm, nor to that of both? then is this a good deed entailing happiness. Such a deed must thou do again and again.*"
—(Rāhulovāda Sutta).

In doing a deed a Buddhist takes into consideration the interests of both himself and others—animals not excluded.

In the Karaṇīya Metta Sutta the Buddha says: "As the mother protects her only child even at the risk of her own life, even so let one cultivate one's boundless thoughts of loving-kindness towards all beings."

The Dhammapada says:—

"All fear punishment; to all life is dear. Comparing others with self, let one neither hurt nor kill."

"As I am, so are these; as these are, so am I. Thus identifying himself with others the wise man should neither kill nor cause others to kill."

It is evident from the above sayings that Buddhism is not egoistic.

It should be mentioned here that an Almighty God or any other external supernatural agency plays no part whatsoever in the moulding of the character

---

1. See Mrs. Rhys Davids—"Buddhism," p.125.

of a Buddhist. In Buddhism there is no one to reward or punish. Pain or happiness are the due results of our own actions. The question of incurring the pleasure or displeasure of a God does not enter the mind of a Buddhist. Neither hope of reward nor fear of punishment acts as an incentive to him to do good or refrain from evil. A Buddhist no doubt is aware of future consequences, but, strictly speaking, he refrains from evil because it retards, does good because it aids, progress to Bodhi—Enlightenment. There may also be some who do good because it is good, refrain from evil because it is bad.

To understand the exceptionally high standards of morality the Buddha expects from His ideal followers, one must carefully read the *Dhammapada*, *Sigālovāda Sutta*, *Mangala Sutta*, *Karaṇīya Metta Sutta*, *Parābhava Sutta*, *Vasala Sutta*, *Dhammika Sutta*, *etc.*

In one sense Buddhism is not, therefore, a philosophy; in another sense it is the *philosophy of philosophies*.

In one sense Buddhism is not a religion; in another sense it is the *religion of religions*.

As a moral teaching it excels all ethical systems, but morality is only the beginning and not the end of Buddhism.

The original Pāli term for Buddhism is *Dhamma*, which literally means that which upholds. There is no English equivalent that exactly conveys the meaning of the Pāli term.

The Dhamma is that which really is. It is the *Doctrine of Reality*. It is a *Means of Deliverance*, and *Deliverance itself*. Whether the Buddhas arise or not the Dhamma exists. It is a Buddha who realises this

Dhamma, which ever lies hidden from the ignorant eyes of gods and men, till He, an Enlightened One comes, and compassionately reveals it to the world.

> "Whether the Tathāgatas appear or not, O Bhikkhus, it remains a fact, an established principle, a natural law that all conditioned things are transient (*Anicca*), sorrowful (*Dukkha*), and everything is soul-less (*Anatta*). This fact the Tathāgata realises, understands, and when He has realised and understood it, He announces, teaches, proclaims, establishes, discloses, analyses, and makes it clear, that all conditioned things are transient, sorrowful, and everything is soul-less."—(Anguttara Nikāya—part 1, p. 286).

In the Majjhima Nikāya the Buddha says:—

> "*One thing only does the Buddha teach, that is suffering and the cessation of suffering.*"

This is the **Doctrine of Reality.**

"Just as, O Bhikkhus, the mighty ocean is of *one flavour*, the flavour of salt; even so, O Bhikkhus, this Dhamma is of one flavour, the *flavour of Deliverance* (*Vimutti*)."—(Udāna p. 67).

This is the **Means of Deliverance.**

This Dhamma is not something apart from oneself, but is closely associated with oneself. As such the Buddha exhorts us:—

"Abide with oneself as an island, with oneself as a refuge; *abide with the Dhamma as an island*, **with the Dhamma as a refuge.** Seek not for external refuge." —(Parinibbāna Sutta)

CHAPTER X

SOME SALIENT FEATURES OF BUDDHISM

THE chief features of Buddhism are the Four Noble Truths which the Buddha Himself discovered and revealed to the world.

They are the Noble Truth of Suffering, (the *raison d'etre* of Buddhism); the Noble Truth of the Cause of Suffering, i.e. Craving; the Noble Truth of the Annihilation of Suffering, i.e. Nibbāna, (the *summum bonum* of Buddhism), and the Path leading to the Annihilation of Suffering.

All are subject to birth, and consequently to disease, old age, and death. No one is exempt from these four causes of suffering.

Impeded volition is also suffering. We do not wish to come in contact with persons or things we do not like, nor do we wish to be separated from persons or things we like most. But our wishes are not always fulfilled. What we least expect or what we least desire is often thrust on us. At times such unpleasant circumstances become so intolerable and painful that weak ignorant folk are compelled to put an end to their own lives.

In brief this body itself is a cause of suffering.

Buddhism rests on this pivot of suffering.[1] But it does not thereby follow that Buddhism is pessimistic. It is neither totally pessimistic nor totally optimistic. On the contrary it teaches a Truth that lies midway between them. One would be justified in calling the Buddha a pessimist if He had merely emphasized this Truth without suggesting a means to get rid of this suffering and gain the Highest Happiness. The Buddha perceived the universality of sorrow and did prescribe a *panacea* for this universal sickness of humanity. The highest conceivable happiness, according to the Buddha, is Nibbāna. "*Nibbānaṁ paramaṁ sukhaṁ*"—Nibbana is bliss suprem

The Buddha, on the other hand, does not expect His followers to be constantly brooding over this fact of suffering and lead a miserable unhappy life. He exhorts them to be always happy, for joy (*pīti*) is one of the factors of Enlightenment.

The ideal Bhikkhus are reputed to be the happiest persons. "*Aho sukhaṁ, Aho sukhaṁ*"—"Oh, happy indeed! Oh, happy indeed!"—"We shall be living in joy," are some of the favourite sayings of His followers.

Although the Disciples of the Buddha constantly meditate on *transiency* and *sorrow*, yet they are always happy and serene. One day a certain deity approached the Blessed One and questioned Him thus:

---

1. "Dukkhe loko patiṭṭhito"—The world rests on suffering.

"Who in the forest make their wonted haunt—
The saintly livers of the holy life—
Who by one daily meal do break their fast:
Tell me how look they so serene of hue?".

To this the Blessed One replied:

"They make no lamentation over the past,
They yearn not after that which is not come,
By what now is do they maintain themselves:
Hence comes it that they look serene of hue."*

In dealing with the Causal Law Formula in terms of happiness the Buddha says: *Suffering* leads to Confidence (*Saddhā*); Confidence, to Rapture (*Pāmojja*); Rapture, to Joy (*Pīti*); Joy, to Tranquillity (*Passaddhi*); Tranquillity, to Happiness (*Sukha*); Happiness, to Concentration (*Samādhi*); Concentration, to Knowledge and Vision of things as they truly are (*Yathābhūta Ñāṇadassana*); the Knowledge and Vision of things as they truly are, to Repulsion (*Nibbidā*); Repulsion, to Passionlessness (*Virāga*); Passionlessness, to Deliverance (*Vimutti*); Deliverance, to the Knowledge of the Extinction (of passions) (*Khaye Ñāṇa*).*

This text clearly shows how suffering leads to happiness and ultimately to Sainthood.

Real happiness is found within, and is not to be defined in terms of wealth, children, honours, or invasions. If such possessions are misdirected, forcibly or unjustly obtained, misappropriated, or even viewed with attachment, they will be a source of pain and sorrow to the possessors.

The so-called happiness of the ordinary man is merely the gratification of some desire. "No sooner

---

* Kindred Sayings.

the desired thing is gained than it begins to be scorned", and we crave for yet other varied pleasures. So insatiate are all worldly selfish desires.

According to the ordinary man the enjoyment of sensual pleasures is his greatest and only happiness.

One is no doubt fascinated by beautiful forms, musical sounds, fragrant odours, delicious tastes, and soft contacts. There is certainly a kind of momentary happiness in the anticipation, gratification and retrospection of such fleeting material pleasures, but, strictly speaking, they are only a prelude to pain.

Suffering exists as long as there is craving or attachment. Says the Buddha in the Dhammapada—

From craving springs grief, from craving springs fear;

For him who is wholly free from craving there is no grief, whence fear?

Both suffering and craving can only be eradicated by treading the Noble Eightfold Path and attaining the Supreme Bliss of Nibbāna.

The Noble Eightfold Path consists of Right Understanding, Right Thoughts, Right Speech, Right Action, Right Livelihood, Right Endeavour, Right Mindfulness, and Right Concentration.

Right Understanding means the knowledge of four Noble Truths or seeing things as they truly are. It is the knowledge of one's own self.

Right Thoughts are three-fold. They are the thoughts free from lust, i.e. renunciation (*Nekkhamma*) the thoughts free from ill-will, i.e. loving-kindness (*Mettā*), and the thoughts free from cruelty, i.e. compassion (*Karuṇā*).

Right Speech deals with abstinence from lying, slander, harsh words, and vain talk.

Right Action pertains to abstinence from killing, stealing, and unchastity.

Right Livelihood deals with the five forms of trades which should be avoided by a disciple. They are trading in arms, in living beings, in flesh,[1] in intoxicating drinks, and in poison.

Right Endeavour is four-fold. It is the effort to discard evil that has arisen, the effort to prevent the arising of unrisen evil, the effort to cultivate unrisen good, and the effort to promote arisen good.

Right Mindfulness consists in the contemplation of the body (*Kāyānupassanā*), the contemplation of the feelings (*Vedanānupassanā*), the contemplation of consciousness (*Cittānupassanā*), and the contemplation of the Dhamma[2] (*Dhammānupassanā*).

Right Concentration is the one-pointedness of the mind.

These Four Truths, which are dependent on this one-fathomed body, exist whether the Buddhas arise or not, and no blind faith is necessary to understand

1. Here trading in flesh means breeding animals to be sold for slaughter.

2. *Dhamma* is a multi-significant term.
Here Dhamma means the five Hindrances (*Nīvaraṇa*), the five Aggregates (*Khandha*), the six Avenues of Sense (*Āyatana*), the seven Factors of Enlightenment (*Bojjhanga*), and the four Noble Truths (*Ariya-sacca*).

them. The Buddha-Dhamma is not based on the fear of the unknown, but is founded on the bed-rock of these facts which could be verified by experience and tested by ourselves. Buddhism is, therefore, rational and practical.

There is nothing in the Dhamma that is impractical or impracticable. The Buddha practised what He taught; He taught what He practised. Practice is the foundation of His teaching.

Such a rational and practical system cannot contain any mysticism or esoteric doctrines. In the Pari-Nibbāna Sutta the Buddha says:

"I have taught the Truth without making any distinction between esoteric and exoteric doctrine; for in respect of the Truth the Tathāgata has no such thing as the closed fist of a teacher, who keeps some things back."

In another place the Buddha remarks:—

"The doctrines and the rules proclaimed by the Perfect Buddha shine before all the world and not in secret."

No coercions or persecutions or fanaticisms play any part in Buddhism. To the unique credit of Buddhism it must be said that throughout its peaceful march of 2,500 years no drop of blood was shed in the name of the Buddha, no mighty monarch wielded his powerful sword to propagate the Dhamma, and no conversion was made either by force or by repulsive methods.

In the name of Buddhism no altar was reddened with the blood of a Hypatia, no Bruno was burnt alive. "Had Torquemada been born a Buddhist," says Mr. Blatchford, "he never would have taken to roasting heretics."

Buddhism appeals more to the intellect than to the emotion. It is concerned more with the character of the devotees than with their numerical strength.

On one occasion Upāli, a follower of. Nigaṇṭha Nātaputta, approached the Buddha and was so pleased with the Buddha's exposition of the Dhamma that he instantly expressed his desire to become a follower of the Buddha. But the Buddha cautioned him, saying:

"Of a verity, O householder, make a thorough investigation. It is well for a distinguished man like you to (first) make a thorough investigation."

Upāli who was overjoyed at this unexpected remark of the Buddha, said: "Lord, if I had become a follower of another teacher, his followers would have taken me round the streets in procession proclaiming that such and such a millionaire had renounced his former religion and embraced theirs. But, Lord, you advise me to investigate further. The more pleased am I with this remark of yours."

And he appreciatively repeated: "For the second time I seek refuge in the Buddha, Dhamma, and the Sangha."

Buddhism is saturated with this spirit of free inquiry and complete tolerance. It is the teaching of the open mind and the sympathetic heart which, lighting and warming the whole Universe with its twin rays of wisdom and compassion, sheds its genial glow on every being struggling in the ocean of birth and death.

The Buddha was so tolerant that He did not even exercise His power to give commandments to His followers. Instead of using the imperative, He says: "It behoves you to do this—It behoves you not to do this."

Even the precepts which Buddhists are expected to observe are not commandments but modes of discipline *(Sikkhāpada)* which they take of their own accord.

This tolerance the Buddha extended to men, women, and all living beings.

It was the Buddha who first abolished slavery and vehemently protested against the degrading caste-system which was firmly rooted in the soil of India. In the word of the Buddha it is not by mere birth that one becomes either an outcaste or a Brahmin, but by one's deeds.[1]

In the *Vāseṭṭha Sutta* it is stated that two young Brahmins had a discussion with regard to what constitutes a Brahmin. One maintained that birth made a Brahmin, whilst the other contended that conduct made a Brahmin. As neither could convince the other both of them agreed to refer the matter to the Buddha.

So they approached the Buddha and presented their case before Him.

In reply the Buddha at first reminded the questioners that although in the case of plants, insects,

1. Na jaccā vasalo hoti—na jaccā hoti brahmaṇo
Kammanā vasalo hoti—Kammanā hoti brahmaṇo.

quadrupeds, serpents, fish and birds there are many species and marks by which they could be distinguished, yet in the case of men there are no such species and marks. Then He explained how men differentiated themselves according to their various occupations. In concluding the Buddha said:

> "Birth makes no Brahman, nor non-Brahman makes;
> 'Tis life and doing that mould the Brahman true.
> Their lives mould farmers, tradesmen, merchants, serfs;
> Their lives mould robbers, soldiers, chaplains, kings."

Another interesting dialogue concerning this very problem of caste appears in the *Madhura Sutta.* The King of Madhura makes the following report to the venerable Kaccāna:

"The Brahmins say thus, Kaccāna, 'The Brahmins are the most distinguished of the four divisions into which the people are classified; every other division is inferior. The Brahmins alone are accounted pure, not those who are not Brahmins. The Brahmins are the legitimate sons of Brahma, born from his mouth, specially made by him, heirs of Brahma!' What do you, Sir, say to this?"

The venerable Kaccāna replies that it is an empty assertion and points out at first how a wealthy person could get as his servant member of any class or caste. Secondly, he points out how a wicked person of any caste could be born in a state of misery and a good person in a state of bliss, in spite of their castes. Thirdly, he says that a criminal, to whatever caste he may belong, would, without any distinction, be punished for his crime. Lastly, he emphasizes the fact that all joining the Order receive equal honour and reverence, irrespective of their castes.

Thus, according to Buddhism, caste or colour does not preclude one from becoming a Buddhist or entering the Order. Fishermen, scavengers, courtesans together with the warriors and the Brahmins were freely admitted to the Order and enjoyed equal privileges and were also given positions of rank.

Upāli, the barber, for instance, was made in preference to all others, the chief in matters pertaining to the rules and regulations of the Order. The timid *Sunīta*, the scavenger, was admitted by the Buddha Himself into the Order and enabled him to attain Saintship. *Angulimāla*, the robber and murderer, was converted to a compassionate Saint. The fierce *Ālavaka* sought refuge in the Buddha and entered the first stage of Sainthood. The courtesan, *Ambapāli*, entered the Order and attained Arahantship. *Sāti*, the monk, who maintained a deadly heresy, was the son of a fisherman. *Subhā* was the daughter of a smith. *Puṇṇā* was a slave girl. *Cāpā* was the daughter of a deer-stalker. Such instances could easily be multiplied from the Tipitaka to show that the portals of Buddhism were wide open to all without any distinction.

It was also the Buddha who raised the status of womem and brought them to a realisation of their importance to society.

The Buddha did not humiliate women, but only regarded them as feeble by nature. He saw the innate good of both men and women and assigned to them their due places in His Teaching. Sex is no barrier to attaining Sainthood.

Referring to the Chariot of the Dhamma the Buddha says—

"And be it woman, be it man for whom
Such chariot doth wait, by that same car
Into Nibbāna's presence shall they come."

(Kindred Sayings)

Sometimes the Pāli term used to denote women is "*Mātu-gāma*"—which means "mother-folk," or "society of mothers." As a mother woman holds an honourable place in Buddhism. Even the wife is regarded as the "best friend" *(paramā sakhā)* of the husband.

Hasty critics are only making *ex parte* statements when they reproach Buddhism with being inimical to woman. Although at first the Buddha refused to admit women into the Order on reasonable grounds yet later He yielded to the entreaties of the venerable *Ānanda* and His foster-mother, *Pajāpati Gotami*, and founded the Order of Bhikkunis (Nuns).

Just as the Arahants *Sāriputta* and *Moggallāna* were made the two chief disciples in the Order of Monks, even so the Arahants *Khemā* and *Uppalavaṇṇā* were made the two chief female disciples in the Order of Nuns. Many other female disciples too were named by the Buddha Himself as amongst His most distinguished and pious followers. Even amongst the Vajjis freedom to women was regarded as one of the causes that led to their prosperity. Before the advent of the Buddha Indian women did not enjoy sufficient freedom and were deprived of the opportunities to display their spiritual nature and their knowledge. Even the birth of a daughter to a family was considered an unwelcome addition.

On one occasion when the Buddha was conversing with King Kosala a messenger came and informed the king that a daughter was born unto him. Hearing which the king was displeased. But the Buddha consoled him, saying:

" A woman child, O Lord of men, may prove
Even a better offspring than a male."

To women who were placed under such unfavourable circumstances this establishment of the new Order must have no doubt been a great blessing. In this Order, queens, princesses, daughters of noble families, widows, bereaved mothers, helpless women, courtesans —all despite their caste or rank—met on a common platform, enjoyed perfect consolation and peace, and breathed that free atmosphere which is denied to those cloistered in cottages and palatial mansions. Many who otherwise would have fallen into oblivion distinguished themselves in various ways and gained their emancipation by seeking refuge in the Order.

Khema, the first chief female disciple, was the beautiful consort of King Bimbisāra. She was at first reluctant even to see the Buddha as He used to refer to external beauty in disparaging terms. One day she was however attracted to the monastery. The Buddha seeing her preached a suitable discourse to her. Soon she became a convert, entered the Order and rose to the position of first chief female disciple.

Patacara, who lost her children, husband, parents and brother, attained Arahantship after hearing the Dhamma from the Buddha. She afterwards became a source of consolation to many a bereaved mother.

Dhammadinna was one of the ablest exponents of the Dhamma.

It was **Soma**, a daughter of the chaplain of King Bimbisāra, who bravely remarked:—

"What should the woman-nature count for us, in her who with mind well set, and knowledge advancing, has right insight into the Dhamma? To one for whom the question arises, 'Am I a woman in those matters, or am I a man, or what then am I?' such as are you, you Evil One are fit to talk."

Amongst the laity too there were many ladies who were distinguished for their piety, generosity, devotion, learning, loving-kindness, etc.

Visakha stands foremost amongst them all. She was a noble example to her lesser sisters. At a very early age she entered the first stage of Sainthood, and although she was married to a mis-believer she was able to convert her parents-in-law to Buddhism. She bacame the chief benefactress of the Order.

Suppiya was a very devout lady who, being unable to procure some flesh from the market, cut a piece of flesh from her thigh to prepare a soup for a sick monk.

Nakulamata was a faithful wife who, by reciting her virtues, rescued her husband from the jaws of death.

Samavati was a pious and lovable queen, who extended her thoughts of loving-kindness towards her rival even when she was burnt to death through her machination.

Khujjuttara was a maid-servant who was distinguished as an able exponent of the Dhamma.

Mallika was a wise queen who counselled her husband, King Pasenadi, on many occasions and secured many converts by teaching the Dhamma.

Punabbasu's mothers was so intent on hearing the Dhamma that she hushed her children thus:—

"O silence, little Uttara! Be still,
Punabbasu, that I may hear the Norm

Taught by the Master, by the Wisest Man.
Dear unto us is our own child and dear

Our husband; dearer still than those to me
Is't of this Doctrine to explore the Path".

A mother, when asked why she did not weep at the loss of her child, said:

"Uncalled he hither came, unbidden soon to go;
E'en as he came, he went. What cause is here for woe?"

Sumana and **Subhadda** were two young ladies of exemplary character who had implicit faith in the Buddha.

These few instances will suffice to illustrate the great part played by women in the time of the Buddha.[1]

This tolerance of the Buddha was extended not only to men and women but also to the dumb creation as well. For it was the Buddha who put a stop to the sacrifice of poor beasts and admonished His followers to extend their loving-kindness or Maitrī to all living beings,—even to the tiniest creature that crawls at our feet. No man has the power or the right to destroy the life of another as life is precious to all.

A monk should exercise this loving-kindness to such an extent that he is forbidden by his rules even to dig or cause to dig the ground. He cannot even destroy a plant. Nor can he drink water without being filtered.

1. See "Psalms of the Sisters" and "Women under Primitive Buddhism."

Asoka, 'the greatest of kings', wrote on rock and monolith, saying: "The living must not be nourished with the living. Even chaff with insects must not be burnt."

A genuine Buddhist should practise his Maitrī towards every living being and identify himself with all, making no distinction whatsoever with regard to caste, creed, colour, or sex. It is this Buddhist *Mettā* that attempts to break all the barriers which separate one from another. There is no necessity for one to keep aloof from others merely because they belong to another persuasion or another nationality. In that noble *Toleration Edict*, which is based on the *Culla-Viyūha* and *Mahā-Viyūha Suttas*, Asoka says: "Concourse alone is best, that is, all should hearken willingly to the doctrines professed by others."

Buddhism is not confined to any country or any particular nation. It is universal. It is not nationalism, which, in other words, is another form of caste system founded on a wider basis. Buddhism, if it be permitted to say so, is supernationalism.

To the Buddhist there is no far or near, no enemy or foreigner, no renegade or untouchable since universal love, realised through understanding, has established the brotherhood of all living beings. A real Buddhist is a citizen of the world.

Buddhism is, therefore, unique, mainly owing to its rationality, practicability, efficacy, and universality. It is the noblest of all unifying influences and the only lever that can uplift the world.

CHAPTER XI

KAMMA, OR THE BUDDHIST LAW OF CAUSATION

Inequality

WE are faced with a totally ill-balanced world. We perceive the inequalities and the manifold destinies of men and the various gradations of beings prevalent in the world. We see one born into a condition of affluence, endowed with fine mental, moral and physical qualities, and another into a condition of absolute poverty and wretchedness. Here is a man virtuous and holy but, contrary to his expectations, ill-luck is ever ready to greet him. The wicked world runs counter to his ambitions and desires. He is poor and miserable in spite of his honest dealings and piety. There is another vicious and foolish, but is accounted to be fortune's darling, despite his short-comings and evil modes of life.

Why, it may be questioned, should one be an inferior and another a superior? Why should one be wrested from the hands of a fond mother when one has scarcely seen a few summers and another perish in the flower of manhood, or at the ripe age of eighty or hundred? Why should one be congenitally sick and infirm and another strong and healthy? Why should one be handsome and another ugly and hideous, repulsive to all? Why should one be brought up in the lap of luxury, surrounded with amusements and pleasures, and another in tears, steeped to the lips in misery? Why should one be born a millionaire and another a pauper? Why should one be made a mental prodigy and another an idiot? Why should one be born with saintly characteristics and another with criminal tendencies? Why should some be linguists, artists, mathematicians or musicians from their very cradle? Why should some be born blind, deaf, and deformed?

These are some problems that perplex the minds of all thinking men. How are we to account for this inequality of man?

* * * *

Is it due to blind chance or accident?

To those who hold the view that everything is due to chance the Buddha says:—"So then, owing to no cause or condition at all, men will become murderers, thieves, unchaste, liars, slanderers, abusive, babblers, covetous, malicious, and perverse in view. Thus for those who fall back on the uncaused and unconditioned as the essential, there is neither desire to do, nor effort to do, nor necessity to do this deed or to abstain from that deed."[1]

There is nothing in this world that happens by blind chance or accident. To say that anything happens by chance, is no more true than that this book has come here of itself. Strictly speaking nothing happens to any man that he does not deserve for some reason or other.

---

1. "Gradual Sayings"—Vol. 1. p. 158.

Could this be the *fiat* of an irresponsible God-Creator?

We, Buddhists, would not think it right or reasonable to attribute this injustice to an almighty, all-loving Father in Heaven.

"What kind of a Deity must it be who creates a baby-soul, born of diseased parents, foredoomed to ill-health and a life of poverty, misery, probably crime? In these days surely no one could for a moment entertain such a lame explanation or consider it in anyway satisfactory."[1]

There are some who say that there is a *Mahesvara God* who is absolute, omnipresent, and eternal; and that (he) is the Creator of all Dharmas.

As the *Vijñaptimātratā Siddhi Śāstra* of the Buddhist Idealistic school says, this theory is illogical.

"That which creates is not eternal; that which is not eternal is not omnipresent; that which is not omnipresent is not the absolute."

As Charles Bradlaugh says "the existence of evil is a terrible stumbling-block to the Theist. Pain, misery, crime, poverty confront the advocate of eternal goodness, and challenge with unanswerable potency his declaration of Deity as all-good, all-wise, and all powerful."[2]

---

1. A. E. Powell.

2. See his essay on "A Plea for Atheism", "Humanity's Gain from Unbelief"—p. 23.

"One might say the variation is due to heredity and environment. No doubt they are partly instrumental; but surely they cannot be solely responsible for the subtle distinctions that exist between individuals. Otherwise we fail to understand why twins, physically alike, sharing equal privileges of upbringing, are often *temperamentally*, *intellectually*, and *morally totally different*."

Dealing with this question of heredity Dr. Th. Pascal writes in his interesting book on "Reincarnation":—

"To return to the role played by the germ in the question of heredity we repeat that the physical germ, of itself alone, explains only a portion of man; it throws light on the physical side of heredity, but leaves in as great darkness as ever the problem of moral and intellectual faculty. If it represented the whole man, one would expect to find in any individual the qualities manifested in his progenitors and parents—never any other; these qualities could not exceed the amount possessed by the parents, whereas we find criminals from birth in the most respectable families and saints born to parents who are the very scum of society. You may come across twins, i.e., beings born from the same germs, under the same conditions of time and environment, one of whom is an angel and the other a demon, though their physical forms closely resemble each other.

"Child prodigies are sufficiently numerous to frequently trouble the thinker with the problem of heredity.

"In the lineage of these prodigies has there been found a single ancestor capable of explaining these faculties, as astonishing as they are premature? If to the absence of a cause in their progenitors is added the fact that genius is not hereditary,[1] that Mozarts, Beethovens, and Dantes have left no children stamped from birth as prodigies or genius, we shall be forced to the conclusion that, within the limits it has taken up, materialism is unable to explain heredity.

"Nor is heredity always realised; many a physical characteristic is not reproduced; in families tainted with dangerous physiological defects, many children escape the evil, and the diseased tendencies of the tissues remain latent in them, although they often afflict their descendants. On the other hand extremely divergent mental types are often met with in the same family, and many a virtuous parent is torn with grief on seeing the vicious tendencies of the child.........

"This is the reason we find that heredity and environment either fail to fulfil their promise or else give what was not their's to give."[2]

According to Buddhism this *variation* is due not only to heredity, environment, "nature and nurture",[3] but also to our own Kamma or, in other words, to our own inherited past actions and present deeds. We ourselves are responsible for our own deeds, happiness, and misery. We create our own heavens. We

---

1. Of Shakespeare, Col. Ingersold writes:
   "Neither of his parents could read or write. He grew up in a small and ignorant village."
2. Dr. Th. Pascal in *Reincarnation*.
3. "Human inequality springs from two sources, nature and nurture."—J. B. S. Haldane—"The Inequality of Man"—p. 23.

build our own hells. We are the architects of our own fate. In short we ourselves are our own Kamma.

[1] On one occasion a certain young man named *Subha* approached the Buddha, and questioned why and wherefore it was that among human beings there are low and high states.

"For," said he, "we find amongst mankind the *short-lived* and the *long-lived*, the *sickly* and the *healthy*, the *ill-looking* and the *good-looking*, the *unfluential* and the *influential*, the *poor* and the *rich*, the *low-born* and the *high-born*, the *ignorant* and the *intelligent*."

The Buddha briefly replied: "Every living being has Kamma as its own, its inheritance, its cause, its kinsman, its refuge. Kamma is that which differentiates all living beings into low and high states."

He then enumerated the causes of such differences:

If a person destroys life, is a hunter, besmears his hands with blood, is engaged in killing and wounding, and is not merciful towards living beings, he, as a result of his killing, when born amongst mankind, will have a *brief life*.

If a person avoids killing, leaves aside cudgel and weapon, and is merciful and compassionate towards all living beings, he, as a result of his non-killing, when born amongst mankind, will enjoy *long life*.

---

1 Cullakamma Vibhanga Sutta—Majjhima Nikāya No. 135. Compare the Venerable Nāgasena's reply to the identical question put by King Milinda. See Warren's "Buddhism in Translation"—p. 214.

If a person is in the habit of harming others with fist or clod, with cudgel or sword, he, as a result of his harmfulness, when born amongst mankind, will *suffer from various diseases.*

If a person is not in the habit of harming others, he, as a result of his harmlessness, when born amongst mankind, will *enjoy good health.*

If a person is wrathful and turbulent, is irritated by a trivial word, gives vent to anger, ill-will, and resentment, he, as a result of his irritability, when born amongst mankind, will be *ill-looking.*

If a person is not wrathful and turbulent, is not irritated even by a torrent of abuse, does not give vent to anger, ill-will, and resentment, he, as a result of his amiability, when born amongst mankind, will be *good-looking.*

If a person is jealous, envies the gains of others, marks of respect and honour shown to others, stores jealousy in his heart, he, as a result of his jealousy, when born amongst mankind, will be *uninfluential.*

If a person is not jealous, does not envy the gains of others, marks of respect and honour shown to others, stores not jealousy in his heart, he, as a result of his non-jealousy, when born amongst mankind, will be *influential.*

If a person does not give anything for charity, he, as a result of his greediness, when born amongst mankind, will be *poor.*

If a person is bent on charitable giving, he, as a result of his generosity, when born amongst mankind, will be *rich.*

If a person is stubborn, haughty, honours not those who are worthy of honour, he, as a result of his arrogance and irreverence, when born amongst mankind, will have a *birth* in a *low family.*

If a person is not stubborn, not haughty, honours those who are worthy of honour, he, as a result of his humility and deference, when born amongst mankind, will have a *birth* in a *high family.*

If a person does not approach the learned and the virtuous and inquire what is good and what is evil, what is right and what is wrong, what should be practised and what should not be practised, what should be done and what should not be done, what conduces to one's welfare and what to the reverse, he, as a result of his non-inquiring spirit, when born amongst mankind, will be *ignorant.*

If a person does approach the learned and the virtuous and make the above inquiries, he, as a result of his inquiring spirit, when born amongst mankind, will be *intelligent.*

* * * *

In connection with this variation the *Atthasālinī* states[1]:—

"Depending on *this* difference in Kamma appears the difference in the birth of beings, high and low, base and exalted, happy and miserable. Depending on the difference in Kamma appears the difference in the individual features of beings as beautiful and ugly, high-born or low-born, well-built or deformed.

1. See "The Expositor," pt. 1, p. 87.

Depending on the difference on Kamma appears the difference in the worldly conditions of beings as gain and loss, fame and disgrace, blame and praise, happiness and misery.

> "*By Kamma the world moves,*
> *by Kamma men live,*
> *and by Kamma are beings bound;*
> *As by its pin the rolling chariot wheel.*
> *By Kamma one attains glory and praise,*
> *By Kamma bondage, ruin, tyranny.*
> *Knowing that Kamma bears fruit manifold,*
> *Why say ye, 'In the world no Kamma is?'*"

Thus we see that our mental, intellectual, and moral differences are mainly due to our own actions and tendencies.

With respect to this similarity of actions and reactions, the following note[1] by Dr. Grimm will perhaps be of interest to the readers:—

"It is not difficult in all these cases also to show the law of affinity as the regulator of the grasping of a new germ that occurs at death.

"Whoso devoid of compassion, can kill men or even animals, carries deep within himself the inclination to shorten life. He finds satisfaction or even pleasure in the short-livedness of other creatures. Short-lived germs have therefore some affinity which makes itself known after his death in the grasping of another germ which then takes place to his own detriment. Even so, germs bearing within themselves

---

1. George Grimm—"The Doctrine of the Buddha," p. 246.

the power of developing into a deformed body, have an affinity for one who finds pleasure in ill-treating and disfiguring others.

"An angry person begets within himself an affinity for ugly bodies and their respective germs, since it is the characteristic mark of anger to disfigure the face.

"Whoever is jealous, niggardly, haughty, carries within himself the tendency to grudge everything to others and to despise them. Accordingly germs that are destined to develop in poor, outward circumstances, possess affinity for him.

"It is, of course, only a consequence of the above, that a change of sex may also ensue.

"Thus it is related in the Dīgha Nikāya No. xxi that Gopikā, a daughter of the Sākya house, was reborn after her death as Gopaka Devaputta, because the female mind has become repulsive to her, and she had formed a male mind within herself."

Although Buddhism attributes this variation to Kamma, yet it does *not* assert that *everything is due to Kamma.*

If everything were due to Kamma, a person must ever be bad for it is his Kamma to be bad. One need not consult a physician to be cured of a disease; for if one's Kamma is such, one will be cured.

In refuting the view that "whatsoever weal or woe or neutral feeling is experienced, all that is due to some previous action", the Buddha says:

"So, then, owing to a previous action, men will become murderers, thieves, unchaste, liars, slanderers, abusive, babblers, covetous, malicious, and perverse in view. Thus for those who fall back on the former deed as the essential reason there is neither desire to do, nor effort to do, nor necessity to do this deed or abstain from that deed." [1]

There are *five orders* or *Niyāmas* according to Buddhism:

(i) *Kamma Niyāma*, order of act and result; e.g., desirable and undesirable results follow good and bad actions respectively.

(ii) *Utu Niyāma*, physical (inorganic) order; e.g., seasonal phenomena of winds and rains.

(iii) *Bīja Niyāma*, order of germs or seeds; e.g., rice produced from rice-seed, sugary taste resulting from sugar-cane or honey, etc.

(iv) *Citta Niyāma*, order of mind; e.g., processes of consciousness *(Citta Vīthi)* etc.

(v) *Dhamma Niyāma*, order of the norm; e.g., the phenomena occuring at the advent of a Bodhisatta in his last birth, gravitation, etc.

Kamma is, therefore, only one of the five orders that prevail in the universe.

This law of Kamma, it must be admitted, can neither be proved nor disproved experimentally.

---

1. Gradual Sayings – Vol. 1, p. 157.

CHAPTER XII

WHAT IS KAMMA?

KAMMA — Sanskrit *Karma* — literally means "*action.*" In its ultimate sense *Kamma* means good and bad volition (*Kusala Akusala Cetanā*).

The Buddha says: "I declare, O Bhikkhus, that volition is Kamma. Having willed, one acts by body, speech, and thought."

Every volitional action, except that of a Buddha and an Arahant, is called Kamma. The Buddhas and Arahants do not accumulate fresh Kamma, as they have destroyed all their passions. They are delivered from evil and good.[1]

There is no Kamma where there is no consciousness (*Nāma*). Plants, for instance, do not accumulate Kamma. Nor is any action a Kamma which is unintentional, for Kamma depends on the will or volition that is involved in the doing. Any deed which is devoid of willing or intention is, therefore, not called a Kamma.

There are some religions that attribute the unevenness of life to Kamma, but they go at a tangent with Buddhism when they propound the irrational theory that even unintentional actions are Kamma. According to them "the unintentional murderer of his mother is a hideous criminal. The man who commits murder or who harasses in any way a living being

---

1. See p. 97.

without intent, is none the less guilty, just as a man who touches fire is burnt."

This astounding theory undoubtedly leads to palpable absurdities. The embryo and the mother would both be guilty of making each other suffer. Further the analogy of the fire is logically fallacious. For instance, a man would not be guilty if he got another person to commit the murder, for one is not burnt if one gets another to put his hand into the fire. Moreover unintentional wrong actions would be much worse than intentional wrong actions, for, according to the comparison, a man who touches fire without knowing that it would burn is likely to be more deeply burnt than the man who knows.[1]

In the working of Kamma mind is the most important factor. All our actions, words, and thoughts are coloured by the mind or consciousness we experience at such particular moments. "When the mind is unguarded, bodily action is unguarded, speech also is unguarded, thought also is unguarded. When the mind is guarded, bodily action is guarded, speech also is guarded and thought also is guarded."

"*By mind the world is led, by mind is drawn:*
And all men own the sovereignty of mind."

"If one speaks or acts with an evil mind, pain follows one as the wheel, the hoof of the ox.

" If one speaks or acts with a good mind, happiness follows one as the shadow that never departs."

One might ask whether this immaterial mind is capable of producing tremendous changes in the

---

1. Poussin—"The Way to Nirvana"—p. 68.

external world. Well, it is neither strange nor wonderful as one might imagine. The most wonderful and powerful machines that tend to revolutionise the whole world today are the direct results of thoughts that originated in the minds of great scientists.

*   *   *   *

Kamma and Vipaka

According to Abhidhamma Kamma constitutes the twelve types of immoral consciousness, eight types of moral consciousness pertaining to the Sentient Realm (*Kāmāvacara*), five types of moral consciousness pertaining to the Realms of Forms (*Rūpāvacara*), and four types of moral consciousness pertaining to the Formless Realms (*Arūpāvacara*).[1]

The volitional activities of the supramundane consciousness (*Lokuttara Citta*) are not regarded as Kamma since they do not cause rebirth. They, on the contrary, tend to eradicate passions that condition rebirth. In the supramundane consciousness wisdom (*Paññā*) is predominant, whilst in the ordinary types of conscousness volition (*cetanā*) is predominant.

The nine types of moral consciousness pertaining to the Realms of Forms and to the Formless Realms are the five *Rūpāvacara* and four *Arūpva cara Jhānas* (Ecstasies). They are purely mental.

Words and deeds are caused by the remaining twenty types of consciousness. Verbal actions are done by mind by means of speech. Bodily actions are

1. See Compendium of Philosophy — Abhidhammattha Sangha, Chapter 1.

done by mind through the instrument of the body. Purely mental actions have no other instrument than the mind.

These twenty-nine types of consciousness are called Kamma because they have the power to produce their due effects (*Vipāka*) quite automatically, independent of any external agency. Just as every object is accompanied by a shadow, even so every volitional activity is accompanied by its due effect.

Those types of consciousness one experiences as inevitable consequences of one's good and bad thoughts are called resultant consciousness (*Vipāka*). The twenty-three types of resultant consciousness pertaining to the Sentient Realm, the five types of resultant consciousness pertaining to the Realms of Form and the four types of resultant consciousness pertaining to the Formless Realms are called the *Vipāka* or fruition of Kamma.

The external differences such as health, wealth, sickness, poverty, etc. are the *Vipākānisaṅsa*—consequences.

A mango seed, for instance, is like the *Kamma;* mango fruit is like the *Vipāka*, effect; the leaves and flowers are like the *Vipākanisaṅsa.*

Kamma, therefore, does not necessarily mean only past actions; it may be both past and present actions.

For instance, at the moment of giving something to the poor, I experience a good thought which will have its reaction at any opportune moment in the form of a gift from another. On receiving the gift I experience a good consciousness which is the result of a past good thought of mine.

We plant a seed today. Sooner or later we will be able to reap its fruit. In the same way, according to the law of Kamma, every good and bad thought will produce its reaction when a suitable occasion arises.

Kamma is action and Vipāka, fruit, is its re-action. It is not fate. It is not pre-destination which is imposed on us by some mysterious unknown power, to which we must helplessly submit ourselves. It is one's own doing which re-acts on one's own self. It is a law in itself. In other words it is the law of cause and effect in the ethical realm.

Hence, it is as clear as daylight that the doctrine of Kamma is the very opposite of fatalism. This just doctrine holds that man can control his future by creating now what will produce good effects in future.

It is this doctrine of Kamma which the mother teaches her child when she says: "Be good and you will be happy, and others will love you. But if you are bad, you will be unhappy, and others will hate you."

The *Sanyutta Nikāya* says:

> *"According to the seed that's sown,*
> *So is the fruit ye reap therefrom,*
> *Doer of good will gather good,*
> *Doer of evil, evil reaps.*
> *Sown is the seed, and thou shalt taste*
> *The fruit thereof."* *

---

* *Sanyutta Nikāya—Vol. I, p. 227.*

What is the Cause of Kamma ?

This so-called "*I*" which is composed of mind and matter is compelled to act. It receives impressions from internal and external stimuli. Sensations arise thereby, and owing to the latent *Ignorance* and *Craving* one accumulates deeds which consequently produce rebirth in states of happiness or states of misery.

Evil acts lead to misery, good acts lead to happiness. Nevertheless, good actions are necessary to escape this cycle of rebirth.

A drowning man would tenaciously cling to a corpse which, ordinarily, he would detest, and save himself. After his escape he would no longer cling to it but throw it away. Even so a person would do good to escape this cycle of birth and death. After gaining Deliverance he would no more accumulate fresh Kammic activities which produce rebirth. He will be beyond both good and evil.

Not knowing things as they truly are does one accumulate Kamma. No Kamma is accumulated by him who has completely eradicted his craving and has understood things as they truly are.

* * * *

The doer of Kamma.

Who is the doer of Kamma? Who reaps the fruit of Kamma? "Is it a sort of accretion about a soul, as is taught in Hinduism, which the soul, a part of the Divine Essence, builds about itself?"

Says the Venerable Buddhaghosa in the Visuddhi Magga:—

> *"No doer is there who does the deed*
> *Nor is there one who feels the fruit;*
> *Constituent parts alone roll on......"*

In the ultimate sense (*Paramattha Sacceno*) a Buddhist cannot conceive of any unchanging entity, any being in the form of a Deva, a man or an animal. These forms are merely temporary manifestations of the Kammic force. "Being" is only a term used for conventional purposes. Strictly speaking, what we call a "being" is nothing but a mere composition of mind and matter.

Matter, according to Buddhism, is merely a manifestation of forces and qualities. Mind, too, is nothing beyond a complex compound of fleeting mental states. Each unit of consciousness consists of three phases—genesis (*Uppāda*), development (*Ṭhiti*), and dissolution (*Bhanga*). One unit of consciousness perishes only to give birth to another. The subsequent thought-moment is neither the same as its predecessor because it is not absolutely identical nor entirely another, being the same stream of Kamma energy.

We Buddhists believe that there is no actor apart from action, no perceiver apart from perception, or, in other words, no conscious subject behind consciousness.

Who, then, is the doer of Kamma? What experiences Kamma?

Volition or will (*Cetanā*) is itself the doer. Feeling (*Vedanā*) is itself the reaper of the fruits of Kamma. Apart from these mental states there is none to sow and none to reap.

Just as, says the Venerable Buddhaghosa, in the case of these elements of matter that go under the name of tree, as soon as at any point the fruit springs up, it is then said "the tree bears fruit" or "thus the tree has fructified"; so also in the case of groups (*Khandas*) which go under the name of Deva or man when a fruition of happiness or misery springs up at any point, then it is said "that Deva or man is happy or miserable." Strictly speaking, there is neither a sower nor a reaper besides the volition and the feeling.

Where is Kamma ?

"Stored within the psyche (mind)," says a certain writer on psycho-analysis, "but usually inaccessible and to be reached only by some, is the whole record, without exception, of every experience the individual has ever passed through, every influence felt, every impression received. The sub-conscious mind is not only an indelible record of individual experiences but also retains the impress of primeval impulses and tendencies which so far from being outgrown as we fondly deem in civilised man, are subconsciously active and apt to break out in disconcerting strength at unexpected moments."

We Buddhists would make the same assertion but with a slight modification. Not stored within the psyche, would we say, for there is neither a receptacle nor a store-house in this ever-changing complex machinery of man but dependent on the Five Groups (*Pañcakkhanda*) or the flux is every experience the individual has passed through, every influence felt, every impression received, every characteristic, divine, human or brutal. In short the whole Kamma force is dependent on the flux, ever ready to manifest itself in multifarious phenomena as occasion arises.

"Where, Reverend Sir," is Kamma?" questions King Milinda from the Venerable Nagasena.

"O Mahārāja," says the Venerable Nagasena, "Kamma is not said to be stored somewhere in this fleeting consciousness or in any other part of the body. But dependent on mind and matter it rests manifesting itself at the opportune moment, just as mangoes are not said to be stored somewhere in the mango tree, but dependent on the mango tree they lie springing up in due season."

Just as wind or fire is not stored in any particular place, even so Kamma is not stored anywhere within or without this body.

Kamma is an individual force, and is transmitted from one existence to another. It plays the chiefest part in the moulding of character and explains that marvellous phenomena of Genius. The clear understanding of this Doctrine is essential for the welfare of the world.

CHAPTER XIII

THE WORKING OF KAMMA

THE working of Kamma is not a subject which could easily be grasped by the ordinary intellect. Only a Buddha can fully comprehend this intricate law. In order to understand the working of Kamma it is necessary to get some idea of the process of consciousness *(Citta Vīthi)* according to the Abhidhamma.

The subject, the consciousness, receives objects from within and without. When a person is in a state of profound sleep his mind is said to be vacant, or, in other words, in a state of Bhavānga. We experience such a sub-conscious state when our minds do not respond to external objects. This sub-conscious state or the flow of Bhavanga is interrupted when objects enter the mind. The Bhavānga consciousness which one always experiences as long as it is uninterrupted by stimuli, vibrates for two thought-moments and pass away. Then the consciousness of the kind that apprehends sensation[1]. (*Pañcadvārāvajjana*) arises and ceases. At this stage the natural flow is checked and turned towards the object. Immediately after which there arises and ceases visual consciousness[1] (*Cakkhu viññāṇa*), but yet knows no more about it. This sense operation is followed by a moment of reception of the object so seen (*Sampaṭicchana*). Next comes the

1. I.e. if the object be a form *(Rūpa)*. This consciousness depends on the object of sense received.

investigating faculty (*Santīrana*) or a momentary examination of the object so received. After this comes that stage of representative cognition termed the determining consciousness (*Votthapana*) on which depends the subsequent psychologically important stage—apperception—or Javana. This Javana stage usually lasts for seven thought-moments, or, at times of death, five. The whole process which happens in an infinitesimal part of time ends with the registering consciousness (*Tadālambana*), lasting for two thought-moments—thus completing one thought process at the expiration of seventeen thought-moments. It must be understood that at this important apperceptional stage one does both good and bad Kamma*.

"The smile of the mango tree may here serve to illustrate the above process. A man, lost in deep sleep, is lying at the foot of a mango tree with his

---

* The thought process runs as follows:

1	2	3
* * *	* * *	* * *
Atīta Bhavānga	*Bhavanga Calana*	*Bhavānga Upaccheda*
"Past Bhavānga"	"Vibrating Bhavānga"	"Arrest Bhavānga"

4	5	6
* * *	* * *	* * *
Āvajjana	*Dassana*	*Sampaṭicchana*
"Sense-door consciousness"	"Visual consciousness"	"Receiving consciousness"

7	8 9 10 11 12 13 14
* * *	*** *** *** *** *** *** ***
Santīrana	*Javana—"Apperception"*
"Investigating consciousness"	

15	16 17
* * *	* * * * * *
Votthapana	*Tadalambana*
"Determining consciousness"	"Registering consciousness"

head covered. A wind now stirs the branches, and a fruit falls besides the sleeping man. He is in consequence aroused from dreamless slumbers. He removes his head-covering in order to ascertain what has awakened him. He sees the newly fallen fruit, picks it up and examines it. Apprehending it to be a fruit with certain constitutive attributes observed in the previous stage of investigation, he eats it, and then, replacing his head-covering, once more resigns himself to sleep.

"The dreamless sleep corresponds to the unperturbed current of the stream of being (*Bhavāṅga*). The striking of the wind against the tree is like the "past" life-moment, during which the object enters the stream and passes down with it, without perturbing it. The swaying of the branches in that wind represents the vibration of the stream of being. The falling of the fruit corresponds to the arrest or interruption of being, the moment at which the stream is "cut off" by thought; the waking of the man to the awakening of attention in the act of cognition on occasion of sense; the removal of the head-covering to the sense re-action of sight. The picking up of the fruit is comparable to the operation of receiving; inspection of it recalls the examining function. The simple apprehension of the fruit as such, with certain constitutive attributes of its own corresponds to the discriminative or determining stage; the eating of the fruit resembles the act of apperception. Finally, the swallowing of the last morsels that are left in the mouth corresponds to the operation of retention, after which the mind subsides into more vital process, even as the man once more falls asleep." (*Compendium of Philosophy by S. Z. Aung—Introductory Essay p. 30*).

If, for instance, A hits B, the latter will consequently experience some pain. This unpleasant sensation is the result of some past bad Kamma. If B is not a self-controlled person, he will, through his indiscrimination, engender thoughts of hatred towards A. The generating of those thoughts occurs in the Javana process. This doing of bad Kamma is his own, even if it be admitted that A acted as the cause, and he, too, did a bad Kamma on his part. Here comes the question of freewill in Buddhism.

The evil effect of the first Javana thought-moment being the weakest, B may reap in this life itself. This is called "immediately effective" (*Diṭṭhadhamma-vedanīya*) Kamma.

If it did not operate in this life, the Kamma becomes "ineffective" (*Ahosi*).

The next weakest is the seventh thought-moment. The evil effect of which B may reap in the second birth. This is called "subsequently effective" (*Upapajjavedanīya*) Kamma.

This, too, becomes ineffective if it did not operate in the second birth.

The effects of the intermediate thought-moments may take place at any time until B attains Nibbāna. The Kamma of this type is known as "indefinitely effective" (*Aparāpariyavedanīya*).

The working of good Kamma is similar to the above. The effect of a good Kamma generally occurs in the form of a pleasant sensation.

It is evident from this classification of Kamma that there are actions which may produce their due effects in this very life, or in a subsequent life, or in any life in the course of one's wanderings in Sansāra.

Illustrations:

A certain Brahman and his wife possessed only one upper garment to wear when they go out of doors. One day the husband went to hear the Dhamma from the Buddha, and was so pleased with the Doctrine that he wanted to offer his only upper garment, but his greed would not permit him to do so. He combated with his passions till morning, and finally overcoming his greed, offered the robe to the Buddha and exclaimed, "I have won, I have won." The king, who was present on the occasion, was delighted to hear his story and in appreciation of his generosity presented him thirty-two robes. The poor Brahman kept one for himself and another for his wife and offered the rest to the Buddha.[1]

This is the result of a good Kamma reaped in this life itself.

The following story illustrates the result of a bad Kamma reaped in this life.

A hunter who was going to the forest, followed by his dogs, met by the wayside a Bhikkhu who was proceeding on his alms round. As the hunter could not procure any game he thought it was because he met the Bhikkhu. Whilst returning home he met the same Bhikkhu, and his anger heightened by his second sight. In spite of the entreaties of the innocent Bhikkhu he set the dogs on him. Finding no escape therefrom the Bhikkhu climbed a tree. The wicked man ran up to the tree, and pierced the soles of his feet with the point of an arrow. The pain was unbearable for the Bhikkhu, and the robe he was wearing fell upon the

1. Buddhist Legends, (Dhammapadaṭṭha Kathā) pt. 2, p. 262.

hunter completely covering him. The dogs thinking that the Bhikkhu had fallen from the tree devoured their own master.[1]

Subsequently Effective Kamma :

An employee of *Anāthapiṇḍika*, the millionaire, returned home in the evening after his laborious work in the field, and found that all were observing the Eight Precepts as it was a full moon day. Learning that he could also observe the Precepts even for half a day he spent the day accordingly, without taking any meal at night. However, he died in the following morning and was born as a Deva owing to his good Kamma.[2]

Ajātasattu was immediately after his death born in a state of misery as the result of his killing the father.

Indefinitely Effective Kamma :

No one, not even the Buddha and Arahants, is exempt from this class of Kamma.

The Arahant Moggallāna, in one of his previous births, killed his mother and father. As a result of which he suffered long in the Avīci, the most woeful state and even in his last birth he was clubbed to death before he finally passed away.

The Buddha was imputed with the murder of a female follower of the naked ascetics as a result of his having insulted a Pacceka Buddha in one of his previous births.

Devadatta attempted to kill Him, and His foot was injured, because in a previous birth of His, He killed a step-brother with the object of appropriating his property.

---

1. Buddhist Legends, (Dhammapadaṭṭha Kathā) pt. 2, p. 282.
2. Buddhist Legends, (Dhammapadaṭṭha Kathā) pt. 1, p. 278.

The above-mentioned classification of Kamma is *with reference to the time in which effects are worked out.*

*   *   *   *

The following classification is according to "*Function*."

Every birth is conditioned by a past good or bad Kamma which predominates at the moment of death. The Kamma that conditions the future birth is called *Reproductive* or *Janaka Kamma.*

Our forms are but the outward manifestations of the invisible Kammic force. This all-pervading force carries with it all our characteristics, which usually lie latent, but may rise to the surface at unexpected moments. Hence it is difficult to judge another as long as one is a worlding. A person may safely be judged by the thought he experiences at a particular moment. As to his future one cannot definitely say.

The death of a person is merely "the temporary end of a temporary phenomenon." Though the present form perishes another form which is neither the same nor entirely different takes place according to the thought that was powerful at the death moment, as the Kammic force which propels the life flux still survives. It is this last thought, which is technically called Reproductive Kamma, that determines the state of a person in his subsequent birth.

This may be either a good or a bad Kamma.

Now another Kamma may step forward to assist or maintain the action of this Reproductive Kamma. Just as this Kamma has the tendency to strengthen the Reproductive Kamma some other action, which tends to weaken, interrupt, or retard the fruition of the Reproductive Kamma, may step in. Such actions are respectively termed "Supportive" (*Upatthambhaka*) and "Counteractive" (*Upapīḍaka*) Kamma.

According to the Law of Kamma the potential energy of the Reproductive Kamma could be nullified by a more powerful opposing Kamma of the past, which, seeking an opportunity, may quite unexpectedly operate, just as a powerful opposing force can check the path of the flying arrow and bring it down to the ground. Such an action is called "Destructive" or *Upaghātaka* Kamma, which is more effective than the above two in that it not only obstructs but also destroys the whole force.

As an instance of the operation of all the four, the case of Devadatta who attempted to kill the Buddha and who caused a schism in the Sangha, may be cited.

His Reproductive good Kamma conditioned him a birth in a royal family. His continued comfort and prosperity were due to the action of the Supportive Kamma. The Counteractive Kamma came into operation when he was subject to much humiliation as a result of his being excommunicated from the Sangha. Finally the Destructive Kamma brought his life to a miserable end.

* * * *

There is another classification of Kamma according to the *priority of effect.*

The first is *Garuka* which means weighty or serious. This Kamma which is either good or bad produces results in this life or in the next for certain. If good, it is purely mental as in the case of Jhānas (Ecstasies). Otherwise it is verbal or bodily. The five kinds of weighty Kamma are:

1. Matricide,
2. Parricide,
3. The murder of an Arahant,
4. The wounding of a Buddha,
5. The creation of a schism in the Sangha.

Permanent Scepticism[1] (*Niyata Micchādiṭṭhi*) is also termed one of the Weighty Kammas.

---

1. PERMANENT SCEPTICISM " As the appearance of scepticism amongst the causes of the most grievous Evil mental Action that a man can generate may give rise to apprehension in some, we must explain what is really involved. The 'Scepticism' referred to is not, of course, the mere disbelief, a state resultant from lack of knowledge,—of the principles of the Buddha Dhamma. In the most tolerant religion in the world such a doctrine would of course be totally out of place. It is the confirmed mental attitude of denial of all Good that is implied ; the steadfast and persistent denial of the existence of any law or power of Righteousness whatever ; the denial of any good or holy or noble purpose in all highest and holiest deeds; the consistent misattribution of all nobility and charity and magnanimity to the basest and most selfish motives. It is this,—and not an attitude of suspended judgment,—which is generally associated with the word 'Scepticism' that is here classified amongst the terrible crimes of matricide etc. And the reason is obvious. Since it is the mental attitude of a man which is constantly building the character of his future flux, and since it is his own mind that he sees as it were projected upon the external world, it follows, first, that whoso is guilty of this mental attitude must himself be devoid of these good qualities which are the means of emancipation, and secondly, by allowing this attitude to become confirmed, he is not only perpetuating in the world a monster devoid of every moral guidance,—but his words and inter-course with mankind tend to poison with the same evil doctrine all weak-minded persons with whom he comes in contact."—Ananda Metteyya—"*Buddhism*"—Vol. II, p. 74

If, for instance, any person were to develop the Jhānas and later were to commit one of these heinous crimes, his good Kamma would get obliterated by the powerful evil Kamma. His subsequent birth will be conditioned by the evil Kamma in spite of his having gained the Jhānas earlier. Devadatta lost his psychic powers and was born in an evil state, because he wounded the Buddha and caused a schism in the Order.

King Ajātasattu would have attained the first stage of Sainthood, if he had not committed parricide. In this case the powerful evil Kamma acted as an obstacle to gaining Sainthood,

In the absence of the Weighty Kamma to condition the future birth, a death-proximate (*Āsanna*) Kamma might operate. This is the Kamma one does immediately before the dying moment. Owing to the great part it plays in determining the future birth much importance is attached to this death-bed Kamma in almost all Buddhist countries. The custom of reminding the dying man of his good deeds and making him do good deeds on his death-bed still prevails in Ceylon, Burma and other Buddhist countries.

Sometimes a bad person may die happily and receive a good birth, if fortunately he remembers or does a good act at the last moment. A story runs that a certain executioner who casually happened to give some alms to the Venerable Sāriputta remembered this good act at the dying moment and was born in a state of happiness. This does not mean that although he enjoys a good birth he will be exempt from the effects of the evil deeds he accumulated during his life-time.

At times a good person may die unhappily by suddenly remembering an evil act of his or by harbouring some unpleasant thought, perchance compelled by unfavourable circumstances. Such unhappy ends are sometimes due to the ignorance of the relatives who may molest or worry the dying person.

Queen Mallikā, the consort of King Kosala, led a righteous life, but as a result of remembering, at her death moment, a lie which she had uttered she had to suffer for about seven days in a state of misery.

These are only some exceptional cases. As a rule the last thought-moment is conditioned by the general conduct of a person. However, it is always advisable to remind the dying person of his good deeds and turn his attention away from all worldly bonds and worries.

"Habitual" (*Āciṇṇa*) Kamma is the next in priority of effect. It is the Kamma that one habitually performs and recollects and for which one has a great liking.

Habits whether good or bad become second nature. They tend to form the character of a person. At leisure moments one often thinks of one's habitual characteristics. In the same way at the death moment, unless influenced by other circumstances, one, as a rule, recalls to mind one's habitual characteristics.

A miser will constantly think of his gold and may not be able to detach his mind from his cherished possessions. A drunkard will be worried with his glass of liquor. A social worker will be interested in his social activities. A spiritual adviser will be always intent on his spiritual work. Thus we may be dominated by our habitual doings, especially at our death moments, in spite of the attempts of friends and relatives to turn our attention otherwise.

Cunda, the butcher, who was living in the vicinity of the Buddha's monastery, died yelling like an animal because he was earning his living by slaughtering pigs.

King Dutthagāmaṇī of Ceylon was in the habit of giving alms to the monks before he takes his meals. It was this habitual Kamma that gladdened him at the dying moment and gave him rebirth in Tusita heaven.

The last in this category is the "Cumulative" (*Kaṭattā*) Kamma in which is included all that cannot be brought under the above-mentioned three. This is as it were the reserve fund of a particular being.

The last classification is according to the place in which the Kamma effects transpire, namely:—

1. Evil Kamma (*Akusala*) which may ripen in the Sentient Existence (Kāmaloka).
2. Good Kamma (*Kusala)* which may ripen in the Sentient Existence.
3. Good Kamma which may ripen in the Realm of Form (*Rūpaloka*).
4. Good Kamma which may ripen in the Formless Realms (*Arūpaloka*).

CHAPTER XIV

THE WORKING OF KAMMA—*(contd.)*

Evil Kamma

THERE are ten evil Kammas which are caused by deed, word, and thought.

Three are caused by deed—namely, killing, stealing, and unchastity.

Four are caused by word—namely, lying, slandering, harsh speech, and frivolous talk.

Three are caused by mind—namely, coveteousness, ill-will, and false view.

Killing means the destruction of any living being. The Pāli term used is *Pāṇa* which means that which breathes. According to Abhidhamma *Pāṇa* is the psycho-physical life confined to a particular existence. The quick destruction of this life force without allowing it to run its due course is *Pāṇātipāta*. Animals are also included in living beings, but not plant life.[1]

The following five conditions are necessary to complete this offence of killing:—a being, consciousness that it is a being, intention of killing, effort, and consequent death.

1. In plants there is no transmission of stimuli by nerves. Nerves are unknown to them as nerve-centres.

—Dr. Karl V. Frisch in *You and Life*, p. 125.

Gravity of the crime depends on the goodness and the size of the being concerned. In the case of a virtuous person or a big animal it is more heinous (Mahā Sāvajja) than in the case of a vicious person or a small animal. Nevertheless, it is a killing which entails suffering.

The evil effects of killing are:—short life, diseasefulness, constant grief caused by the separation from the loved, and constant fear.

Five conditions are necessary to complete the offence of stealing (*Adinnādāna*), viz:—another's property, consciousness that it is so, intention of stealing, effort, and consequent removal.

The evil effects of stealing are:—poverty, wretchedness, unfulfilled desires, dependent livelihood.

Three conditions are necessary to complete the offence of unchastity (*Kāmesu Micchācāra*), viz:—the mind to enjoy the forbidden object, the effort to enjoy, devices to obtain, and possession.

The evil effects of unchastity are:—having many enemies, getting undesirable wives, birth as a woman or as an eunuch.

Four conditions are necessary to complete the offence of lying (*Musāvāda*), viz:—an untrue thing, intention to deceive, corresponding effort, the communication of the matter to others.

The gravity of this evil depends on the loss caused to others by uttering the untruth. It is a small offence, if someone denies the possession of something because he does not wish to give it to another. It becomes a great offence, if people perjure themselves in order to cause loss to others.

The evil effects of lying are:—being tormented by abusive speech, being subject to vilification, incredibility, and stinking mouth.

Four conditions are necessary to complete the offence of slandering (*Pisuṇavācā*), viz:—other persons to be divided, the purpose to separate them, or the desire to endear oneself to another, corresponding effort, and the communication.

The evil effects of slandering are:—the dissolution of friendship without any sufficient cause.

Three conditions are necessary to complete the offence of harsh speech (*Pharusavācā*), viz:—another to be abused, angry thought, and the abuse.

The evil effects of harsh speech are:—being detested by others, although quite blameless, and harsh voice.

Two conditions are necessary to complete the offence of frivolous talk (*Samphappalāpa*), viz:—the inclination towards frivolous talk and its narration.

The evil effects of frivolous talk are:—disorderliness of the bodily organs and unacceptable speech.

Covetousness (*Abhijjhā*) has the characteristic mark of thinking, 'Ah! would this property were mine!' The two conditions necessary to complete this offence are:—another's property and the bending over to it, saying—'Would this were mine!'

---

1. See "The Expositor" pt. 1, p. 128.

The evil effect of covetousness is the nonfulfilment of one's wishes.

Two conditions are necessary to complete the offence of ill-will (*Vyāpādo*), viz:—another being, and the thought of doing harm.

The evil effects of ill-will are:—ugliness, various diseases, and detestable nature.

False view (*Micchādiṭṭhi*) is seeing things wrongly without regarding them as they truly are. Wrong beliefs like the denial of the efficacy of deeds etc., are included under wrong view.

Two conditions are necessary to complete this wrong, viz:—perverted manner in which the object is viewed, and the understanding of it according to that misguided view.

The evil effects of false view are: base attachment, lack of wisdom, dull wit, chronic diseases, and blameworthy ideas.

"False Views" are ten-fold, viz:—

(1) There is no such thing as "alms" (dinnaṁ). (This means that there is no effect in giving alms).

(2) There is no such thing as "sacrifice" (iṭṭhaṁ), or (3) "offering" (hutaṁ). (Here too the implied meaning is that there is no effect in liberal alms-givings and in giving gifts to guests, etc.)

(4) There is neither fruit, nor result of good or evil deeds.

(5) There is no such thing as "this world" or (6) "the next"; i.e., those born here do not accept

a past existence, and those living here do not accept a world beyond.

(7) There is no mother or (8) father. (The implied meaning is that there is no effect in anything done to them).

(9) There are no beings that die and are being born (Opapātikā).

(10) There are no righteous and well-disciplined recluses and brahmins who, having realised by their own super-intellect this world and world beyond, make known the same. (The reference here is to Buddhas and Arahants.)[1]

---

2. Good Kamma which may ripen in the Sentient Existence:—

[2] There are ten moral actions—namely, generosity (*Dāna*), morality, (*Sīla*), meditation, (*Bhāvanā*), reverence, (*Apacāyana*), service (*Veyyāvacca*), transference of merit (*Pattidāna*), rejoicing in others' merit (*Pattānumodana*), hearing the doctrine (*Dhammasavaṇa*), expounding the Doctrine (*Dhammadesana*), straightening one's views (*Diṭṭhijju Kamma*).

These ten are sometimes treated as twelve. In which case 'Praising others' good works' (*Pasaṁsā*) is added to 'Rejoicing in others' merit', and 'Taking the

---

1. The Pāli text runs as follows:—

" *N'atthi dinnaṁ, n'atthi iṭṭhaṁ, n'atthi hutaṁ, n'atthi sukaṭadukkaṭānaṁ Kammānaṁ phalaṁ vipāko, n'atthi ayaṁ loko, n'atthi paraloko, n'atthi mātā, n'atthi pitā, n'atthi sattā opapātikā, n'atthi loke samaṇa-brāhmaṇā sammaggatā sammāpaṭipannā ye imaṁ ca lokaṁ paraṁ ca lokaṁ sayaṁ abhiññā sacchikatvā pavedenti.*

See Dhammasangani—p. 233; "The Expositor"—pt II, p. 493; and "Buddhist Psychology"—p. 355.

2. See "The Expositor" pt. I, p. 209.

Three Refuges' (*Saraṇa*) and 'Mindfulness (*Anussati*) are used instead of 'Straightening of one's views.'

"Generosity" yields wealth. "Morality" gives birth in noble families and in states of happiness. "Meditation" gives birth in Realms of Form and Formless Realms, and helps to gain Higher Knowledge and Emancipation. "Transference of merit" acts as a cause to give in abundance in future births. "Rejoicing in others' merit" is productive of joy wherever one is born. Both "expounding and hearing the Dhamma" are conducive to wisdom. "Reverence" is the cause of noble parentage. "Service" produces large retinue. "Praising others' good works" results in getting praise to oneself. "Seeking the Three Refuges" results in the destruction of passions. "Mindfulness" is conducive to diverse forms of happiness.

3. Good Kamma which may ripen in the Realms of Form.

These are the five kinds[1] of Rūpa Jhānas or ecstasies which are purely mental.

i. Moral consciousness of the first stage of Jhāna. This occurs together with initial application, sustained application, pleasurable interest, happiness, and one-pointedness.

ii. Moral consciousness of the second stage of Jhāna. This occurs together with sustained

1. According to the Abhidhammattha Sangaha there are five Rūpa Jhānas, but according to the Visuddhi Magga there are four Jhānas. There is no great difference between the two interpretations. In the former the Jhānas are divided into five according to the five constituents. In the latter the second Jhāna consists of three constituents.

application, pleasurable interest, happiness, and one-pointedness.

iii. Moral consciousness of the third stage of Jhāna. This occurs together with pleasurable interest, happiness, and one-pointedness.

iv. Moral consciousness of the fourth stage of Jhāna. This occurs together with happiness and one-pointedness.

v. Moral consciousness of the fifth stage of Jhāna. This occurs together with equanimity and one-pointedness.

These Jhānas have their corresponding effects in the Realms of Form.

---

4. Good Kamma which may ripen in the Formless Realms.

These are the four Arūpa Jhānas which have their corresponding effects in the Arūpa (Formless) Realms.

i. Moral consciousness dwelling in the infinity of space (*Ākāsānañcāyatana*).

ii. Moral consciousness dwelling in the infinity of consciousness (*Viññānañcāyatana*).

iii. Moral consciousness dwelling on nothingness (*Ākiñcaññāyatana*).

iv. Moral consciousness wherein perception neither *is* nor *is not*. (*N'eva Saññā Nāsaññā-yatana*).

CHAPTER XV

NATURE OF KAMMA

IS one bound to reap all that one has sown in just proportion? Not necessarily. In the *Anguttara Nikâya* the Buddha states:—

"If any one says, O Bhikkhus, that a man **must** reap according to his deeds, in that case, O Bhikkhus, there is no religious life nor is an opportunity afforded for the entire extinction of sorrow (*Dukkha*). But if any one says, O Bhikkhus, that what a man reaps **accords** with his deeds, in that case, O Bhikkhus, there is a religious life and an opportunity is afforded for the entire extinction of sorrow."

In Buddhism, therefore, there is every possibility to mould one's Kamma. Here one is not always compelled by an iron necessity.

Although it is stated that neither in heaven, nor in the recesses of a cave, there is any place in the world where one could escape evil Kamma, yet one is not bound to pay all the past arrears of one's Kamma. In such case no escape is possible. One is neither the master nor the servant of this Kamma. Even a most vicious person can by his own effort become the most virtuous person. We are always becoming something, and that something depends on our own actions. We may at any moment change for the better or for the worse. Even the most sinful person should not be discouraged or despised on account of his evil nature. We must have compassion on him for we must have also been in that same position at a certain stage. As we have changed for the better he may also change perhaps sooner than ourselves. Who can say what good Kamma he has in store for him? Who knows his potential goodness?

Who thought that Angulimāla—a highway robber and a murderer of more than a thousand of his fellow brethren—would become a Saint, judging him by his external deeds? But he did become an Arahant and erased, so to say, all his past misdeeds.

Who imagined that Ālavaka, the fierce demon who feasted on the flesh of human beings, would ever become a Saint? Yet he did give up his carnivorous habits and attain the first stage of Sainthood.

Who believed that Asoka who was stigmatised Caṇḍa (the Wicked)—on account of the atrocities caused by him to expand his empire, would ever win the noble title—Dhammāsoka or Asoka the Righteous. But he did completely change his career to such an extent that today, "Amidst the tens of thousands of names of monarchs that crowd the columns of history, their majesties and graciousnesses and serenities and royal highnesses and the like, the name of Asoka shines, and shines almost alone, a star." [1]

These are a few instances to illustrate the fact that a complete reformation of character could be brought about by our own actions.

---

1 H. G. Wells in his "Outline of History."

It may so happen that in some cases a lesser evil may produce its due effect, while the effect of a greater evil may be minimised.

The Buddha says:—

"Here, O Bhikkhus, a certain person is not disciplined in body, is not disciplined in morality, is not disciplined in mind, is not disciplined in wisdom, is with little good and less virtue, and lives painfully in consequence of trifles. Even a trivial evil act committed by such a person will lead him to a state of misery."

"Here, O Bhikkhus, a certain person is disciplined in body, is disciplined in morality, is disciplined in mind, is disciplined in wisdom, is with much good, is high-souled, and lives without limitation."

"A similar evil act committed by such a person ripens in this life itself and not even a small effect manifests itself (after death), not to say of a great one."[1]

"It is as if, O Bhikkhus, a man were to put a lump of salt into a small cup of water. What do you think, O Bhikkhus? Would now the small amount of water in this cup become saltish and undrinkable?"

"Yes, Lord."

"And why?"

"Because, Lord, there was very little water in the cup, and so it became saltish and undrinkable by this lump of salt."

---

1. The reference here is to an Arahant who is not subject to any future sorrow.

"Suppose, O Bhikkhus, a man were to put a lump of salt into the river Ganges. What think you, O Bhikkhus? Would now the river Ganges become saltish and undrinkable by the lump of salt?"

"Nay, indeed, Lord."

"And why not?"

"Because, Lord, the mass of water in the river Ganges is great, and so it would not become saltish and undrinkable."

"In exactly the same way, O Bhikkhus, we may have the case of a person who does some slight evil deed which brings him to a state of misery; or, again, O Bhikkhus, we may have the case of another person who does the same trivial misdeed, and expiates in the present life. Not even a small effect manifests itself (after death), not to say of a great one."

"We may have, O Bhikkhus, the case of a person who is cast into a prison for a half-penny, penny, or for a hundred pence; or, again, O Bhikkhus, we may have the case of a person who is not cast into prison for a half-penny, for a penny, or for a hundred pence."

"Who, O Bhikkhus, is cast into prison for a half-penny, for a penny, or for a hundred pence?"

"Whenever, O Bhikkhus, any one is poor, needy and indigent: he, O Bhikkhus, is cast into prison for a half-penny, for a penny, or for a hundred pence."

"Who, O Bhikkhus, is not cast into prison for a half-penny, for a penny, or for a hundred pence?"

"Whenever, O Bhikkhus, any one is rich, wealthy, and affluent: he, O Bhikkhus, is not cast into prison for a half-penny, for a penny, or for a hundred pence?"

"In exactly the same way, O Bhikkhus, we may have the case of a person who does some slight evil deed which brings him to a state of misery; or, again, O Bhikkhus, we may have the case of another person who does the same trivial misdeed, and expiates in the present life. Not even a small effect manifests itself (after death), not to say of a great one."[1]

Good begets good, but any after-repentance on the part of the doer deprives him of the due desirable results.

The following case may be cited in illustration thereof:—

On one occasion King Pasenadi of Kosala approached the Buddha and said:

"Lord, here in Sāvatthi a millionaire householder has died. He has left no son behind him, and now come here, after having conveyed his property to the palace. Lord, a hundred lakhs in gold, to say nothing of the silver! But this millionaire householder, Lord, used to eat broken scraps of food and sour gruel. And thus he clothed himself: for dress he wore a robe of coarse hemp: and as to his coach, he drove in a broken down chariot rigged up with a leaf-awning."

Thereupon the Buddha said:

---

1. Anguttara Nikāya, part 1, p. 249.
See Warren—"Buddhism in Translations"—p. 218.

"Even so, O King, even so. In a former life, O King, this millionaire householder gave alms of food to a *Pacceka Buddha*, called *Tagarasikhi*. And as, after having said, 'Give alms of food to the ascetic!' he rose from his seat and went away, he repented having given the food, saying within himself: 'It would be better if my servants and workmen ate the food I gave for alms!' And besides this he deprived his brother's only son of his life, for the sake of his property.

"And because, O King, this millionaire householder gave alms of food to the *Pacceka Buddha Tagarasikhi*, in requital for his deed, he was reborn seven times to a happy destiny in the heavenly world. And by the residual result of that same action, he became seven times a millionaire in this very Sāvatthi.

"And because, O King, this millionaire householder repented of having given alms, saying to himself: 'It would be better that my servants and workmen ate the food; therefore, as requital for this deed, he had no appreciation of good food, no appreciation of fine dresses, no appreciation of an elegant vehicle, no appreciation of the enjoyments of the five senses.

"And because, O King, this millionaire householder slew the only son of his brother for the sake of his property, as requital for this deed he had to suffer many years, many hundreds of years, many thousands of years, many hundreds of thousands of years of pain in states of misery. And by the residual result of that same action, he is without a son for the seventh time, and in consequence of this, had to leave his property to the royal treasury."[1]

---

1. Saṇyutta Nikāya, part 1, p. 91.
   See Warren—"Buddhism in Translations." p. 296; and Grimm—"The Doctrine of the Buddha"—p. 248.

This millionaire in question obtained his vast fortune as a result of the good act done in a past birth, but since he repented of his good deed, he could not fully enjoy the benefit of the riches which Kamma provided him.

In the working of Kamma it should be understood that there are maleficent and beneficent forces to counteract and support this self-operating law. Birth (Gati), time or conditions (Kāla), beauty (Upadhi), and effort (Payoga), are such aids and hindrances to the fruition of Kamma.

If, for instance, a person is born in a noble family or in a state of happiness, his fortunate birth will act sometimes as a hindrance to the fruition of his evil Kamma.

If, on the other hand, he is born in a state of misery or in an unfortunate family, his unfavourable birth will provide an easy opportunity for his evil Kamma to operate.

This is technically known as Gati Sampatti (Favourable birth) and Gati Vipatti (Unfavourable birth).

An unintelligent person, who, by some good Kamma, is born in a royal family, will, on account of his noble parentage, be honoured by the people. If the same person were to have a less fortunate birth, he would not be similarly treated.

King Duṭṭhagāmani of Ceylon acquired both good and evil Kamma. Owing to good Reproductive Kamma he was born in the Tusita Heaven. It is believed that he will have his last birth in the time of the future Buddha Metteyya. His evil Kamma cannot successfully operate owing to his favourable birth.

King Ajātasattu who committed parricide became distinguished for his piety and devotion owing to his association with the Buddha. He now expiates in a state of misery as a result of his heinous crime. His unfavourable birth would not permit him to enjoy the benefits of his good deeds.

Beauty (Upadhi Sampatti) and ugliness (Upadhi Vipatti) are two other factors that act as aids and hindrances to the working of Kamma.

If by some good Kamma a person obtains a good birth, but is unfortunately deformed, he will not be able to enjoy the beneficial results of his good Kamma. Even a legitimate heir to the throne may not perhaps be raised to that exalted position if he happens to be physically deformed.

Beauty on the other hand will be a valuable asset to the possessor. A good looking son of a poor parent will perhaps attract the attention of a kind person, and might be able to distinguish himself through his influence.

Asokamāla, an ordinary girl, got married to Prince Sāliya, the son of King Duṭṭhagāmaṇī, owing to her beauty.

Prince Kusa was subject to much humiliation owing to his ugly appearance.

Favourable and unfavourable time or occasion (Kāla Sampatti and Kāla Vipatti) are another two factors that aid or impede the working of Kamma.

In the case of a famine all without exception will be compelled to suffer the same fate. Here the unfavourable conditions open up possibilities for evil

Kamma to operate. The favourable conditions, on the other hand, will prevent the operation of evil Kamma.

The fourth and the last is effort (Payoga). If a person makes no effort to cure himself of a disease or to save himself from his difficulties, his evil Kamma will find a suitable opportunity to produce its due effects. If, on the contrary, he endeavours on his part to surmount his difficulties, his good Kamma will come to his succour.

When shipwrecked in deep sea, the Bodhisatta Mahā Janaka made an effort to save himself, whilst the others prayed to the gods and left their fate in their hands. The result was that the Bodhisatta escaped whilst the others got drowned. This is technically known as Payoga Sampatti and Payoga Vipatti.

It is evident from these counteractive and supportive factors that Kamma is sometimes influenced by external circumstances.

It is this doctrine of Kamma that gives consolation, hope, self-reliance, and moral courage to a Buddhist.

When the unexpected happens to him and when he is beset with difficulties almost insurmountable and misfortunes almost unbearable, he consoles himself with the thought that they are the results of his own past doings. He realises that the inevitable must happen. He no doubt reaps what he has sown; he can at the same time turn up weeds and sow useful seeds in their place, for the future is entirely in his hands. Kamma enables him to shape his future as he wills.

When the wicked are successful in every walk of life, whilst the virtuous meet with ill-luck and are compelled to lead a miserable life, a Buddhist would neither accuse another of injustice nor blame the world for its unjust ways, since he knows that they are only reaping what they have sown. The virtuous are thereby not discouraged because they are convinced that their good acts will have their due effects in some future life though not in the present.

Even the most corrupted person is not condemned in Buddhism. On the other hand he is loved and shown the way to a perfect life. He is assured that he has the chance to reform and remodel himself at any moment. Though bound to suffer in states of misery, he has the hope of attaining eternal Peace. For instance, the wicked Devadatta, who now expiates in a state of misery for his heinous crimes, is destined to be a *Pacceka Buddha* in the future.

A Buddhist who is fully convinced of the doctrine of Kamma does not pray to another to be saved but confidently relies on himself for his salvation.

It is this belief in Kamma that validates his effort, and kindles his enthusiasm. It is also this firm belief in Kamma that prompts him to refrain from evil and to do good and be good without being frightened of any punishments or tempted of any rewards. He has no fear of the future, nor does he dread so-called death. He is ever kind, tolerant, and considerate.

This law of Kamma explains the problem of suffering, the mystery of so-called fate or predestination of other religions, and above all the inequality of mankind.

As stated earlier it is a law in itself, but it does not thereby follow that there should be a law-giver. Ordinary laws of nature, like gravitation, need no law-giver. The law of Kamma too demands no law-giver. It operates in its own field without the intervention of an external, independent, ruling agency.

Nobody, for instance, has decreed that fire should burn. Nobody has commanded that water should seek its own level. No scientist has ordered that water should consist of H_2O, and that coldness should be one of its properities. These are their intrinsic characteristics.

Inherent in Kamma is the power of producing its due effect. The cause produces the effect; the effect explains the cause. Seed produces the fruit; the fruit explains the seed as both are inter-related. Even so Kamma and its effect are inter-related; "the effect already blooms in the cause."

Happiness and suffering which are the common lot of humanity are the inevitable effects of some cause or causes. There is no doubt of the fact that both happiness and suffering have their attendant curses and blessings and that they are essential. In that well-known fable the stag admired his horns and blamed his feet, but when the hunter came his swift feet saved him, his beautiful horns, caught in a thicket, destroyed him.

But why should these disparities exist? Are they the "rewards" and "punishments" of an Almighty Being who sits on an imperial throne in heaven above controlling the destinies of the human race[1]. No, they are not. They are the due effects of our own good and bad deeds. Our good actions make us happy; our evil actions make us miserable. We ourselves are responsible for our happiness and misery. We are the architects of our own fate. We are our own creators. We are our own destroyers. We build our own heavens. We build our own hells.

What we think, speak, and do, become our own. It is these thoughts, words, and deeds that assume the name of Kamma and pass from life to life, exalting and degrading us in the course of our wanderings in Sansāra.

Says the Buddha:—

"Man's merits and the sins he here hath wrought:—
That is the thing he owns, that takes he hence,
That dogs his steps, like shadows in pursuit.
Hence let him make good store for life elsewhere.
Sure platform in some other future world,
Rewards of virtue on good beings wait."

("Kindred Sayings"—Vol. 1, p. 98)

---

1 "If this Being (God) is omnipotent, then every occurrence, including every human action, every human thought, and every human feeling and aspiration is also His work; how it is possible to think of holding men responsible for their deeds and thoughts before such an Almight Being?

"In giving out punishment and rewards, He would to a certain extent be passing judgment on Himself. How can this be combined with the goodness and righteousness ascribed to Him."—*Einstein*

CHAPTER XVI

REBIRTH

The Origin of Life

What is the ultimate origin of life?

THIS is a question which perplexes the mind of every profound thinker. The expected answer has not yet been obtained, despite the fact that it has received the attention of all scientists and philosophers.

It is doubtful whether this mysterious problem will ever be solved to the satisfaction of all.

Hinduism, in endeavouring to solve the problem, traces the origin of life to a mystical *Paramātma* from which emanate all *Ātmas* or souls that transmigrate from existence to existence, until they are finally re-absorbed in *Paramātma*.

Christianity, in attempting to give an explanation, attributes everything to the *fiat* of an Almighty God.

According to the Christian conception all life was created out of nothing.

"Whoever," as Schopenhaeur says, "regards himself as having become out of nothing must also think that he will again become nothing; for that an eternity has passed before he was, and then a second eternity had begun, through which he will never cease to be, is a monstrous thought."[1]

1. "The World as Will and Idea."

Moreover, "If birth is the absolute beginning, then death must be his absolute end; and the assumption that man is made out of nothing leads necessarily to the assumption that death is his absolute end." [1]

"According to the Theological principles man is created arbitrarily and without his desire, and at the moment of creation is either *blessed* or *damned* eternally. Hence, man is either good or evil, fortunate or unfortunate, noble or depraved, from the first step in the process of his physical creation to the moment of his last breath, regardless of his individual desires, hopes, ambitions, struggles or devoted prayers. Such is theological fatalism." *

"The doctrine that all men are sinners and have the essential sin of Adam is a challenge to justice, mercy, love, and omnipotent fairness." *

The First Cause in Christianity is as mysterious as the First Cause in Hinduism.

"Unfettered by any religious belief, freed from all dogmatic assertions, but solely relying on common sense," and confining itself to sense-data, modern science endeavours to tackle the problem with its systematised knowledge based on observations and experiments.

According to the scientific point of view we are the direct products of the sperm and ovum cells provided by our parents. But science does not claim to give a satisfactory explanation with regard to the development of the mind which is infinitely more important than the mere machinery of man's material body.

---

1. "The World as Will and Idea."
* A. Spencer Lewis.

Materialists, on the other hand, while asserting *omne vivum e vivo*—"all life from life," maintain that life and mind gradually evolved from the lifeless.

Now, what is the attitude of Buddhism with regard to the origin of life?

At the outset it should be mentioned that the Buddha is not concerned either with the First Cause or with the Last Effect. Such speculations are absolutely fruitless.

As Bradlaugh says the conception of a first cause is as ridiculous as a round triangle.

On one occasion a certain Bhikkhu named *Mālunkyaputta*, not content to lead the Holy Life and achieve by degrees his Emancipation, approached the Buddha and impatiently demanded an immediate solution of some speculative problems on the threat of discarding the robe forthwith.

"Lord," he said, "these theories have not been elucidated, have been set aside and rejected by the Blessed One—whether the world is eternal or not eternal; whether the world is finite or infinite...... If the Blessed One will elucidate these questions to me, then I will lead the Holy Life under Him. If He will not, then I will abandon the precepts and return to the lay life."

"If the Blessed One knows that the world is eternal, let the Blessed One elucidate to me that the world is eternal; if the Blessed One knows that the world is not eternal, let the Blessed One elucidate that the world is not eternal. If the Blessed One does not know whether the world is eternal or not—in that case, certainly, for one who does not know and lacks the insight, the only upright thing is to say: I do not know; I have not the insight."

Calmly the Buddha questioned the erring Bhikkhu whether his adoption of the Holy life was in any way conditional upon the solution of such problems.

"Nay, Lord!" the Bhikkhu replied.

The Buddha then admonished him not to waste time and energy over such idle speculation which was detrimental to his spiritual progress, and said:—

"Whoever, *Mālunkyaputta*, should say: I will not lead the Holy Life under the Blessed One until the Blessed One elucidates these questions to me—that person would die, *Mālunkyaputta*, before these questions had ever been elucidated by the Accomplished One.

"It is as if, *Mālunkyaputta*, a person were pierced by an arrow thickly smeared with poison, and his friends and relatives were to procure a surgeon, and then he were to say I will not have this arrow taken out until I know the details of the person by whom I was wounded, nature of the arrow with which I was pierced, etc., that person would die, *Mālunkyaputta*, before this would ever be known by him.

"In exactly the same way, *Mālunkyaputta*, whoever should say:—'I will not lead the Holy Life under the Blessed One until the Blessed One elucidates to me whether the world is eternal or not eternal;

whether the world is finite or infinite.........' that person would die, *Mālunkyaputta*, before these questions had ever been elucidated by the Accomplished One.

"If it be the belief, *Mālunkyaputta*, that the world is eternal, will there be the observance of the Holy Life? In such a case—No! If it be the belief, *Mālunkyaputta*, that the world is not eternal, will there be the observance of the Holy Life? In that case also—No! But, *Mālunkyaputta*, whether the belief be that the world is eternal or that it is not eternal, undoubtedly, there is birth, there is old age, there is death,...... —the extinction of which in this life itself I make known.

"*Mālunkyaputta*, I have not revealed whether the world is eternal or not eternal; whether the world is finite or infinite. Why have I not revealed these? Because these are not profitable, do not concern the bases of holiness, are not conducive to aversion, to passionlessness, to cessation, to tranquillity, to intuitive wisdom, to enlightenment, or to Nibbāna. Therefore I have not revealed these." *

Buddhism does not profess to provide an explanation to all ethical and philosophical problems that interest mankind. Neither does it deal with idle speculations and theorisings that do not tend to edification. Nor does it demand faith from its adherents with regard to a First Cause. It is a Means of Deliverance or a Doctrine of Reality. It has a practical and specific purpose—the cessation of sorrow—and with that Goal in view all irrelevant side issues are

1. Majjhima Nikāya—Cūla Mālunkya Sutta No. 63.

completely ignored. Nevertheless, every encouragement is given to keen investigation into the real nature of life. To have right knowledge or to gain Deliverance from sorrow, one need not be troubled with a First Cause.

Suppose "X" be the first cause. Now, does this knowledge bring us any nearer to our goal? Nay, it only tends to gratify childish curiosity.

Whatever other religions and science may teach with regard to the ultimate origin of life, Buddhism pertinently says:—

"Without cognisable end is this *Sansāra*. A first beginning of beings, who, *obstructed by ignorance* and *fettered by craving*, wander and fare on, is not to be perceived." [1]

It seems further to address the enthusiastic seekers after truth and say: Young friends, worry not in vain seeking for a beginning in a beginningless past. Life is not an identity, but a process of becoming. It is a flux or force like electricity, and, as such, necessitates a beginningless past. Whether you are descended from an arboreal or ground ape, created by God or Brahma, birth, death, and suffering, to which all are

---

1. *Anamataggo 'yam Bhikkave Samsāro. Pubbākoti na paññāyati avijjānīvaraṇāṇam sattānam taṇhāsamyojanānam sandhāvatam.*

"Incalculable is the beginning, brethren, of this faring on. The earliest point is not revealed of the running on, the faring on, of beings cloaked in ignorance, tied to craving."

Woodward—
Kindred Sayings—Part ii, p. 118.

"Inconceivable is the beginning of this Sansāra, not to be discovered a first beginning of beings, who, obstructed by ignorance and ensnared by craving, are hurrying and hastening through this round of rebirths."—Nyanatiloka.

subject in the long run, are inevitable. Seek, therefore, the cause of this "faring on" that concerns all humanity, and utilise your valuable energy to transfer this life stream to the sorrowless and peaceful state, Nibbāna.

To those who love to speculate for the mere sake of argument, these words will of course be of no avail. Well, it makes no great difference to Buddhism.

One might argue that life must have had a beginning in the infinite past and that beginning or the First Cause is the Creator.

In that case there is no reason why the same demand may not be made of this postulated God-Creator.[1]

---

1. "A strict demonstration of the existence of God is utterly impossible. Almost all the proofs that have been offered assume in the very premises the conclusion to be proved."

—Rev. W Kirkus in "Orthodoxy Scripture and Reason", p. 34.

"We have got to recognize that evil falls within a universe for which God is responsible. We cannot absolve God for permitting the existence of sin and pain."

—Canon C. E. Raven in "The Grounds of Christian Assumption."

CHAPTER XVII

THE BUDDHA ON THE SO-CALLED GOD-CREATOR?

THE Pāli equivalent for a God-Creator in other religions is either *Issara* (Sanskrit *Īśvara*-Lord) or Brahma.

However much one may plumb the depths of Buddhist literature one will not find even a faint trace of any reference by the Buddha or His disciples to the existence of a God-Creator. Nowhere has the Buddha placed a supernatural God over man.

Evidently the question of a God-Creator was not so seriously discussed as the more intricate problem of soul. On several occasions has the Buddha denied the existence of a permanent soul—Atta. As to the denial of a God-Creator there are only a few references. In no place, however, has the Buddha admitted the existence of a God-Creator—whether in the form of a force or being.

In the Anguttara Nikaya the Buddha speaks of three views prevalent in His time. One of which is:—

> "Whatsoever happiness or pain or neutral feeling this person experiences, all that is due to the creation of an Issara (Supreme Deity)."

To those who hold this view the Buddha says:—

"So, then, owing to the creation of an Issara, men will become murderers, thieves, unchaste, liars, slanderers, abusive, babblers, covetous, malicious, and perverse in view. Thus for those who fall back on the creation of an Issara as the essential reason there is neither desire to do, nor effort to do, nor necessity to do this deed or abstain from that deed. So, then, the necessity for action or inaction not being found to exist in truth and verity, the term recluse cannot reasonably be applied to yourselves, since you live in a state of bewilderment with faculties unwarded.

"Such is my rebuke to those recluses and brahmins who thus teach, who hold such views."[1]

According to this argument we are what we were willed to be by a Creator. Our destinies are in his hands. Our fate is determined by him. The supposed freewill granted to his creation is a farce.

Again in the Devadaha Sutta (Majjhima Nikāya—No. 101) the Buddha criticises the view of a God-Creator in the same strain.

Referring to the self-mortification of naked ascetics, the Buddha says:—

"If, O Bhikkhus, beings experience pain and happiness as the result of God's (Issara) creation,[2] then certainly these naked ascetics must have been created by a wicked God, since they are at present experiencing such severe terrible pain."

Further in the Kevaḍḍha Sutta (Dīgha Nikāya—No. 11) the Buddha makes a humorous reference to a God-Creator.

---

1. Woodward—Gradual Sayings—Vol. 1., p. 158.
2. Issara-nimmāna-hetu.

An inquisitive Bhikkhu, desiring to know the end of elements, approached Mahā Brahma and questioned him:—

"Where, my friend, do the four great elements—earth, water, fire, and air—cease, leaving no trace behind?"

To this the Great Brahma replied:—

"I, brother, am Brahma, Great Brahma, the Supreme Being, the Unsurpassed, the Perceiver of all things, the Controller, the Lord of all, the Maker, the Fashioner, the Chief, the Victor, the Ruler, the Father of all beings who have been and are to be."

For the second time the Bhikkhu asked the same question.

For the second time the Great Brahma replied in the same manner.

For the third time the Bhikkhu questioned him.

Then Great Brahma took the Bhikkhu by the arm, led him aside and spoke as follows:—

"O brother, these gods of my suite believe as follows:—'Brahma sees all things; knows all things; has penetrated all things.' Therefore was it that I did not answer you in their presence. I do not know, O brother, where these four great elements—earth, water, fire, and air—cease, leaving no trace behind. Therefore it was an evil and a crime, O brother, that you left the Blessed One, and went elsewhere in quest of an answer to this question. Turn back, O brother, and having drawn near to the Blessed One, ask him this question, and as the Blessed One shall explain to you, so believe."[1]

With regard to the origin of Mahā Brahma, the so-called Creator, the Buddha says in the *Pāṭika Sutta* (Dīgha Nikāya—No. 24):—

"On this, friends, that being who was first reborn thinks thus: I am Brahma, the Great Brahma, the Vanquisher, the Unvanquished, the All-seeing, the Disposer, the Lord, the Maker, the Creator, the Chief, the Assigner, the Master of Myself, the Father of all that are and are to be. By me are these beings created. And why is that so? A while ago I thought: Would that other beings too might come to this state of being! Such was the aspiration of my mind, and lo these beings did come.

"And those beings themselves who arose after him, they too think thus: This worthy must be Brahma, the Great Brahma, the Vanquisher, the Unvanquished, the All-seeing, the Disposer, the Lord, the Maker, the Creator, the Chief, the Assigner, the Master of Himself, the Father of all that are and are to be.

"On this, friends, that being who first arose becomes longer lived, handsomer, and more powerful, but those who appeared after him become shorter lived, less comely, less powerful. And it might well be, friends, that some other being, on deceasing from that

1. See Warren—Buddhism in Translations—p. 311; and Prof Rys Davids—Dialogues of the Buddha, Vol. i., p 282.

state, should come to this state (on earth). So come he might go forth from the household life into the homeless state. And having thus gone forth by reason of ardour, effort, devotion, earnestness, perfect intellection, he reaches up to such rapt concentration, that with rapt mind he calls to mind his former dwelling place, but remembers not what went before. He says thus: That Worshipful Brahma, the Vanquisher, the Unvanquished... .. ...Father of all that are and are to be, he by whom we were created, he is permanent, constant, eternal, unchanging, and he will remain so for ever and ever. But we who were created by that Brahma, we have come hither all impermanent, transient, unstable, short-lived, destined to pass away.

"Thus was appointed the beginning of things which ye, sirs, declare as your traditional doctrine; to wit, that it has been wrought by an overlord, by Brahma."[1]

In the Bhūridatta Jātaka (No. 543) the Bodhisatta expresses his views about a Creator, and complains of his injustice in the following words:—

"He who has eyes can see the sickening sight;
Why does not Brahma set his creatures right?

"If his wide power no limits can restrain,
Why is his hand so rarely spread to bless?

"Why are his creatures all condemned to pain?
Why does he not to all give happiness?

---

1. Prof. Rys Davids—Dialogues of the Buddha—Vol. iii., p. 26.

"Why do fraud, lies, and ignorance prevail?
Why triumphs falsehood,—truth and justice fail?

"I count your Brahma one th'unjust among,
Who made a world in which to shelter wrong."*

(Jataka Stories—Vol. VI., p. 110.)

Refuting the theory that everything is the creation of a Supreme Being, the Bodhisatta says in the Mahābodhi Jātaka (No. 528):—

"If there exists some Lord all powerful to fulfil
In every creature bliss or woe, and action good or ill,
That Lord is stained with sin. Man does but work his will."

(Jātaka Stories—Vol. V., p. 122.)

---

* Commenting on human suffering and God Professor J.B.S. Haldane says:—

"Either suffering is needed to perfect human character, or God is not almighty. The former theory is disproved by the fact that some people who have suffered very little, but have been fortunate in their ancestry and education have very fine characters. The objection to the second is that it is only in connection with the universe as a whole that there is any intellectual gap to be filled by the postulation of a deity. And a creator could presumably create whatever he or it wanted."
"The Inequality of Man"—p. 183.

God, perchance, is in heaven, but all's wrong with the world.
—Mr. A. G. Gardiner's Essay on George Bernard Shaw. *Prophets, Priests and Kings*, p. 18.

In "Despair", a poem of his old age, Lord Tennyson thus bodly attacks God, who, as recorded by Isiah, says: "I CREATE EVIL." (Isiah xlv.7.)

What! I should call on that infinite Love that has served us so well?
Infinite cruelty, rather, that made everlasting hell,
Made us, foreknew us, foredoom'd us, and does what he will with his own;
Better our dead brute mother who never has heard us groan.

CHAPTER XVIII

CAUSE OF BIRTH AND DEATH

IN the search after the cause of birth and death Buddhism takes for its starting point the *being as it is*, here and now, and traces back the causes of its conditioned existence.

From the Buddhist point of view all men and animals are composed of inter-related mind and matter (*Nāma* and *Rūpa*).

Though all are identical inasmuch as they possess the two common factors, mind and matter, yet they are all so varied that, leaving animals aside, even amongst mankind, no two persons are found to be alike in any respect—each person having his own psychological characteristics.

Could this variation be due to heredity and environment? If so, we fail to understand why twins who are physically alike, and who enjoy equal privileges of upbringing, should often exhibit totally different characteristics.

No doubt these two factors play an important part in the formation of our character, and they are certainly partly instrumental, but not solely responsible for the subtle distinctions that exist amongst individuals. Besides, why should an innocent child suffer because its parents are diseased or miserable?

The theory of heredity cannot account for the birth of a criminal in a long line of honourable ancestors, nor the birth of a saint or a noble man in a family "rotten to the trees."

Tracing back the individual, therefore, to the foetus in the womb to see where lies the cause, we discover two more common factors—the sperm-cell and the ovum-cell.

Now a question might arise as to whether those two are the only materials for the production of the foetus. If so, we cannot comprehend why precisely "A" should fortunately or unfortunately spring from the particular sperm and ovum-cell and not "B", since one has equal claims as the other.

Buddhism offers a solution to this intricate problem by attributing the appropriation of this cell-matter to the existence of a third factor which is vital for the formation of the foetus.*

There is reason to believe that a foetus is not produced by the mere combination of the sperm and ovum-cell. There they remain and will die and pass away unless joined by the third element which is mainly responsible for the subtle distinction prevalent amongst beings.

The Buddha says: "Where, O Bhikkhus, three are found in combination, there a germ of life is planted. If mother and father come together, but it is not the mother's period, and the 'being-to-be-born' (*Gandhabba*) is not present, then no germ of life is planted. If mother and father come together, and it is the mother's period, but the 'being-to-be-born' is not

* See Dhalke—"Buddhism and Science."

present, then again no germ of life is planted. If mother and father come together, and it is the mother's period, and the 'being-to-be-born' is also present, then by the conjunction of these three, a germ of life is there planted."[1]

For a "being-to-be-born" here, a being must die somewhere. The birth of a person in this life means the death of a person in a previous life. Birth and death are only two phases of the same process. Thus birth precedes death, and death, on the other hand, precedes birth. This constant succession of birth and death in connection with each individual life-flux constitutes what is technically known as Saṃsāra.[2]

This newly discovered third element is, in the words of the Abhidhamma, termed *Paṭisandhi Viññāṇa* (Re-linking consciousness).

The first term of the life's progression is now found, but our limited knowledge does not permit us to proceed further and determine the cause of this re-linking consciousness, which is the essential factor for the being-to-be-born.

The Buddha, however, developing a supernormal insight so as to penetrate into the realms beyond the reach of normal sense, comprehended also the root of this third element. He tells us that the coming into being of the re-linking consciousness is dependent upon the pasing away of another consciousness in a past birth, and that the process of becoming and passing away is the result of Karma, or, in other words, one's own action. This is the cause (*Kammayoni*) of this becoming.

1. Majjhima Nikāya—Mahātaṇhā Samkhaya Sutta No. 38.
2. "The unbroken line of organs, elements, and aggregates—'*Sansāra*' is its name."—The Expositor Part—I., p. 13.

CHAPTER XIX

REASONS TO BELIEVE IN A PAST BIRTH

HOW are we to believe that there is a past birth?

The most valuable evidence Buddhists cite in favour of rebirth is the Buddha, for He developed a knowledge which enabled Him to perceive the past and future lives. Says He: "With clairvoyant vision, purified and supernormal, I perceived beings disappearing from one state of existence and re-appearing in another: I beheld the base and the noble, the beautiful and the ugly, the happy and the miserable, and beings passing according to their deeds."

Following His instructions His disciples also developed this knowledge and were able to read their past lives to a great extent.

The acquisition of this faculty is not restricted only to the Buddha and His disciples. Any person, whether Buddhist or not, could possess this power.[1]

Some Indian Rshis, even before the advent of the Buddha, were distinguished for such powers as clairaudience, clairvoyance, thought reading, remembering past births, etc. For instance, the ascetic

1. "Psalms of the Brethren" (*Theragatha*) gives an interesting account of a Brahmin, named *Vangisa*, "who won favour as a teacher by tapping on skulls with his finger-nails and discovering thereby where their former occupants were reborn."

Asita, also known as *Kāla Devala*, who foretold that prince Siddhattha would become a Buddha, was able to read both the past and the future to some extent.

One might doubt whether it is possible to possess such a memory. But when we consider the miraculous inventions and stupendous discoveries of science that are presented to us to-day there is left no room to deny the possibility of acquiring such a memory.

Thanks to the indefatigable efforts of scientists, we are now in a position to sit at our table and hear distant voices with the greatest ease, and before long television will probably introduce to us distant scenes. All these are the products of the human mind. If so, why cannot one's mind be so trained as to read one's past without any mechanical aid just as we would recall a past incident of our present life?

Well, then, how is it that we do not often find persons with such wonderful memories to-day?

Do we behold Buddhas and Arahants to-day? Are there Krishnas and Christs amongst us? Where are Platos and Shakespeares?

The fact that they do not exist at present is no reason to disbelieve that they existed in the past.

There are also some persons who in an unaccountable way suddenly develop the memory of their past birth and remember fragments of their previous lives. Such exceptional cases are reported from Burma, India, Germany, England, etc.[1]

---

1. See "The Christian Doctrine of Rebirth"—by Dr. W. T. Evans-Wentz, p. 36, "The Soul of a People" by Fielding Hall, "The Rationale of Reincarnation" by A. E. Powell.

In parenthesis, it may be said that the experiences of some modern reliable psychists and strange cases of alternating and multiple personalities[1] tend to throw light upon this belief in rebirth.

This phenomenon of secondary personalities has to be explained either as remnants of past individual experiences or as "being possessed." The former explanation sounds more reasonable, but the latter cannot totally be discarded.[2]

Sometimes we get strange experiences[3] which cannot be explained but by rebirth.

---

1. Prof. James cites some remarkable cases in his Principles of Psychology.

2. The Visuddhimagga mentions an interesting incident of a *deva* "entering into the body" of a layman—See "The Path of Purity." Part I, p. 48.

The writer himself has come across persons who were adopted as mediums by invisible beings to convey their thoughts, and some others who were actually possessed by evil spirits. When in this hypnotic state they speak and do things of which normally they are totally ignorant.

3. "It was such experiences that led Sir Walter Scott to a sense of metempsychosis. From his diary, February 17, 1828, his biographer, Lockhart, in his 'Life of Scott' records:

" 'I cannot, I am sure, tell if it is worth marking down, that yesterday, at dinner time, I was strangely haunted by what I would call the sense of pre-existences, viz., a confused idea that nothing that passed was said for the first time; that the same topics had been discussed and the persons had stated the same opinions on them. The sensation was so strong as to resemble what is called a mirage in the desert and *calenture* on board ship.'

"Bulwer Lytton describes these mysterious experiences as that strange kind of inner and spiritual memory which often recalls to us places and persons we have never seen before, and which Plantonists would resolve to be the unquenched and struggling consciousness of a former life."

"The Theory of Reincarnation"—explained by H. M. Kitchener—p. 7.

How often do we meet persons whom we have never before met, and yet inwardly feel that they are quite familiar to us? How often do we visit places, and yet feel impressed that we are perfectly acquainted with their surroundings?

The Dhammapada commentary relates the story of a husband and wife, who, seeing the Buddha, fell at His feet and saluted Him, saying:—"Dear son, is it not the duty of sons to care for their mother and father when they have grown old? Why is it that for so long a time you have not shown yourself to us? This is the first time we have seen you."[1]

The Buddha attributed this sudden out-burst of parental love to the fact that they had been His parents several times during His past lives and remarked:

> "*Through previous associations or present advantage,*
>
> *That old love springs up again like the lotus in the water.*"

Into this world come Perfect Ones like the Buddhas and highly developed saintly personalities. Do they evolve suddenly? Can they be the products of a single existence?

How are we to account for colossal characters like Homer and Plato, men of genius like Shakespeare, infant prodigies like Pascal, Mozart, Beethoven, Raphael, etc.?

---

1. See "Buddhist Legends"—Vol. 3, p. 108.

Heredity alone cannot account for them, "else their ancestry would disclose it, their posterity, even greater than themselves, demonstrate it."

Could they rise to such lofty heights if they had not lived noble lives and gained similar experiences in the past? Is it by mere chance that they are born of those particular parents and placed under those favourable circumstances?

The theory of heredity should be supplemented by the doctrine of Kamma and rebirth for an adequate explanation of these puzzling problems.

Says a certain Western writer:

"Whether we believe in a past existence or not, it forms the only reasonable hypothesis which bridges certain gaps in human knowledge concerning facts of every day life. Our reason tells us that this idea of past birth and Kamma alone can explain the degrees of differences that exist between twins, how men like Shakespeare with a very limited experience are able to potray with marvellous exactitude, the most diverse types of human character, scenes and so forth, of which they could have no actual knowledge, why the work of the genius invariably transcends his experience, the existence of infant precocity, the vast diversity in mind and morals, in brain and physique, in conditions, circumstances, and environments, observable throughout the world, and so forth."

Is it reasonable to believe that the present brief span of life is the only existence before two eternities of happiness and misery?

The few years we are privileged to spend here, or for the most five score years, must certainly be an inadequate preparation for eternity.

If one believes in the present and in the future, it is quite logical to believe in the past.[1]

If there be reasons to believe that we have existed in the past, then surely there are no reasons to disbelieve that we shall continue to exist after our present life has apparently ceased.

It is indeed a strong argument in favour of past and future lives that "in this world virtuous persons are very often unfortunate and vicious persons prosperous." [2]

We are born into the state created by ourselves. If, in spite of our virtue, we are destined to lead an unfortunate life, it is due to our own past evil Kamma. If, in spite of our wickedness, we are prosperous, it is also due to our good Kamma of the past. The present deeds will, however, have their due consequences at the earliest possible opportunity.

---

1. "We have come to look upon the present as the child of the past and as the parent of the future."—T. H. Huxley.
2. "It is a strong argument for a state of retribution hereafter, that in this world virtuous persons are very often unfortunate and vicious persons prosperous."—Addison.

CHAPTER XX

THE WHEEL OF LIFE

WHAT does Buddhism say with regard to the *cause* of this rebirth process?

In short, Kamma, which is rooted in ignorance, is the cause of birth and death. As long as this Kammic force survives there is rebirth.

This process of becoming is fully explained in the *Paṭicca Samuppāda.*

Paṭicca means because of or dependent upon; *Samuppāda*, arising or origination. *Paṭicca Samuppāda* therefore means—"Dependent-Arising" or "Dependent Origination."

It must be borne in mind that *Paṭicca Samuppāda* is only a discourse on Sansāra or the process of birth and death, and not a theory of the evolution of the world from primordial matter. It deals with the cause of rebirth and suffering, but it does not in the least attempt to show the absolute origin of life.

Ignorance *(Avijjā)* is the first link or cause of the wheel of life. It clouds all right understanding.

Dependent on ignorance of the Four Noble Truths[1] arise volitional activities (*Sankhārā*)—both moral and immoral. The activities whether good or bad, which

1. Viz: Suffering, its cause, its destruction, and the path leading to its destruction.

are rooted in ignorance, and which must necessarily produce their due effects, tend to prolong wandering in *Sansāra*. Nevertheless, good actions are essential to get rid of the Ills of *Sansāra*.

Dependent on volitional activities arises re-linking consciousness (*Viññāṇa*). This links the past with the present.

Simultaneous with the arising of re-linking consciousness there come into being mind and matter (*Nāma Rūpa*).

The six senses (*Salāyatana*) are the inevitable consequences of mind and matter.

Because of the six senses contact (*Phassa*) sets in.

Contact leads to sensations (*Vedanā*).

Those five—namely, consciousness, mind and matter, six senses, contact, and sensation are the effects of past actions, and are called the passive side of life.

Dependent on sensations arises craving (*Taṇhā*).

Craving results in attachment (*Upādāna*).

Attachment causes Kamma (*Bhava*) which, in its turn, conditions future birth (*Jāti*).

Old age and death (*Jarā-Maraṇa*) are the natural results of birth.

If on account of a cause the effect comes to be, then if the cause ceases, the effect also must cease.

The reverse order of the *Paṭicca Samuppāda* will make the matter clear.

PATICCA SAMUPPADA

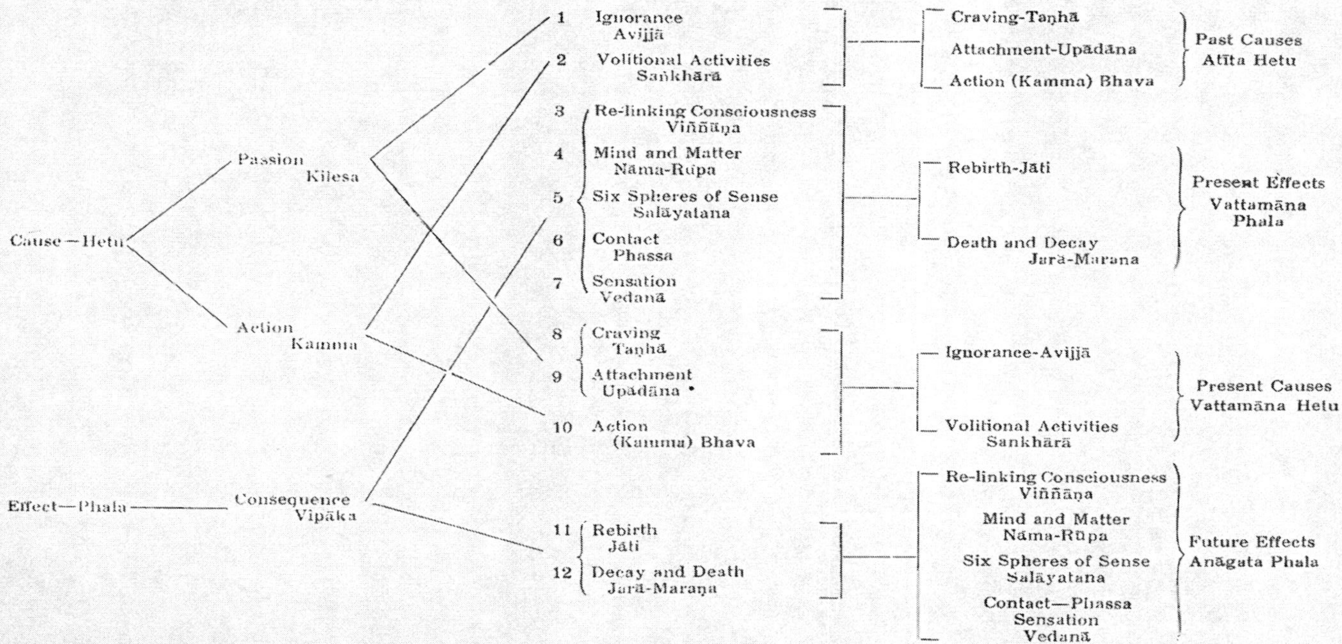

DIAGRAM—i.

Old age and death are only possible in and with a corporeal organism, that is to say as a six-sense machine. Such an organism must be born, therefore it presupposes birth. But birth is the inevitableresult of past action or *Kamma*, which is conditioned by attachment, due to craving. Such craving can appear only where sensation is. Sensation is the outcome of contact between the senses and objects. Therefore it presupposes organs of sense which cannot exist without mind and body. Where there is a mind there is a consciousness. It is the result of past activities which are due to ignorance of things as they truly are.

The whole formula may be summed up thus:—

Dependent on Ignorance arise Volitional Activities.
„ „ Volitional Activities arises Consciousness.
„ „ Consciousness arise Mind and Matter.
„ „ Mind and Matter arise the six Spheres of Sense.
„ „ the six Spheres of Sense arises Contact.
„ „ Contact arises Sensation.
„ „ Sensation arises Craving.
„ „ Craving arises Attachment.
„ „ Attachment arise Actions (Kamma Bhava).
„ „ Actions arises Birth.
„ „ Birth arise Decay, Death, Sorrow, Lamentation, Pain, Grief, and Despair.[1]

Thus does the entire aggregate of suffering arise.

The first two of those twelve pertain to the past, the middle eight to the present, and the last two to the future.

---

1. See Diagram i.

The complete cessation of Ignorance leads to the Cessation of Activities.

The cessation of Activities leads to the cessation of Consciousness.

The cessation of Consciousness leads to the cessation of Mind and Matter.

The cessation of Mind and Matter leads to the cessation of the six Spheres of Sense.

The cessation of the six Spheres of Sense leads to the cessation of Contact.

The cessation of Contact leads to the cessation of Sensation.

The cessation of Sensation leads to the cessation of Craving.

The cessation of Craving leads to the cessation of Attachment.

The cessation of Attachment leads to the cessation of Actions.

The cessation of Actions leads to the cessation of Birth.

The cessation of Birth leads to the cessation of Decay, Death, Sorrow, Lamentation, Pain, Grief, and Despair.

Thus does the cessation of this entire aggregate of suffering result.

This process of cause and effect continues *ad infinitum*. The beginning of this process cannot be determined as it is impossible to say whence this life-flux was encompassed by ignorance. But when this ignorance is turned into knowledge, and the life-flux is diverted into *Nibbāna Dhātu*, then the end of the life-process or *Sansāra* comes about.

CHAPTER XXI

MODES OF BIRTH AND DEATH

BRIEFLY expounding the cause of *Sansāra* in such enigmatic terms, and dealing with the more interesting problem of life's last scene, we find Buddhism assigning death to one of the following four causes:—

(1) The exhaustion of the force of Reproductive Kamma (*Janaka Kamma*) that gives rise to the birth in question.

This kind of death is technically known as *Kammakkhaya*—the exhaustion of Reproductive Kamma energy.

The Buddhist belief is that, as a rule, the thought, volition, or desire which is extremely strong during life-time, becomes predominant at the point of death and conditions the subsequent birth. In this last thought moment is present a special potentiality. When the potential energy of this Reproductive Kamma is exhausted, the organic activities of the material form in which is corporealised the life-force, cease even before the approach of old age.

(2) The expiration of the life term (*Āyukkhaya*).

What are commonly understood to be natural deaths due to old age, may be classed under this category. There are various planes of existence according to Buddhism, and to each plane is naturally assigned a definite age-limit. Irrespective of the Kamma force that has yet to run, one must, however, succumb to death when the maximum age-limit is reached. It may also be said, if the force is extremely powerful, the Kamma-energy rematerialises itself in the same plane or in some higher realm as in the case of *Devas*.

(3) The simultaneous exhaustion of the Reprodutive Kamma-energy and the expiration of the life-term. (*Ubhayakkhaya Maraṇa*).

(4) The action of a stronger Kamma (*Upacchedaka*) that suddenly cuts off the Reproductive Kamma before the expiry of the life-term.

A more powerful opposing force can check the path of the flying arrow and bring it down to the ground. Similarly a very powerful Kammic force of the past is capable of nullifying the potential energy of the last thought-moment, and thus destroy the psychic life of the being. The death of Devadatta was due to an *Upacchedaka Kamma* which he committed during his life time.

The first three types of deaths are collectively called *Kālamaraṇa* (timely death), and the last one is known as *Akālamaraṇa* (untimely death).

An oil lamp, for instance, may get extinguished owing to any of the following four causes—namely, the exhaustion of the wick, the exhaustion of oil, simultaneous exhaustion of both wick and oil, and some extraneous cause like wind.

Death of a person may similarly be caused by any of the above-mentioned four ways.

Explaining the cause of death in the foregoing manner Buddhism tells us that there are also four modes of births, viz., egg-born creatures (*Aṇḍaja*), womb-born creatures (*Jalābuja*), moisture-born creatures (*Sansedaja*), and creatures having spontaneous births (*Opapātika*). This broad classification embraces the entire range of beings that possess life.

Birds and snakes that are born of eggs belong to the first division.

The womb-born creatures comprise all human beings, some Devas inhabiting the earth, and those animals that take their conception in a mother's womb.

Those embryos that take moisture as material for their growth, like certain insects, belong to the third class.

Creatures having a spontaneous birth are generally invisible to the naked eye. Conditioned by their past Kamma they appear suddenly independently of parents. Since they do not pass through the embryonic period, which tends to obliterate the memories of the past, they are capable of recollecting their past birth. "Passing thence he was born amongst Devas and looked into the past to see what good act conditioned him to be born thus," is a passage which often recurs in the Suttas. Brahmas, Devas of heavenly realms, Petas, and the miserable ones who are subject to torments and sufferings in states of woe (*Nirayas*) are included in this last division.

CHAPTER XXII

PLANES OF EXISTENCE*

BIRTHS may take place in different spheres.* There are altogether thirty-one planes of existence in which beings manifest themselves according to their Kammic energy.

They are:—

The four states of unhappiness (*Duggati*)—namely,

1. *Niraya*—woeful states, which are temporary but not everlasting.

2. *Tiracchāna yoni*—the animal kingdom.

3. *Peta yoni*—the place of Petas or ghost-beings.

4. *Asura yoni*—the place of the Asura demons.

These four are the lower unhappy planes of re-birth. Beings are born in these miserable states on account of their evil Kamma. After their period of atonement, which is determined by their own Kamma, they may be re-born in another plane.

Petas, it should be understood, are not spirits or mere disembodied souls. They possess ugly or deformed bodies of varying magnitude. There is a special book, called Petavatthu, which exclusively deals with the stories of those unfortunate beings. Sanyutta

---

* See Diagram ii.

Nikāya also gives some interesting accounts of those *Petas.*[1]

Speaking of a Peta the Venerable Moggallāna says:—

"Just now as I was descending Vulture's Peak hill, I saw a skeleton going through the air, and vultures, crows, and falcons kept flying after it, pecking at its ribs, pulling it apart while it uttered cries of pain. To me came this thought:—Oh, but this is wonderful! Oh, but this is marvellous that a person will come to have such a shape, that the individuality acquired will come to have such a shape!"

This being, the Buddha said, was a cattle butcher in his previous birth, and as the result of his evil Kamma he was born in such a state.

Asura-demons are also another class of unhappy beings, similar to the Petas. They should be distinguished from the Asuras who are opposed to the Devas.

According to the *Milinda Pañha* there are four kinds of Petas:—the *Vantāsikas* who feed on vomit, the *Khuppipāsino* who hunger and thirst, the *Nijjhāmataṇhikā* who are consumed by thirst, and the *Paradattūpajīvino* who live on the gifts of others.

As stated in the *Tirokuḍḍa Suttā* these last mentioned Petas share the merits performed by their living relatives in their names, and could thereby pass on to better states of happiness.

---

1. Kindred Sayings, part 2., p. 170.

Next to the four unhappy states are the seven happy states—*Sugati*. They are:—

1. *Manussa*—the realm of human beings.

This realm is a mixture of both happiness and misery. The Bodhisattas prefer this state as it is the best field to practise the Pāramis (perfections). The Buddhas are born only in the realm of human beings.

2. *Cātummahārājika*—the realms of the four kings who are the guardian deities of the four quarters of the firmament.

3. *Tāvatiṃsa*[1]—'the realm of the Thirty-three Devas.' The Deva Sakka is the chief of this realm.

4. *Yāma*—'the realm of the Yāma Devas.'

5. *Tusita*—'the realm of Delight.'

   The Bodhisattas who have perfected the *pāramis* reside in this Plane until the opportune moment comes for them to appear in the human realm to attain Buddhahood. The Bodhisatta Metteyya, the future Buddha, is at present residing in this realm.

6. *Nimmānarati*—'the realm of the Devas who rejoice in their own creations.'

7. *Paranimmita Vasavatti*—'the realm of the Devas who make others' creation serve their own ends.

---

1. A Chinese Buddhist book states that on each of the four sides of this realm are eight heavens (32) and a central one where King Sakka dwells—" Guide to Buddhahood."

The last six are the realms of the gods or Devas who are also a class of beings that possess more refined bodies than human beings. They are not eternal but subject to birth and death. In some respects, such as in their constitution, habitat, food, they are superior to human beings, but as a rule in wisdom they do not transcend them. These celestial beings have spontaneous births appearing like youths of fifteen or sixteen years of age.

The four *Apāyas*, the realm of human beings, and these six celestial realms are collectively called *Kāmaloka*—the sentient existence.

Above the plane of *Kāmaloka* is the *Rūpaloka* plane which consists of sixteen grades, viz:—

(a) The plane of first Jhāna, to wit,

1. *Brahma Pārisajja*—'the realm of the Brahma's retinue.'

2. *Brahma Purohita*—'the realm of the Brahma's ministers,'

3. *Mahā Brahma*—'the realm of the great Brahmas,'

(b) the plane of second *Jhāna*, to wit,

4. *Parittabhā*—'the realm of minor lustre,'

5. *Appamaṇabha*—'the realm of infinite lustre,'

6. *Ābhassara*—'the realm of the radiant Brahmas,'

(c) the plane of third *Jhāna*, to wit,

7. *Parittasubha*—'the realm of the Brahmas of minor aura,'

8. *Appamāṇasubha*—'the realm of the Brahmas of infinite aura,'

9. *Subhakiṇha*—'the realm of the Brahmas full of steady aura,'

(d) the plane of fourth *Jhāna*, to wit,

10. *Vehapphala*—'the realm of the Brahmas of the great reward,'

11. *Asañña Satta*—'the realm of beings devoid of consciousness,'

12. *Suddhāvāsa*—'the Pure Abodes.' These are further sub-divided into five, viz:—

    i. *Aviha*—'the abode of the immobile,'
    ii. *Atappa*—'Serene,'
    iii. *Sudassa*—'Beautiful,'
    iv. *Sudassi*—'Clear-sighted,'
    v. *Akaṇiṭṭha*—'Superior Beings.'

It is only those who have developed the Jhānas or Ecstasies that are born in these higher planes. Yogis who have developed the first Jhāna are born in the first plane, those who have developed the second and third Jhānas are born in the second plane, and those who have developed the fourth and fifth Jhānas are born in the third and fourth planes, respectively.

The first grade of each plane is assigned to those who have developed the Jhānas to an ordinary degree, the second to those who have developed the Jhānas to a moderate extent, and the third to those who have gained a complete mastery over the Jhānas.

In the eleventh plane called the *Asaññā Satta* there is no consciousness but only matter. Here the mind is temporarily suspended while the force of the Jhāna lasts.

The *Suddhāvāsa* or the Pure Abodes are the camping places of *Arahants* and *Anāgāmīs*. Ordinary beings are not born in these states. Those who attain *Anāgāmi* in the sentient existence are, after death, born in these abodes, and reside there until they attain *Arahantship*.

There are four other planes called the *Arūpaloka* realms which are devoid of matter or bodies. Buddhists maintain that there are realms where mind exists without matter. "Just as it is possible for an iron bar to float in the air because it has been flung there, and there it remains as long as it retains any unexpended momentum, even so the 'Formless being' appears through being flung into that state by powerful mind-force, and there it remains till that momentum is expended. This is a temporary separation of mind from matter, which, normally, co-exist."[1]

It should be mentioned that there is no sex distinction in the *Rūpaloka* and the *Arūpaloka*.

The *Arūpaloka is* divided into four grades, according to the four Arūpa Jhānas. They are:—

1. *Ākāsānañcāyatana*—'the sphere of the conception of infinite space,'

---

1. Dr. Cassius A. Pereira

2. *Viññaṇañcayatana*—'the sphere of the conception of infinite consciousness,'

3. *Ākincannayatana*—'the sphere of the conception of Nothingness,'

4. *N'eva sanna N'asannayatana*—'the sphere of neither perception nor non-perception.'

The Abhidhammattha Sangaha gives the age limit of these planes of existence as follows:

"There is no fixed limit to the duration of life in beings reborn to misfortune in the four planes of misery, in human beings and in degraded *Asuras*. The life-term in the case of the gods called the Four Kings is 500 celestial years--that is to say, as men reckon years, 9,000,000. The life-term of the Thirty-three gods is four times this amount. That of the *Yama* gods is again four times the life term of the Thirty-three; and so on for the gods of the Heavens of Delight, for those of the gods who rejoice in their own creations, and for those of the gods who make others' creations serve their own ends.

"The life-term of gods in the heaven of Brahma's retinue is the third of an æon (*Kappa*); of gods in that of Brahma's ministers, half an æon; of the Great Brahmas, one æon; of the gods of minor lustre, two (great) æons; of the gods of infinite lustre, four great æons; of the radiant gods, eight æons; of the gods of minor aura, sixteen æons; of the gods full of steady aura, sixty-four æons; of the gods of great reward, and of the unconscious beings, five hundred great æons; of the immobile gods, a thousand great æons; of the

PLANES OF EXISTENCE

Loka	Realm	Group	Plane	AGE LIMIT
Arūpaloka (4) Formless Realms			Neva Saññā Nāsaññāyatana	84,000 M. Kappas
			Ākiñcaññāyatana	60,000 M. Kappas
			Viññāṇañcāyatana	40,000 M. Kappas
			Ākāsānañcāyatana	20,000 M. Kappas
Rūpaloka (16) Realms of Form	Catuttha Jhāna Bhūmi (Fourth Jhāna Realm)	Suddhāvāsa	Akaṇiṭṭha	16,000 M. Kappas
			Sudassī	8000 M. Kappas
			Sudassa	4000 M. Kappas
			Atappa	2000 M. Kappas
			Aviha	1000 M. Kappas
			Asaññasatta	500 Maha Kappas
			Vehapphala	500 Maha Kappas
	Tatiya Jhāna Bhūmi (Third Jhāna Realm)		Subhakiṇha	64 Maha Kappas
			Appamāṇasubha	32 Maha Kappas
			Parittasubha	16 Maha Kappas
	Dutiya Jhāna Bhūmi (Second Jhāna Realm)		Ābhassara	8 Maha Kappas
			Appamāṇābha	4 Maha Kappas
			Parittābha	2 Maha Kappas
	Paṭhama Jhāna Bhūmi (First Jhāna Realm)		Mahā Brahma	1 Asankheyya Kappa
			Brahmapurohita	½ Asankheyya Kappa
			Brahmapārisajja	⅓ Asankheyya Kappa
Kāmaloka (11) (Sentient Existence)	Sugati (7)	Devaloka (6)	Paranimmita Vasavatti	16000 Celestial Years
			Nimmānarati	8000 "
			Tusita	4000 "
			Yāma	2000 "
			Tāvatimsa	1000 "
			Cātummahārājika	500 "
			MANUSSA	No.
	Duggati (4)		Asurayoni	"
			Petayoni	"
			Tiracchānayoni	"
			Niraya	"

DIAGRAM—ii.

serene gods, two thousand great æons; of the beautiful gods, four thousand great æons; of the clear sighted gods, eight thousand great æons; of the superior gods, sixteen thousand great æons.

"The life-term of *Ākasanañcayatana* is twenty thousand great æons; that of *Viññānañcāyatana* is forty thousand great æons; that of *Ākiñcaññayatana* is sixty thousand great æons; that of *N'eva sanna N'asaññāyatana* is eighty-four thousand great æons."[1]

---

1. See Compendium of Philosophy—pp. 140—143.

CHAPTER XXIII

HOW REBIRTH TAKES PLACE

LET us now come to the most interesting and extremely subtle point of our subject:—

Suppose a person is about to die. From the seventeenth thought-moment reckoned backward from the point of death no renewed physical functioning recurs. Material qualities born of Kamma (*Kammaja Rūpa*) arise no more, but those which come into being before the static phase of that thought-moment persist till the time of dying-thought and then cease.*

This critical stage may be compared to the flickering of a lamp just before it is extinguished.

To this dying man is presented a *Kamma*, *Kamma Nimitta*, or *Gati Nimitta*. By *Kamma* is here meant some action of his whether good or bad. It may be either meritorious or demeritorious weighty action (*Garuka Kamma*), such as *Jhānas* (Ecstasies), or parricide, and so forth.

---

* According to Buddhism material qualities are produced in four ways:—

1. *Kamma*, i. e. past moral and immoral actions.
2. *Utu*, i e. phyiscal change or *Tejo*-element which includes both heat and cold.
3. *Citta*, i. e. mind and mental properties.
4. *Āhāra*, i e. nutriment that exists in food— See "Compendium of Philosophy," p. 161.

These are so powerful that they totally eclipse all other actions and appear very vividly before the mind's eye. If experience has afforded him nothing weighty, he may take for his object of the dying-thought a Kamma done immediately before death (*Āsanna Kamma*).

It is not presumptuous to suppose that most of the soldiers who die fighting, would be having a death-proximate Kamma, like the killing of their fellow-men. Consequently their rebirth cannot possibly be good.

In the absence of an *Āsanna Kamma*, a habitual meritorious or demeritorious act (*Āciṇṇa Kamma*) is presented, such as stealing in the case of a robber, or the healing of the sick in the case of a good physician. Failing all these, some casual act, that is one of the accumulative reserves of the endless past (*Kaṭattā*) Kamma—becomes the object of the dying-thought.

Kamma Nimitta is any sight, sound, smell, taste, touch, or idea which was obtained at the time of the commission of the Kamma, such as knives in the case of a butcher, patients in the case of a physician, an object of worship in the case of a devotee, etc.

By Gati Nimitta is meant some sign of the place where he is to take birth—a thing which invariably happens to dying persons. When these indications of the future birth occur, and if they are bad, they can be turned into good. This is done by influencing the thoughts of the dying man, so that his good thoughts may now act as the proximate Kamma and counteract the influence of the Reproductive *Kamma* which would otherwise affect his subsequent birth.

These symbols of one's destiny may be hellish fires, forests, mountainous regions, mother's womb, celestial mansions, etc.[1]

Taking for the object one of the above, a thought process runs its course even if the death be an instantaneous one. It is said that even the fly which is crushed by a hammer on the anvil also experiences such a process of thought before it actually dies.

Let us imagine for the sake of convenience that the dying person is to be reborn in the human kingdom and that the object is some good Kamma.

His *Bhavanga* consciousness is interrupted, vibrates for two thought-moments and passes away, after which the mind-door consciousness (*Manodvārāvajjana*) rises and passes away. Then comes the psychologically important stage—*Javana* process, which here runs only for five thought-moments by reason of its weakness, instead of the normal seven. As such it lacks all reproductive power, its main function being the mere regulation of the new existence—*Abhinavakaraṇa*. The object in the present case being desirable, the consciousness he experiences is a moral one—automatic or volitional, accompanied by pleasure, and associated with wisdom or not as the case may be. The *Tadālambana* consciousness which has for its function a registering or identifying for two moments of the object so perceived may or may not follow. After this occurs the death-consciousness (Cuti-Citta) the last thought-moment to be experienced in this present life.[2]

---

1. For details with regard to these "premonitory visions of the place of rebirth"—See Dr. W. T. Evans-Wentz, "*The Tibetan Book of the Dead*" p. 183.

2. See Diagram iii.

The process of the decease-consciousness is as follows:—

1	2	3	4	5	6	7	8	9	10	11	12	13	14
***	***	***	***	***	***	***	***	***	***	***	***	***	***
Atīta Bhavānga (Past Sub-Consciousness)	*Bhavānga Calana* (Vibrating Sub-Consciousness)	*Bhavānga Upaccheda* (Arrest Sub-Consciousness)	*Manodvārāvajjana* (Mind-door Consciousness)	**JAVANA**						*Tadālambana* (Registering Consciousness)	*Cuti* (Decease Consciousness)	*Paṭisandhi* (Re-linking Consciousness)	*Bhavānga* (Sub-Consciousness)

DIAGRAM—iii

fresh one in another birth. In the present case the thought experienced whilst dying being a moral one, the rebirth resultant consciousness takes for its material an appropriate sperm and ovum-cell of human parents. The rebirth-consciousness (*Paṭisandhi Viññāṇa*) then lapses into the sub-conscious states (Bhavānga).

Simultaneous with the arising of the rebirth consciousness there spring up the '*body-decad*,' '*sex-decad*,' and '*base-decad*' (*Kāya-Bhāva-Vatthu Dasaka*).[1]

From this it is evident that the sex is determined at the very conception of the being. It is conditioned by Kamma and not by a fortuitous combination of sperm and ovum-cells.

The passing away of the consciousness of the past birth gave occasion to the arising of the new consciousness in the subsequent birth, but nothing unchangeable or permanent passed from the past to the present.

Just as the wheel rests on the ground only at one point, even so we live only for one thought-moment. We are always in the present, and this present is ever slipping into the irrevocable past. Each consciousness, on passing away, gives up its whole energy or all the

---

1. The 'body-decad' is composed of the four elements—namely, 1. the element of hardness (*Paṭhavi*), 2. the element of cohesion, (*Āpo*). 3 the element of heat (*Tejo*), 4 the element of motion (*Vāyo*); its four derivatives (*Upādā Rūpa* —namely, 5. colour (*Vaṇṇa*), 6. odour (*Gandha*), 7. taste (*Rasa*), 8. Nutritive essence (*Ojā*), 9. vitality (*Jīvitindriya*), and 10. body (*Kāya*).

"Sex-decad" and "base-decad" also consist of the first nine and sex (*Bhava*) and seat of consciousness (*Vatthu*), respectively.

impressions received to its successor. Each successive consciousness therefore consists of the potentialities of all its predecessors and something more.

Now this stream of consciousness flows on *ad infinitum*. At death the consciousness perishes only to give birth to another in a subsequent birth. This renewed consciousness inherits all the past experiences.

"This new being which is the present manifestation of the stream of Kamma-energy is not the same as, and has no identity with the previous one in its line; the aggregate that makes up its composition being different from, and having no identity with, those that make up the being of its predecessor. And yet it is not an entirely different being, since it has the same stream of Kamma-energy, though modified perchance just by having shown itself in that last manifestation, which is now making its presence known in the sense perceptible world as the new being."[1]

The transition of the flux is also instantaneous and leaves no room whatever for an intermediate state (*antara bhava*). Buddhists do not believe that the spirit of the deceased person takes lodgment in a certain state until it finds a suitable place for its reincarnation.[2]

The continuity of the flux at death is unbroken in point of time, and there is no breach in the stream of

---

1. Silācāra.

2. According to Tibetan Buddhist works there is an intermediate state where beings remain ' either for one, two, three, four, five, six, or seven weeks, until the forty-ninth day." See Dr W Y. Evans-Wentz. *The Tibetan Book of the Dead*, pp xlii-xliii, 6 8, 160-165.

consciousness. The only difference between the passing of one thought to another and of the dying thought-moment to the rebirth-consciousness is that in the latter case a marked perceptible death is visible.

Rebirth takes place immediately, and there is no difference in time whether one is born in a heaven, a state of misery, animal kingdom, or human realm.

This is well expressed in the Milinda Pañha:—

The King Milinda questions:

Venerable Nāgasena, if somebody dies here and is reborn in the world of Brahma, and another one who dies here and is reborn in Kashmir, which of them would arrive first?"

"They would arive at the same time, O King."

"Give me a simile."

"In which town were you born, O King?"

"In a village called Kalasi, venerable Sir."

"How far is Kalasi from here, O King?"

"About two hundred miles, venerable Sir."

"And how far is Kashmir from here, O King?"

"About twelve miles, venerable Sir."

"Now think of the village of Kalasi, O King."

"I have done so, venerable Sir."

"And now think of Kashmir, O King."

"It is done, venerable Sir."

"Which of these two, O King, did you think the more slowly and which the more quickly?

"Both equally quickly, venerable Sir."

"Just so, O King, he who dies here and is reborn in the world of Brahma, is not reborn later than he who dies here and is reborn in Kashmir."

"Give me one more simile."

"What do you think, O King? Suppose two birds were flying in the air, and they should settle at the same time, one upon a high, and the other upon a low tree,—which bird's shade would first fall upon the earth, and which bird's later?"

"Both shadows would appear at the same time, not one of them earlier and the other later.

* * * *

A question might arise—Are the sperm and ovum-cells always ready waiting to take up this rebirth thought?

As Dr. Dhalke puts it "this taking hold is not something that has law that runs its appointed course according to definite laws, but it is law in itself. A point in the ground is always ready to receive the falling stone."

It should be understood that, according to Buddhism, living beings are indefinite, and so are world-systems. It is not, therefore, so difficult to believe that there will always be an appropriate place to receive the rebirth thought or, in other words, the relinking consciousness which is conditioned by Kamma.

CHAPTER XXIV

WHAT IS IT THAT IS REBORN?

(No-Soul)

APART from mind and matter which constitute this so-called being there is no place for an immortal soul or an eternal ego, which man is either gifted with or has obtained in a mysterious way from an equally mysterious Being or force.

At the outset this Buddhist doctrine of rebirth should be distinguished from the theory of reincarnation or transmigration, for Buddhism denies the existence of an unchanging or eternal soul.

A soul which is eternal must necessarily remain always the same without any change whatsoever. If the soul which is supposed to be the essence of man is eternal, there cannot be either a rise or fall. Besides one cannot understand why "different souls are so variously constituted at the outset." Buddhism denies the existence of such a permanent entity.

In the ultimate sense (Paramattha-saccena) a Buddhist cannot think of an unchanging soul, any being in the form of a Deva, a man, or an animal. These forms are merely the temporary manifestations of the Kammic force. "Being" is only a concept used for conventional purposes. Strictly speaking a being is nothing but a mere composition of mind and matter.

To prove the existence of endless felicity in an eternal heaven and unending torments in an eternal hell, an immortal soul is absolutely necessary. Otherwise, what is it that sinned on earth and punished in hell?

"It should be said," writes Bertrand Russell, "that the old distinction between soul and body has evaporated quite as much because 'matter' has lost it solidity as because mind has lost its spirituality. Psychology is just beginning to be scientific. In the present state of psychology belief in immortality can at any rate claim no support from science."

According to the learned author of "The Riddle of the Universe"—"the *theological proof*—that a personal creator has breathed an immortal soul (generally regarded as portion of the divine soul) into man is a *pure myth.* The *cosmological proof*—that the moral order of the world demands the eternal duration of the human soul—is a *baseless dogma.* The *teleological proof* that the higher destiny of man involves the perfecting of his defective, earthly soul beyond the grave, rests on a false *anthropism.* The *moral proof*—that the defects and the unsatisfied desires of earthly existence must be fulfilled by compensative justice on the other side of eternity—is nothing more than a *pious wish.* The *ethnological proof* that the belief in immortality, like the belief in God, is an innate truth, common to all humanity—is an *error in fact.* The *ontological proof* that the soul, being a simple, immaterial, and indivisible entity, cannot be involved in the corruption of death—is based in an entirely, erroneous view of the psychic phenomena; it is a *spiritualistic fallacy.* All these and similar 'proofs of athanatism' are in a parlous condition; they are definitely annulled by the scientific criticism of the last few decades."

If nothing in the form of a spirit or soul passes from this life to the other, what is it that is reborn?

In asking this question one takes for granted that there is something to be reborn.

In the past too it was argued "*Cogito ergo sum*"— I think, therefore I am. True indeed, but it has to be proved first that there is an I to think.

"I say that there is no 'I' to think." Preposterous! you exclaim. "In one breadth you contradict yourself." Yes, it has to be admitted that we cannot avoid using conventional terms.

We say that the sun arises in the East and sets in the West, despite what scientists prove to us. We cannot strike the same place twice although to all appearance we have done so. Everything has changed so soon. Even space has changed at the second moment.

Buddhists do agree with Russel when he says "there is obviously some reason in which I am the same person as I was yesterday, and, to take an even more obvious example, if I simultaneously see a man and hear him speaking, there is some sense in which the I that sees is the same as the I that hears."

Until recently scientists believed in an indivisible and indestructible atom. "For sufficient reasons pysicists have reduced this atom to a series of events;

for equally good reasons psychologists find that mind has not the identity of single continuing thing but is a series of occurrences bound together by certain intimate relations. The question of immortality, therefore, has become the question whether these intimate relations exist between occurrences connected with a living body and other occurrences which take place after that body is dead."

As C. E. M. Joad says in *The Meaning of Life* "matter has since disintegrated under our very eyes. It is no longer solid; it is no longer enduring; it is no longer determined by compulsive causal laws; and more important than all it is no longer known."

The so-called atoms, it seems, are both "divisible and destructible." The electrons and protons that compose atoms "can meet and annihilate one another, while their persistence, such as it is, is rather that of a wave lacking fixed boundaries, and in process of continual change both as regards shape and position, than that of a thing."[1]

Bishop Berkeley who proved that this so-called atom is a metaphysical fiction held that there exists a spiritual substance called the soul.

Hume closely investigated this consciousness and perceived nothing but fleeting mental states. He, therefore, concluded that the supposed permanent ego is non-existent.

"There are some philosophers," he says, "who imagine we are every moment conscious of what we call ourselves; that we feel its existence and its continuance in existence and so we are certain--both of its

1. C. E. M. Joad, *The Meaning of Life*.

perfect identity and simplicity. For my part when I enter most intimately into what I call myself I always stumble on some particular perception or the other—of heat or cold, light or shade, love or hatred, pain or pleasure. I never catch myself—never can observe anything but the perception—nor do I conceive what is further requisite to make me a perfect non-entity."

Bergson says, "All consciousness is time existence; and a conscious state is not a state that endures without changing. It is a change without ceasing; when change ceases it ceases; it is itself nothing but change."

Dealing with this question of soul Prof. James says:—"The soul-theory is a complete superfluity, so far as accounting for the actually verified facts of conscious experience goes. So far no one can be compelled to subscribe to it for definite scientific reasons.

"This me is an empirical aggregate of things objectively known. The I which knows them cannot itself be an aggregate, neither for psychological purpose need it be considered to be an unchanging metaphysical entity like the soul, or a principle like the pure Ego viewed as out of time. It is a thought, at each moment different from that of the last moment, but appropriative of the latter, together with all that the latter called its own. All the experimental facts find their place in this description, unencumbered with any hypothesis save that of the existence of passing thoughts or states of mind."

In concluding his interesting chapter on the soul he says:—"And in this book the provisional solution which we have reached must be the final word: the *thoughts themselves are the thinkers.*"

The Buddha propounded these facts some 2500 years ago whilst He was sojourning in the valley of the Ganges.

According to Buddhism the so-called being is composed of mind and matter—*Nāma* and *Rūpa*.

Rūpa or matter is merely the manifestation of forces and qualities.

In the ancient days the Indian sages too believed in an indivisible atom—*paramānu*. The Buddha analysed this so-called indivisible *paramānu* and declared that it is only a manifestation of particular inter-related forces which He termed *Paramatthas* or essentials of matter.

These Paramatthas are *Paṭhavi*, *Āpo*, *Tejo* and *Vāyo*. One must not understand, as was believed by some Greek thinkers of the past, that these elements are earth, water, fire, and air.

"*Paṭhavi*" means the element of extension, the substratum of matter. Without it objects cannot occupy space. The qualities of hardness and softness which are purely relative are two phases of this element. It must be understood that this element of extension is present in earth, water, fire, and air. For instance, the water above is supported by water below. It is this element of extension in conjunction with the element of motion (Vāyo) that produces the upward pressure.

"*Āpo*" is the element of cohesion. Unlike *Paṭhavi* it is intangible. It is this element which coheres the scattered atoms of matter and gives us the idea of "body."

"*Tejo*" is the element of heat. Cold is also a form of Tejo. Both heat and cold are included in Tejo because they possess the power of maturing bodies or, in other words, the vitalising energy. Preservation and decay are due to this element.

"*Vāyo*" is the element of motion. The movements are caused by this element. Motion is regarded as the force or the generator of heat. "Both motion and heat in the material realm correspond respectively to consciousness and Kamma in the mental."

These four are the fundamental units of matter and are invariably combined with the four derivatives —namely, colour (*Vaṇṇa*), odour (*Gandha*), taste (*Rasa*), and nutritive essence (*Ojā*).

The four elements and the derivatives are inseparable and inter-related, but one element may preponderate over another, as for instance, the element of extension preponderates in earth; cohesion, in water; heat, in fire; and motion, in air.

Thus, according to Buddhism, matter consists of forces and qualities which are in a state of constant flux.

Mind which is the most important part in the machinery of man is also a complex compound of fleeting mental states. There are fifty-two such mental states. *Vedanā* or sensation is one, *Saññā* or perception is another. The remaining fifty mental states are collectively called *Sankhārā* or volitional activities. These immaterial states arise in a consciousness (*Viññāṇa*).

Each unit of consciousness consists of three phases—genesis (*Uppāda*), development (*Ṭhiti*) and dissolution (*Bhanga*). One unit of consciousness perishes only to give birth to another. The subsequent thought-moment is neither absolutely the same as its predecessor—since its composition is not identical—nor entirely another—being the same continuity of *Kamma* energy.

It must not be misunderstood that a consciousness is chopped up in bits and joined together like a train or a chain. But, on the contrary, "it constantly flows on like a river receiving from the tributary streams of sense constant accretions to its flood, and ever dispensing to the world around it the thought-stuff it has gathered up by the way."[1] It has birth for its source and death for its mouth. The rapidity of the flow is such that hardly is there any standard whereby it can be measured even approximately. However, it pleases the commentators to say that the time duration of one thought-moment is even less than the one-millionth part of the time occupied by a flash of lightning.

Here we find a juxtaposition of fleeting mental states of consciousness opposed to a superposition of such states as some appear to believe. No state once gone ever recurs, nor is absolutely identical with what goes before. These states constantly change not remaining for two consecutive moments the same. We worldlings, veiled by the web of illusion, mistake this apparent continuity to be something eternal and go to the extent of introducing an unchanging soul, an Attā (*Ātma*), the supposed doer and receptacle of all actions, to this ever changing consciousness.

1. See Compendium of Philosophy—Introduction p 12.

"The so-called being is like a flash of lightning that is resolved into a succession of sparks that follow upon one another with such rapidity that the human retina cannot perceive them separately, nor can the uninstructed conceive of such succession of separate sparks."—(*Dhalke*).

We see a vast expanse of water in the sea, but the waters of the ocean consist of countless drops. An infinite number of particles of sand constitute the sea-beach, but it appears as one long sheet. Waves arise and dash against the shore, but actually speaking no single wave came from the deep sea to lose its identity on the shore. In the cinematograph we see a picture in motion, but to represent that picture a series of momentary motions must appear on the film.

In exactly the same way there is no one permanent soul that resides in this so-called being, which is only a composition of the five Aggregates.

One cannot say that the perfume of a flower rests on the petal or on the pistil or on the colour, for the perfume is in the flower.

In the same way one's individuality is the combination of all these five. If one were to say that by soul or self is meant the process of this psycho-physical phenomenon that is constantly becoming and passing away, then there would be no objection to the term. For the Buddha Himself uses the term Atta—soul or self—to indicate the collection of the Khandas or aggregates.

Buddhism does not totally deny the existence of a personality in an empirical sense. It attempts to show that it does not exist in an ultimate sense. The Buddhist philosophical term for an individual is *Santati*, i. e., a flux or continuity. It includes the mental and physical elements as well. The Kammic force of each individual binds these elements together. This uninterrupted flux or continuity of psycho-physical phenomenon, which is conditioned by Kamma, and not limited only to the present life, but having its source in the beginningless past and its continuation in the future—is the Buddhist substitute for the permanent ego or immortal soul of other religions.

In fact this doctrine of no-soul is the crux of Buddhism.

How is rebirth possible without a soul to be reborn?

Birth, according to Buddhism, is simply the coming—into—being of the Khandhas, the aggregates (*Khandhānaṁ pātubhāvo*).

Just as the arising of a physical state is conditioned by a preceding state as its cause, even so the coming-into-being of this psycho-physical life is conditioned by causes anterior to its birth. The present process of becoming is the result of the craving for becoming in the last birth, and the present craving for becoming conditions the life in a future birth.

As one life-process is possible without a permanent thing passing from one thought-moment to another, a series of life-processes is possible without anything to transmigrate from one life to another.

This Buddhist doctrine of rebirth should be differentiated from the theory of re-incarnation which implies the transmigration of a soul and its invariable fleshly rebirth.

According to Buddhism no permanent soul or any unchanging spiritual substance transmigrates from one life to another. If one prefers, one may say that we inherit our Kammic activities. Our natural abilities and our inherent characteristics are due to this Kamma.

In the Milinda Pañha and Visuddhi Magga the Venerable Nāgasena and the Venerable Buddhaghosa have employed several similes to show that nothing transmigrates from one life to another.

The simile of the flame is very striking. This life is a flame. Rebirth is the transmitting of this flame from one group to another. The flame of life is continuous although there is an apparent break at so-called death.

King Milinda questions—

"Venerable Nāgasena, does rebirth take place without anything transmigrating?

"Yes, O King. Rebirth takes place without anything transmigrating.

"Give me an illustration, Venerable Sir."

"Suppose, O King, a man were to light a light from another light; pray, would the one light have passed over to the other light?"

"Nay, indeed, Venerable Sir."

"In exactly the same way, O King, does rebirth take place without anything transmigrating."

"Give another illustration."

"Do you remember, O King, having learnt, when you were a boy, some verse or other from your teacher of poetry?"

"Yes, Venerable Sir."

"Pray, O King, did the verse pass over to you from your teacher."

"Nay, indeed, Venerable Sir."

"In exactly the same way, O King, does rebirth take place without anything transmigrating."

Again King Milinda questions—

"Venerable Nāgasena, what is it that is born into the next existence?"

"O King, it is mind and body that is born into the next existence?"

"Is it this same mind and body that is born into the next existence."

"O King, it is not this same mind and body that is born into the next existence, but with this mind and body, O King, one does a deed—it may be good, or it may be evil—and by reason of this deed another mind and body is born into the next existence."

"Venerable Sir, if it is not this mind and body that is born into the next existence, is one not freed from one's evil deeds?"

"If one were not born into another existence, one would be freed from one's evil deeds; but, O King, inasmuch as one is born into another existence, therefore is one not freed from one's evil deeds."

"Give an illustration."

"O King, it is as if a man were to take away another man's mangoes, and the owner of the mangoes were to seize him, and show him to the king, and say —'Sire, this man hath taken away my mangoes;' and the other were to say, 'Sire, I did not take away this man's mangoes. The mangoes which this man planted were different from those which I took away. I am not liable to punishment.' Pray, O King, would the man be liable to punishment?"

"Assuredly, Venerable Sir, would he be liable to punishment."

"For what reason?"

"Because, in spite of what he might say, he would be liable to punishment for the reason that the last mangoes derived from the first mangoes."

"In exactly the same way, O King, with this mind and body one does a deed—it may be good, or it may be bad—and by reason of this deed another mind and body is born into the next existence. Therefore is one not freed from one's evil deeds." [1]

The venerable Buddhaghosa elucidates this point by citing the similes of *echo*, *light*, *impression of a seal*, and *reflection in a mirror*.

---

1. See Warren—*Buddhism in Translations*, pp. 234, 235.

A modern writer illustrates this process by a series of billiard balls in close contact.

"If, for instance, another ball is rolled against the last stationary ball, the moving ball will stop dead, and the foremost stationary ball will move on. The first moving ball does not pass over, it remains behind, it dies; but it is undeniably the movement of that ball, its *momentum*, its Kamma, and not any newly created movement, which is reborn in the foremost ball."[1]

In like manner—to use conventional terms—the body dies transmitting its Kammic force to another without anything transmigrating from this life to the other. The future being there will be conditioned by the present Kamma here. The new being is neither absolutely the same nor totally different, being the same stream of Kamma energy. There is, therefore, a continuity of a particular life-flux; just that and nothing more.

---

1. Dr. Ananda Coomaraswami, *Buddha and the Gospel of Buddhism*, p. 106.

CHAPTER XXV

MORAL RESPONSIBILITY

IS it one who does the act in this birth and another who reaps its results in the other birth?

To say that he who sows is absolutely the same as he who reaps, is one end; and to say that he who sows is totally different from he who reaps, is the other end. Overcoming these two ends the Buddha teaches the Doctrine in the middle in terms of cause and effect.

This important point the venerable Buddhaghosa has elaborated in the *Visuddhi Magga*. He states—*Na ca so na ca añño—neither the same nor another.*

As an illustration let us take the case of the butterfly. It was first an egg, and then it became a caterpillar. Later it developed into a chrysalis, and finally evolved into a butterfly. This process occurs in the course of one lifetime. The butterfly is neither the same as, nor totally different from, the caterpillar. Here also there is a flux of life or a continuity.

[1]Venerable Nagasena explains this point by citing the illustration of the lamp that burns throughout the night. The flame of the first watch is not identical with that of the last watch, yet in dependence upon

1. See "The Questions of Milinda"—Part I, p. 111 and Dr. Dahlke—"Buddnism and Science", p. 64.

the one and the same lamp the light burns throughout the night. In the same way there is a continuity of life—each succeeding state depending upon the preceding one.

If there is no soul, can there be any moral responsibility.

Yes, because there is a continuity. Identity is set aside and is substituted by a continuity.

A child, for instance, becomes a man, yet the latter neither absolutely the same as the former nor totally different, since the cells that formed his body in manhood have undergone a complete change. This constant change applies not only to body but also to mind. In the latter the change is more marked. Nevertheless, the individual as man is responsible for whatever he did in his childhood.

Quite so, man continues to exist in the same life. Yes, the most important point here is this *continuity* and not the identity.

Suppose a person was "X" in his last birth, and "Y" in this birth, and will be "Z" in his future birth.

Now "Y" is the continuation of "X," and "Z" will be the continuation of "Y." With the death of "X" his physical vehicle, which is the outward manifestation of the Kammic energy, is relinquished, and with the birth of "Y" a fresh physical vehicle arises. Despite the changes the material forms have undergone the invisible life current continues to flow, uninterrupted

---

1. See "Anatta and Moral Responsibility" written by Mr. A. D Jayasundara to the "Mahabodhi" Journal, Vol. 41, p. 93.

by death, carrying along with it all the impressions received from the tributary streams of sense.

Must not therefore "Y" be responsible for the actions of "X" who is his predecessor?"

But there is no memory in this case.

Well, then, that makes the only difference between the first and second instances.

In the first case of the child who attained manhood there is memory, whilst in the other case "Y" does not remember his actions as "X" owing to the intervening death.

Is identity or memory absolutely essential in assessing moral responsibility?

Strictly speaking neither is essential.

If, for instance, a person were to commit a crime and by sudden loss of memory he were to forget the incident, would he not be responsible for his act? His forgetfulness would surely be immaterial for the operation of the laws of the country.

But, what is the use of punishing him for he is not aware that he is being punished for his misdemeanour?

Is there any justice here?

Of course, there is not, if we are arbitrarily governed by a God who rewards and punishes us.

According to Buddhism the world is not so constituted. Instead of an arbitrary personal Almighty Being there is the just and rational law of Kamma that operates quite automatically without any external agency. Whatever pain or happiness we experience is the inevitable consequence of a past act. There are no rewards and punishments in Buddhism. Buddhists speak in terms of cause and effect.

In the words of Silācāra:—"If a person does something in his sleep, gets out of bed and walks over the edge of a verandah, he will fall into the road below and in all likelihood break an arm or leg or something worse. But this will happen not at all as a punishment for his sleep-walking, but merely as its result. And the fact that he did not remember going out on the verandah would not make the slightest difference to the result of his fall from it, in the shape of broken bones. So the follower of the Buddha takes measures to see that he does not walk over verandahs or other dangerous places, asleep or awake, so as to avoid hurting himself or anybody who might be below and on whom he might fall."

The fact that a person does not remember his past is no hindrance for the intelligent working of the Kammic law. It is this knowledge of the inevitability of the consequence of Kamma in the course of one's life in Sansāra that more or less moulds the character of a Buddhist.

CHAPTER XXVI

KAMMIC DESCENT AND KAMMIC ASCENT

IS there any possibility for a Kammic descent, or, in other words, for a man to be born as an animal?

Yes, there is the possibility for a Kammic descent.

Material forms such as Deva, man or animal, through which the life-continuum expresses itself, are, as stated earlier, merely temporary visible manifestations of the Kammic energy. The present physical vehicle is not directly evolved from the past physical vehicle, but is no doubt the successor of its past—being the same stream of Kammic energy. Just as an electric current can successively manifest itself in the form of heat, light, or motion—one without necessarily being evolved from the other—even so this Kammic energy may manifest itself in the form of man, animal, Deva, etc.,—one form having no physical connection with the other. It is one's Kamma that determines the nature of the material form, which varies according to the so-called evolutionary scale of beings.

Instead of saying that man becomes an animal or *vice versa*, it would be more correct to say that the Kammic force that manifested itself in the form of man may manifest itself in the form of an animal.

As we wander in *Sansāra*—to speak in conventional terms—we gather various experiences, receive

29

manifold impressions, acquire diverse characteristics. Every thought, word, or deed of ours is indelibly recorded in our palimpsest-like mind. The different natures we thus acquire in the course of our births as men, Devas, animals, Petas, etc., lie dormant within us, and as long as we are worldlings these undestroyed natures may, at unexpected moments, rise to the surface, "in disconcerting strength", and reveal our latent Kammic tendencies.

It is quite natural for us to remark after witnessing an unexpected outburst of passion in a highly civilised person—Oh, how could he have committed such an act! We never thought that he would do such an immoral thing!

There is nothing strange in this misdemeanour of his, for he only revealed a hidden part of his intricate self. This is the reason why men actuated by high moral standards are sometimes tempted to do things which can be least expected of them.

Devadatta, for example, was a noble prince of the aristocratic Sakya clan and a leading member of the Holy Order, possessed of supernormal powers. But, overcome by jealousy, latent in him, he made unsuccessful attempts to kill his own Master the Buddha.

Such is the intricate nature of mankind. One's past is not always a true index to one's future. For we are creating fresh Kamma every moment. In one sense we are truly what we were, and we will be what we are. But in another sense we are not what we were, and we will not be what we are. Who was yesterday a criminal may become a saint today; who is today a holy man may turn out to be a wretched sinner tomorrow.

We can safely and rightly be judged by this eternal present. Now we sow the seeds of our future. At this very moment we may act the part of a brute and create our own hell, or, on the other hand, act the part of a superman and create our own heaven. This present thought-moment conditions our second thought-moment. The subsequent birth, too, according to Buddhist philosophy, is determined by the last thought-moment we experience in this life. Just as in the course of one life one thought perishes giving up all its potentialities to its successor, even so the last thought-moment of this life perishes giving up all the acquired characteristics and natures to the succeeding moment in the subsequent birth.

Now, if the dying person cherishes a base desire or idea, or experiences a thought, or does an act which befits only an animal, his evil Kamma will condition him a birth in animal form. The Kammic force which manifested itself in the form of a man will then manifest itself in the form of an animal. It must not be misunderstood that thereby all his past good Kammic tendencies are lost. They also lie in a dormant state seeking an opportunity to rise to the surface. It is such a good Kamma that will later effect a birth as a human being.

This last thought-moment does not, as a rule, depend on the sum total of our actions in our lifetime. Generally a good person gets a good birth, and a bad person gets a bad birth. Under exceptional circumstances, however, the unexpected may also take place.

Queen Mallikā, to take an example from our Books, was a very good lady, but as the result of experiencing an evil thought at her dying moment, she was born in a state of misery. As her good Kamma was more powerful she had to expiate only for seven days.

Is this justifiable? one might ask.

If a holy person, due to some provocation, were to commit a murder, he would be charged as a murderer. His past good will no doubt stand to his credit and will have its due effect, but the present brutal act cannot be obliterated by his past good. Perhaps his past good record will tend to mitigate the sentence, but is totally powerless in acquitting him of his heinous crime. As a result of this unexpected incident he will be compelled to live in an uncongenial atmosphere amongst similar criminals. Is *this* fair? Just consider how one single immoral act could reduce a great man to such a state of degradation, totally regardless of his past!

On one occasion two ascetics *Punna* and *Seniyā* who were practising ox-asceticism and dog-asceticism came to the Buddha and questioned Him as to their future destiny:—

The Buddha replied:—

"In this world a certain individual cultivates thoroughly and constantly the practices, habits, mentality, and manners of a dog. He having cultivated the canine practices, habits, mentality, and manners thoroughly and constantly—upon the breaking up of the body after death, is reborn amongst dogs. Certainly if he holds such a belief as this: 'By virtue of this practice, austerity or noble life, I shall become a god or a deity of some kind,' that is a false belief of his, for one who holds a false belief I declare there is one of two future states: - either the state of torment or the animal kingdom. Thus failing a state of torment, successful canine asceticism only delivers one to companionship with dogs.

In the same way the Buddha declared that he who observes ox-asceticism will after death be born amongst oxen.

As there is the possibility for a Kammic descent in one bound in the so-called evolutionary scale of beings, so there is also the possibility for the contrary, a Kammic ascent.

When, for instance, an animal is about to die, it will experience a moral consciousness that will ripen into a human birth. This last thought-moment does not wholly depend on any action or thought of the animal, for generally it is dull and is incapable of doing any moral action. It depends on some past good deed which it has done during its round of existence and which, for a long time, has been prevented from producing its results. In its last moment the animal therefore cherishes ideas, desires, or images which will cause a human birth.

Poussin, a French writer, illustrates this fact by the law of heredity: "A man may be like his grandfather but not like his father. The germs of a disease have been introduced into the organism of an ancestor, for some generation they remain dormant: but suddenly they manifest themselves in actual diseases."

Such is the intricate nature of this doctrine of Kamma and rebirth.

* * * *

Whence we came, whither we go, and when we go, we know not. The fact that we must go we know for certain.

Our cherished possessions, our kith and kin follow us not—nay, not even our bodies which we call our own. From elements they came, to elements they return. Empty fame and vain glory vanish in thin air.

Alone we wander in this tempest-tossed sea of Sansāra wafted hither and thither by our own Kamma, appearing here as an animal or man and there perchance as a god or Brahma.

We meet and part and yet we may meet again incognito. For seldom do we find a being who, in the course of our wandering, had not at one time been a mother, a father, a sister, a son, a daughter.

"If a man," says the Buddha, "were to prune out the grasses, sticks, boughs, and twigs in this India and collecting them together, should make a pile laying them in a four inch stack, saying for each: 'This is my mother; this is my mother's mother,—' the grasses, sticks, boughs, twigs in this India would be used up, ended, but not the mothers of that man's mother.

"If a man were to make this great earth into clayballs each the size of only a *kola* kernel and lay them down, saying: 'This is my father, this is my father's father,—' this great earth would be used up, ended, but not the fathers of that man's father."

So closely bound are we during our journeyings in Sansāra.

The countless lives we have led and the innumerable sufferings we were subject to in the infinite past are such that the Buddha remarks:—"The bones of a single person wandering in Sansāra would be a cairn, a pile, a heap as great as Mount Vēpulla, were there a collector of these bones and were the collections not destroyed.

"Long time have you suffered the death of father and mother, of sons, daughters, brothers and sisters, and whilst you were thus suffering, you have verily shed tears upon this long way, more than there is water in the four oceans.

"Long time did your blood flow by the loss of your heads when you were born as oxen, buffaloes, rams, goats, etc.

"Long time have you been caught as dacoits or highwaymen or adulterers; and through your being beheaded, verily more blood has flowed upon this long way than there is water in the four oceans.

"And thus have you for long time undergone sufferings, undergone torment, undergone misfortune, and filled the graveyards full, verily long enough to be dissatisfied with every form of existence, long enough to turn away and free yourself from them all."

Bhagavad Gita--

"As a man, casting off worn-out garments, taketh new ones, so the dweller in the body, casting off worn-out bodies, entereth into others that are new.

"For certain is death for the born and certain is birth for the dead."

The Bible—

"Whom do the people think that I am the son of?

"Some say that thou art John the Baptist; some Elias; and others, Jeremias or one of the prophets."

Shelley:—

"If there be no reasons to suppose that we have existed before that period at which existence apparently commences, then there are no grounds for supposing that we shall continue to exist after our existence has apparently ceased."

Tennyson:—

"Or if through lower lives I came—
Tho' all experience past became
Consolidate in *mind* and frame
I might forget my weaker lot,
For is not our first year forgot
The haunts of memory echo not."

Wordsworth:—

"Our birth is but a sleep and a forgetting:
The Soul that rises with us, our life's star,
Hath had elsewhere its setting,
And cometh from afar:
Not in entire forgetfulness,
And not in utter nakedness,
……………………………………"

Professor Francis Bowen of Harward University in urging the Christians to accept rebirth writes:—

"Our life on earth is rightly held to be a discipline and a preparation for a higher and eternal life hereafter, but if limited to the duration of a single moral body, it is so brief as to seem hardly sufficient for so grand a purpose. Three score years and ten must surely be an inadequate preparation for eternity. But what assurance have we that the probation of the soul is confined within so narrow limits? Why may it not be continued or repeated through a long series of successive generations, the same personality animating one after another an indefinite number of tenements of flesh and carry forward into each the training it has received, the character it has formed, the temper and dispositions it has indulged, in the steps of existence immediately preceding. It need not remember its past history even whilst bearing the fruits and the consequence of that history deeply ingrained into its present nature. How many long passages of any one life are now completely lost to memory, though they may have contributed largely to build up the heart and the intellect which distinguish one man from another? Our responsibility surely is now lessened by such forgetfulness. We still see accountable for the misuse of time, though we have forgotten how or on what we have wasted it. We are even now repeating the bitter fruits, through enfeebled health and vitiated desires and capacities, of many forgotten acts of self-indulgence, wilfulness and sin-forgotten just because they were so numerous.

"If every soul were an act of absolute creation, the introduction to life of an entirely new creature, we might reasonably ask why different souls are so variously constituted at the outset... .....if metempsychosis is included in the scheme of the divine government of the world, this difficulty disappears altogether. Considered from this point of view, every one is born into the state which he has fairly earned by his own previous history... The Doctrine of inherited sin and its consequence is a hard lesson to be learned .....But no one can complain of the dispositions and endowments which he has inherited so to speak from himself, that is from his former self in a previous state of existence.........What we call death is only the introduction of another life on earth, and if this be not a higher and better life than the one just ended, it is our own fault."[1]

Herodotus says:—

"The Egyptians propounded the theory that the human soul is imperishable, and that where the body of any one dies it enters into some other creature that may be ready to receive it."

1. H. M. Kitchener, *The Theory of Re-incarnation.*

Pythagoras:—

"All have souls, all is soul, wandering in the organic world and obeying eternal will or law."[1]

Plato:—

"Soul is older than body. Souls are continually born over again into this life."

Ovid on Pythagoras: translated by Dryden—

"Death so called, is but old matter dressed
In some new form: and in varied vest
From tenement to tenement though tossed,
The soul is still the same, the figure only lost.
And as the softened wax new seals receives,
This face assumes, and that impression leaves,
Now called by one, now by another name.
The form is only changed the wax is still the same.
Then, to be born is to begin to be
Some other thing we were not formerly.
That forms are changed I grant;
That nothing can continue in the figure it began."

Hume:—

"Metempsychosis is the only system of immortality that philosophy can hearken to."

Disraeli:—

"There is no system so simple, and so little repugnant to our understanding as that of metempsychosis. The pains and pleasures of this life are by this system considered as the recompense or the punishment of our actions in another state.

---

1. Pythagoras remembered having fought, as Euphorbus' in the Trojan War.
Empedocles had been in past births 'a boy, a girl, a bird, and a scaly fish in the ocean'. (Frag. 117; Diels.)

Dante:—

"And then son, who through thy mortal weight shall again return below."

Huxley:—

"Like the doctrine of evolution itself, that of transmigration has its roots in the realm of reality."

"Everyday experience familiarises us with the facts which are grouped under the name of heredity. Everyone of us bears upon him obvious marks of his parentage, perhaps of remoter relationships. More particularly the sum of tendencies to act in a certain way, which we call 'character', is often to be traced through a long series of progenitors and collaterals. So we may justly say that this character, this moral and intellectual essence of a man does veritably pass over from one fleshly tabernacle to another, and does really transmigrate from generation to generation. In the new-born infant the character of the stock lies latent, and the ego is little more than a bundle of potentialities, but, very early, these become actualities: from childhood to age they manifest themselves in dullness or brightness, weakness or strength, viciousness or uprightness; and with each feature modified by confluence with another character, if by nothing else, the character passes on to its incarnation in new bodies.

"The Indian philosophers called character, as thus defined, 'Karma.' It is this Karma which passed from life to life and linked them in the chain of transmigrations; and they held that it is modified in each life, not merely by confidence of parantage but by its own acts."

Emerson:—

"We must infer our destiny from the preparation we are driven by instinct to have innumerable experiences which are of no visible value, and we may receive through many lives before we shall assimilate or exhaust them."

Lessing:—

"Why should I not come back as often as I am capable of acquiring fresh knowledge, fresh experience? Do I bring away so much from once that there is nothing to repay the trouble of coming back.

Schopenhaeur:—

"We find the doctrine of metempsychosis, springing from the earliest and noblest ages of the human race, always spread abroad in the earth as the belief of the great majority of mankind, nay really as the teaching of all religions, with the exception of that of the Jews and the two which have proceeded from it in the most subtle form, however, and coming nearest to the truth as has already been mentioned in Buddhism. Accordingly while Christians console themselves with the thought of meeting in another world in which one regains one's complete personality and knows oneself at once, in these other religions the meetings again is already going on only incognito. In the succession of births now stand in close connection or contact with us will also be born along with us at the next birth, and will have the same or analogous relations and sentiments towards us as now, whether these are of a friendly or hostile description......

"Taught already in the Vedas, as in all sacred books of India, mentempsychosis is well knowp to be the kernel of Brahmanism and Buddhism. It accordingly prevails at the present day in the whole of the non-Mohammedan Asia, thus among more than half of the whole human race, as the firmest conviction and with an incredibly strong practical influence. It was also the belief of the Egyptians from whom it was received with enthusiasm by Orpheus, Pythagoras and Plato: the Pythagoreans, however, specially retain it. That it was also taught in the mysteries of the Greeks undeniably follows the ninth book of Plato's Laws......

"The 'Edda' also especially in the 'Volusna' teaches metempsychosis, not less was it the foundation of the Druids.........

"According to all this, the belief in metempsychosis presents itself as the natural conviction of man, whenever he reflected at all in an unprejudiced manner........."

"The World as Will and Hea"

Pre-existence

"I laid me down upon the shore
and dreamed a little space;
I heard the great waves break and roar;
The sun was on my face.

"My idle hands and fingers brown
Played with the pebbles grey;
The waves came up, the waves went down.
Most thundering and gay.

"The pebbles they were smooth and round
And warm upon my hands,
Like little people I had found
Sitting among the sands.

"The grains of sand so shining-small
Soft through my fingers ran;
The sun shone down upon it all,
And so my dream began;

"How all of this had been befor :
How ages far away
I lay on some unforgotten shore
As here I lie to-day.

"The waves came up shining up the sands,
As here to-day they shine;
And in my pre-Pelasgian hands
The sands was warm and fine.

"I have forgotten whence I came
Or what my home might be,
Or by what strange and savage name
I called that thundering sea.

"I only know the sun shone down
As still it shines to-day,
And in my fingers long and brown
The little pebbles lay."

FRANCES CORNFORD
in *An Anthology of Modern Verse*,
Chosen by A. Methuen, London.
Methuen & Co., and reproduced in the
"*Buddhist Annual of Ceylon*," 1927

A Note on the Doctrine of Kamma and Rebirth in the West

The *Doctrine of Kamma and Rebirth* is the keystone of the philosophy of Plato. Beings are for ever travelling through a 'cycle of necessity'; the evil they do in one semicircle of their pilgrimage is expiated in the other. In the *Republic*, we find Kamma personified as 'Lachesis, the daughter of necessity,' at whose hands disembodied beings choose their incarnations.' Orpheus chooses the body of a swan. Thersites that of an ape, Agamemnon that of an eagle, '*In like manner, some of the animals passed into men, and into one another, the unjust passing into the wild, and the just into the tame.*'

When, in the period preceding the Persian wars, the West came in contact with the East, there arose a revolt against the simple eschatology of Homer, and the search began for a deeper explanation of life. This quest, it is interesting to note, was begun by the Ionian Greeks of Asia Minor, who were influenced by India.

Pythagoras, who was born about 580 B. C. in the island of Samos, travelled widely and, according to his biographer, studied the teaching of the Indians. He taught to the West the doctrine of Kamma and Rebirth.

"It is not too much," says Garbe in his *Greek Thinkers* (i, 127), "to assume that the curious Greek, who was a contemporary of Buddha....., would have accquired a more or less exact knowledge of the East, in that age of intellectual fermentation, through the medium of Persia."

CHAPTER XXVII

NIBBĀNA

BUDDHISM is unique in the quest of the Eternal Peace of Nibbāna as its **Summum Bonum.**

This, indeed, is the sole thought that moves about 500,000,000 co-religionists to-day to follow the sublime Teaching of the Buddha.

However clearly and descriptively one may write on this important subject, with whatever glowing terms one may describe its peaceful state, one can never know what Nibbāna actually is by a mere perusal of books. The genuine Nibbāna is not something to be set down in print, nor is it a subject to be grasped by intellect alone; it is something **transcendental,** and to be realised by one's intuitive wisdom.

A purely intellectual comprehension of Nibbāna is certainly impossible, because it is not within the scope of logic (*atakkāvacara*). Nevertheless, reflecting on the positive and negative aspects of life, one can logically conclude that there must exist a sorrowless and deathless Nibbāna which is opposed to a sorrowful and changing Sansāra or, in other words, that there must be an absolute existence in contradistinction to phenomenal existence.

For instance, the Buddha Himself in His birth as ascetic Sumedha contemplated thus:—

"Even as, although *Misery* is,
Yet *happiness* is also found;
So, though indeed *existence* is,
A *non-existence* should be sought.

"Even as although there may be *heat;*
Yet grateful *cold* is also found;
So, though the three-fold *fire* exists,
Likewise *Nirvāna* should be sought.

"Even as, although there *evil* is,
That which is *good* is also found;
So, though 'tis true that birth exists,
That which is not birth should be sought."[1]

* * * *

The Pāli word Nibbāna—(Sanskrt—*Nirvāna*) is composed of "Ni" and "Vāna." **Ni** is a particle implying negation. **Vana** means weaving or craving. It is this craving which acts as a cord to connect one life with another.

The venerable Anuruddha defines it in his Compendium of Philosophy (Abhidhammattha Sangaha) thus:—"It is called Nibbāna in that it is a 'departure' (*ni*) from that craving which is called Vāna, lusting."

As long as one is bound up by craving one accumulates fresh Kammic forces which must materialise in one form or other in the eternal cycle of birth and death. When all forms of craving are extirpated, Kammic forces cease to operate, and one attains Nibbāna, escaping the cycle of birth and death. The Buddhist conception of salvation is this escape from

1. Warren, *Buddhism in Translations, p. 6.*

the ever-recurring cycle of life and death which implies more than escape merely from sin and hell.

Nibbāna is also explained as the extinction of the fire of lust (Lobha), hatred (Dosa), and delusion (Moha.)

"The whole world is in flames," says the Buddha. "By what fire is it kindled? By the fire of lust, hatred, and delusion; by the fire of birth, old age, death, sorrow, lamentation, pain, grief, and despair is it kindled."

Nibbāna, in one sense, may be interpreted as the extinction of these flames. In reply to the question put by Jambukhādaka, venerable Sāriputta says—"Nibbāna is the extinction of lust, hatred, and delusion.[1]" But one must not thereby infer that Nibbāna is nothing but the extinction of these passions. **"Khayamattam 'eva na Nibbanan'-ti vattabbam"**[2] "One must not say that Nibbāna is mere extinction." It should be noted that the venerable Sāriputta was here indicating the means of attaining Nibbāna.

To say that Nibbāna is nothingness simply because one cannot perceive it with the five senses, is as illogical as to say that light does not exist simply because the blind do not see it. In the well-known fable, too, the fish arguing with its friend, the turtle, triumphantly concluded that there existed no land.

"Once upon a time[1] there was a fish. And just because it was a fish, it had lived all its life in the water and knew nothing whatever about anything else but water. And one day as it swam about in the pond

1. Sanyutta Nikaya Book.IV, p. 251.
2. Abhidhammāvatāra.
1. This fable is quoted from Bhikkhu Silācāra's booklet, —"The Four Noble Truths."

where all its days had been spent, it happened to meet a turtle of its acquaintance who had just come back from a little excursion on the land.

"'Good day, Mr. turtle!' said the fish; 'I have not seen you for a long time. Where have you been?'

"'O, said the turtle, I've just been for a trip on dry land.'

"'*On dry land!*' exclaimed the fish; 'What do you mean by on dry land? There is no dry land. I had never seen such a thing. Dry land is nothing.'

"'Well' said the turtle good-naturedly, 'if you want to think so, of course you may; there's no one who can hinder you. But that's where I've been, all the same.'

"'O come,' said the fish, 'try to talk sense. Just tell me now what is this land of yours like? Is it all wet?'

" No, it is not wet,' said the turtle.

"'Is it nice and fresh and cool?' asked the fish.

"'No, it is not nice and fresh and cool,' the turtle replied.

"'Is it clear, so that light can come through it?'

"'No, it is not clear; light cannot come through it.'

"'Is it soft and yielding; so that I could move my fins about in it and push my nose through it?'

"'No, it is not soft and yielding; you could not swim in it.'

"'Does it move or flow in streams?'

"'No, it neither moves nor flows in streams.'

"'Does it ever rise up into waves, then, with white foams in them?' asked the fish, becoming just a little impatient at this string of *Noes*.

"'No,' replied the turtle truthfully; 'it never rises up into waves that I have seen.'

"'There now!' exclaimed the fish triumphantly. 'Didn't I tell that this land of yours was just nothing? I have just asked, and you have answered me that it is neither wet nor cool, not clear nor soft and that it does not flow in streams nor rise up into waves. And if it isn't a single one of these things what else is it but nothing? Don't tell me!'

"'Well, well,' said the turtle, 'if you are determined to think that dry land is nothing, I suppose you must just go on thinking so. But any one who knows what is water and what is land would say you were just a very silly fish, for you think that anything you have never known is nothing just because you have never known it.'

"And with that the turtle turned away and, leaving the fish behind in its little pond of water, set out on another excursion over the land that was nothing."

It is evident from this fable that neither the turtle, which is acquainted with both land and sea, could explain to the fish the real nature of the land, nor could the fish understand what land is as it is acquainted only with the sea. In the same way the Arahants who are acquainted with both the mundane and the supramundane cannot explain to a worldling what the supramundane exactly is by mundane terms, nor can a worldling understand the supramundane merely by mundane knowledge.

If Nibbāna is nothingness, then it must necessarily coincide with space (*Ākāsa*.)

In the Anguttara Nikāya the Buddha says:—

"There are, O Bhikkhus, two Dhammas permanent, eternal, everlasting, not changing—namely, Space (*Ākāsa*) and Nibbāna."

The former is eternal because it is nothing in itself. The latter is spaceless and timeless. With regard to the difference between space and Nibbana, it may briefly be said that the former is *not*, but the latter *is*.

Speaking of the different modes of existence, too, the Buddha makes a special reference to a "Realm of Nothingness" (Ākiñcaññāyatana).

The fact that Nibbāna is realised as an object, one of the *Vatthu Dhammas*, decidedly proves that it is not a state of Nothingness. If it were so, there would be no necessity for the Buddha to describe its state in various terms, such as "Endless" (*Ananta*), "Non-conditioned" (*Asankhata*), "Incomparable" (*Anūpameya*), "Supreme" (*Anuttara*), "Highest" (*Para*), "Highest Refuge" (*Parāyana*), "Safety" (*Tāna*) "Happiness" (*Siva*), "Further Shore" (*Pāra*), "Unique" (*Kevala*), "Abodeless" (*Anālaya*), "Indestructible" (*Akkhara*), "Absolute Purity" (*Visuddha*). "Supramundane" (*Lokuttara*), "Security" (*Khema*), "Immortality" (*Amata*), "Emancipation" (*Mutti*), "Peace" (*Santi*), and so forth.

In the *Udāna* and *Itivuttaka* the Buddha refers to Nibbāna as follows:-

"There is, O Bhikkhus, an Unborn (*Ajāta*). Unoriginated (*Abhūta*), Unmade (*Akata*) and Non-conditioned (*Asaṅkhata*). If, O Bhikkhus, there were not this Unborn, Unoriginated, Unmade, and Non-conditioned, an escape to the born, originated, made, and conditioned, would not be possible here. As there is, O Bhikkhus, an Unborn, Unoriginated, Unmade, and Non-conditioned, an escape to the born, originated, made, conditioned is possible."[1]

Says the Itivuttaka :—

"The born, become, produced, compounded, made,
And thus not lasting, but of birth-and-death
An aggregate, a nest of sickness, brittle,
A thing by food supported, come to be,—
'Twere no fit thing to take delight in such.
Th'escape therefrom, the real, beyond the sphere
Of reason, lasting, unborn, unproduced,
The sorrowless, the stainless path that ends
The things of woe, the peace from worries,—bliss."

Woodward—"As it was said"—p. 142.

The Nibbāna of the Buddha is, therefore, neither a state of nothingness nor a mere cessation. What it is not, one can definitely say; but what it precisely is, cannot adequately be expressed in conventional language as it is unique.

---

1. According to the commentary all these four terms are used as synonyms.

Ajāta means that it has not sprung up on account of causes or conditions *(Hetu-paccaya)*. *Abhūta* (lit. not-become) means that it has not arisen. As it has not sprung up from a cause and has not come into being, it is not made *(akata)* by any means. Becoming and arising are the characteristics of conditioned things such as mind and matter; but Nibbāna, being not subject to those conditions, is non-conditioned *(asankhata)*.

Sopadisesa and Anupadisesa Nibbana Dhatu

References are frequently made in the Books to Nibbāna as *Sopādisesa* and *Anupādisesa* Nibbāna Dhātu. These in fact are not two kinds of Nibbāna, but the one single Nibbāna receiving its name according to the way it is experienced before and after death.

Nibbāna is attainable even in this present life. Buddhism does not state that its ultimate goal could be reached only in a life beyond. Here lies the difference between the Buddhist conception of Nibbāna and the non-Buddhist conception of an eternal heaven which is attainable only after death. When Nibbāna is realised in this life with the body remaining, it is called Sopādisesa Nibbāna Dhātu.[1] When an Arahant attains Pari Nibbāna, after the dissolution of his body, without any remainder of physical existence, it is called Anupādisesa Nibbāna Dhātu.

In the Itivuttaka the Buddha says:—

There are, O Bhikkhus, two elements of Nibbāna (*Nibbāna-Dhātu*). What two? The element of Nibbāna with the basis still remaining and that without basis.

What, O Bhikkhus, is "the element of Nibbāna with the basis still remaining?"

Herein, O Bhikkhus, a Bhikkhu is an Arahant, one who has destroyed the Defilements, who has lived the life, done what was to be done, laid aside the burden, who has attained his goal, who has destroyed

---

1. Sa—with *upādi*—aggregates (Mind and Body).
Sesa—remaining. The aggregates are called *upādi* because they are firmly grasped by craving and false view.

the fetters of existence, who rightly understanding is delivered. His five sense organs still remain, and as he is not devoid of them he undergoes the pleasant and the unpleasant, experiences pleasure and pain. That destruction of attachment, hatred, and delusion of his, O Bhikkhus, is called the "element of Nibbāna with the basis still remaining."

What, O Bhikkhus, is "the element of Nibbāna without the basis"?

Herein, O Bhikkhus, a Bhikkhu is an Arahant ....is delivered. In this very life, O Bhikkhus, all his sensations will have no delight for him, they will be cooled.[1] This is called, O Bhikkhus, "the element of Nibbāna without a basis.

"These two Nibbāna-states are shown by him
Who seeth, who is such and unattached.
One state is that in this same life possessed
With base remaining, tho' becoming's stream
Be cut off. While the state without a base
Belongeth to the future, wherein all
Becomings utterly do come to cease.
They who, by knowing this state uncompounded
Have heart's release, by cutting off the stream,
They who have reached the core of dhamma, glad
To end,—such have abandoned all becomings."[2]

---

1 Since he will not be reborn.

2. Itivuttaka—p. 38. Woodward—As it was said — p. 143.

CHAPTER XXVIII

THREE DISTINCT CHARACTERISTICS OF NIBBĀNA

CONTRASTING Nibbāna with Sansāra the Buddha says that the former is eternal (*Dhuva*), desirable (*Subha*), and happy (*Sukha*).

According to Buddhism everything cosmic and hypercosmic is classed under two divisions—namely, things conditioned by causes (*Saṅkhata*) and things not conditioned by any cause (*Asaṅkhata*).

Nibbāna is not conditioned by any cause. Hence there is neither an arising nor a passing away. It is birthless, decayless, and deathless. It is neither a cause nor an effect.

All conditioned things—and to this category belongs everything in the universe—are, on the contrary, constantly changing without remaining for two consecutive moments the same.

Becoming is the characteristic of all that are caused or formed or created. Where there is becoming there is change. The universal law of change applies to every conditioned thing, ranging from the minute germ or particle to the highest being or the most massive object.

To illustrate this all-pervading law of transiency one need not multiply instances. The past history of nations, the fall of powerful Empires, the rapid changes a person undergoes during his brief lifetime, the transitoriness of mind and matter, convincingly prove to us the fleeting nature of life.

Everything that has sprung from a cause must inevitably pass away, and as such is undesirable (*Asubha*).

Life is our dearest possession, but when it is confronted with insuperable difficulties, unbearable misfortunes, and unthinkable worries, then that very life becomes an intolerable burden to many. Such miserable souls foolishly seek delight in putting an end to their unfortunate lives. Our foul bodies we adorn and adore. But those charming and adorable objects, when disfigured by time and disease, would not present such an enticing sight. We desire to live peacefully and happily with our near and dear ones, surrounded by amusements and pleasures, but, if by some misfortune, the wicked world were to thwart our ambitions and desires, then the inevitable sorrow would be almost in-describable.

The following beautiful allegory aptly illustrates the fleeting nature of life and its alluring pleasures.

A certain man was passing through a thick forest with great difficulty owing to the thorns and stones that beset his way. Suddenly he noticed an elephant giving chase to him. Through fear he fled, and seeing a well he desired to descend into it and hide himself. Then to his great surprise and misfortune he observed a viper in the bottom of the well. As he had no other alternative, he jumped into the well, and clung to a thorny creeper that was growing in it. On looking up he saw two mice—a white one and a black one—

gnawing at the creeper. Above his face he noticed a beehive from which occasionally drops of honey were trickling.

This foolish man without caring for the elephant that was standing outside, the viper at the bottom, the mice that were gnawing, the bees that were stinging, was greedily tasting the honey.

The thorny path through the forest is Sansāra. Elephant is death, viper is old age, the creeper is birth. The two mice are the night and day. The drops of honey refer to the fleeting sensual pleasures.

* * * *

That which is transient and undesirable certainly cannot be happy (*Sukha*).

What we call happiness or pleasure here is merely the gratification of some desire. No sooner is the desired thing gained than it begins to be scorned. Insatiate are all desires.

Worldly bliss, heavenly bliss not excluded, is only a prelude to pain. Sorrow is essential to life, and cannot be evaded.

But Nibbāna being non-conditioned, that which has not arisen from a cause, is, in contradistinction to phenomenal existence (*Sansāra*), eternal (*Dhuva*), desirable (*Subha*), and happy (*Sukha*).

Happiness of Nibbāna should be differentiated from ordinary happiness. Bliss of Nibbāna grows neither stale nor monotonous. It is a form of happiness that never wearies, never fluctuates. It arises as the result of calming down passions (*Vūpasama*) unlike that worldly happiness which results from the gratification of some desire (*Vedayita*).

In the Bahuvedaniya Suttanta (No. 57, Majjhima Nikāya) the Buddha enumerates ten grades of happiness beginning with the gross material pleasures which result from the pleasant stimulation of the five senses. As one ascends higher and higher in the spiritual plane the so-called happiness becomes more and more exalted, sublime and subtle, so much so that it is scarcely recognisable as happiness by the man of the world. One in the first Jhāna experiences a spiritual happiness which is absolutely independent of the five senses. This happiness is gained by inhibiting the desire for the pleasures of the senses, so highly prized by the materialist. In the fourth Jhāna, however, even this type of happiness is discarded as coarse and unprofitable, and equanimity (upekkhā) is termed happiness.

The Buddha says:—

"Fivefold, Ananda, are sensual bonds. What are the five? Forms cognisable by the eye—desirable, lovely, charming, infatuating, accompanied with thirst, and arousing the dust of the passions; sounds cognisable by the ear; odours cognisable by the nose; flavours cognisable by the tongue; contacts cognisable by the body—desirable, lovely, charming, infatuating, accompanied with thirst, and arousing the dust of passions. These, Ānanda, are the five sensual bonds. Whatever happiness or pleasure that arises from these sensual bonds, is known as sensual happiness.

"Whoso should declare: 'This is the highest happiness and pleasure which beings may experience—'

I do not grant him that; and for what reason? Because there is other happiness which is more exalted and sublime than that.

"And what is that other happiness which is more exalted and sublime than that? Here a Bhikkhu lives completely separated from sense desires, remote from immoral states, exercising the reflection and investigation born of seclusion, in joy and happiness abiding in the First Ecstasy. This is the happiness which is more exalted and sublime than that.

"But should anyone declare: 'This is the highest happiness and pleasure which beings may experience—' I do not grant him that; and for what reason? Because there is another happiness which is more exalted and sublime than that.

"Here a Bhikkhu stilling reflection and investigation, having tranquillity within, mind predominating, reflection and investigation having ceased, as a result of peace, lives in joy and happiness, abiding in the Second Ecstasy. This is the other happiness which is more exalted and sublime than that.

"Yet should anyone declare that this is the highest happiness and pleasure experienced by beings— I do not grant it. There is happiness more exalted.

"Here a Bhikkhu from absence of desire for joy abides serene, mindful, and completely conscious, experiencing in the body of that of which the Ariyas say: 'Endowed with equanimity and mindfulness, he abides in bliss.' Thus he lives abiding in the Third Ecstasy. This is the other happiness and pleasure which is more exalted and sublime than that.

"Still should anyone declare that this is the highest happiness—I do not grant it. There is happiness more exalted.

"Here a Bhikkhu abandoning pleasure and pain, leaving behind former joy and grief—painless, pleasureless, perfect in equanimity and mindfulness—lives abiding in the Fourth Esctasy. This is the other happiness which is more exalted and sublime than that.

"However, were this declared to be the highest happiness—I do not grant it. There is happiness more sublime.

"Here a Bhikkhu passing entirely beyond the perception of form with the disappearance of sense reaction, freed from attention to perceptions of diversity, thinks: 'Infinity is Space'—and lives abiding in the Realm of Infinite Space. This is the other happiness which is more exalted and sublime than that.

"Nevertheless, if this were declared the highest happiness—I do not grant it. There is happiness more sublime than that.

"Here a Bhikkhu transcending entirely the Realm of Infinite Space, thinks: 'Infinite is Consciousness'—and lives abiding in the Realm of Infinite Consciousness. This is the other happiness which is more exalted and sublime than that.

"And yet should this be declared the highest happiness—I do not grant it. There is higher happiness.

"Here a Bhikkhu transcending the Realm of Infinite Consciousness thinks: 'There is nothing whatsoever'—and lives abiding in the Realm of Nothingness. This is the other happiness which is more exalted and sublime than that.

"And still were this declared the highest happiness—I do not grant it. There is happiness more exalted.

"Here a Bhikkhu passing entirely beyond the Realm of Nothingness lives abiding in the Realm of Neither perception nor Non-Perception. This is the other happiness which is more exalted and sublime than that.

"Yet whoso should declare: 'This is the highest bliss and pleasure which beings may experience'—I do not grant him that; and for what reason? Because there is yet another happiness which is more exalted and sublime than that.

"And what is this other happiness which is more exalted and sublime than that? Here a Bhikkhu utterly transcending the Realm of neither Perception nor Non-Perception lives, having attained to the Cessation of perception and sensation. This, Ānanda, is the other happiness which is more exalted and sublime than that." [1]

Of all the ten grades of happiness this is the highest and the most sublime. This state is in other words known as Nirodha Samāpatti; i.e. experiencing Nibbāna in this life itself.

---

1. See "The Blessing"—No. 4, pp. 129-132

As the Buddha has anticipated one may ask,—"How can that state be called highest happiness when there is no consciousness to experience it?"

The Buddha replies:—"Nay, friends, the Blessed One does not recognise bliss merely because of a pleasurable sensation; but, friends, wheresoever bliss is attained, there and there only does the Accomplished one recognise bliss."[1]

I proclaim, says the Buddha, "that everything experienced by the senses is sorrow." But why? Because one in sorrow craves to be happy, and the so-called happy crave to be happier still. So insatiate is worldly happiness!

In conventional terms the Buddha says:

Nibbānaṅ paramaṅ sukhaṅ—Nibbāna is the highest bliss. It is bliss supreme because it is not a kind of happiness that is experienced by the senses.

The very fact of the cessation of this life flux is ordinarily termed happiness, which too is no appropriate word to depict is real nature.

* * * *

Where is this Nibbana?

In the Milinda Pañha the venerable Nāgasena answers the question in the following words:—

---

1. Majjhima Nikāya—Bahuvedaniya Sutta—No. 59. See "The Blessing" No. 4, p. 132.

"There is no spot looking East, South, West, or North, above, below, or beyond, where Nibbāna is situate; and yet *Nibbāna is*; and he who orders his life aright, grounded in virtue, and with rational attention, may realise it whether he lives in Greece, China, Alexandria, or in Kosala".

In illustration thereof he says:—

"Just as fire is not stored up in any particular place but arises when the necessary conditions exist, so Nibbāna is not said to be existing in a *particular* place, but *it is attained* when the necessary conditions are fulfilled."

It may be said that though Nibbāna is not stored anywhere, it is dependent upon this one-fathom body. So states the Teacher in the Rohitassa Sutta.

"In this very one-fathom-long body, along with its perceptions and thoughts, I proclaim the world, the origin of the world, the cessation of the world, and the path leading to the cessation of the world." (Ang. N. IV. V.)

Here world means suffering. The cessation of the world, therefore, means the cessation of suffering, that is Nibbāna.

One's Nibbāna depends on oneself, but is not within one's mind. It is not something that created itself, nor is it something to be produced[1].

---

1. "*Pattabbaṁ'eva h'etaṅ maggena, na uppādetabbaṅ*"—Verily this (Nibbāna) is to be attained (or realised) by means of the Four Paths such as Sotāpatti, Sakadāgāmi, Anāgāmi, and Arahants and is not to be *produced*.

—Visuddhi Magga.

Nibbāna is there where the four elements of cohesion (*Āpo*), extension, (*Paṭhavi*) heat (*Tejo*), and motion (*Vāyo*) find no footing.

The Sanyutta Nikāya states—

"Where the four elements that cleave, and stretch, and burn, and move, no further footing find............"[1]

In the Udāna the Buddha says:—

"Just as, O Bhikkhus, notwithstanding those rivers that reach the great ocean and the torrents of rain that fall from the sky, neither a deficit nor a surplus is perceptible in the great ocean, even so despite the many Bhikkhus that enter the remainderless Parinibbāna there is neither a deficit nor a surplus in the element of Nibbāna."

It, therefore, follows that Nibbāna is not a sort of Heaven where a transcendental ego resides, but an attainment (Dhamma) which is within the reach of all.

An eternal heaven, which provides all forms of pleasures that man desires, and where one enjoys happiness to one's heart's content, is practically inconceivable. It is absolutely impossible to think that such a permanent place could exist anywhere.

Granting that there is no place where Nibbāna is stored up, King Milinda questions venerable Nāgasena whether there is any basis whereon a man may stand and, ordering his life aright, realise Nibbāna.

"Yes, O King, there is such a basis," replies the venerable Nāgasena.

---

1. *Kindred Sayings*, pt 1, p. 23.

"Which, then, venerable Nāgasena is that basis?"

"Virtue, O King, is that basis. For, if grounded in virtue, and careful in attention,—whether in the land of the Scythians, or the Greeks, whether in China or in Tartary, whether in Alexandria or in Nikumba, whether in Benares or in Kosala, whether in Kashmir or in Gandhāra, whether on a mountain top or in the highest heavens,—wheresoever he may be, the man who orders his life aright will attain Nibbāna."

Questions of King Milinda, pp. 202—204.

* * * *

What attains Nibbana, is another question which, on careful consideration, must necessarily be set aside as irrelevant; for Buddhism denies the existence of a permanent entity or an immortal soul.

The so-called being of which we often hear as the "vestment of the soul" is a mere bundle of conditioned factors.

The Arahant Bhikkhunī Vajirā says:—

"And just as when the parts are rightly set,
The word "chariot" ariseth (in our minds);
So doth our usage covenant to say,
A being when the aggregates are there."

According to Buddhism there is an individual life-flux, (*santati*) but no personal identity.[1] This life-flux includes both physical and mental elements. It is the Kammic force of each individual that binds these elements together.

As right now, and here, there is neither a permanent ego nor an identical being, it is needless to point out that there can be no "I" in Nibbāna.

---

1. See p. 135 and chapter xxiv, p 214

Thus hath it been said in the Visuddhi Magga:—

"Misery only doth exist, none miserable;
No doer is there, nought save the deed is found;
Nibbāna *is*, but not the man who seeks it;
The path exists, but not the traveller on it."

The chief difference between the Buddhist conception of Nibbāna and the Hindu conception of Nirvāna or Mukti lies in the fact that Buddhists view their goal without an eternal soul and creator, whilst Hindus do.

This is the reason why Buddhism can neither be called Eternalism nor Nihilism.

In Nibbāna nothing is "eternalised," nor is anything "annihilated."

It must be admitted that this question of Nibbāna is the most difficult in the Teaching of the Buddha. However much we may speculate we shall never be in a position to comprehend its real nature. The best way to understand Nibbāna is to try to realise it with our own intuitive knowledge.

Although Nibbāna cannot be perceived by the five senses and lies in obscurity in so far as the average man is concerned, the only straight path that leads to Nibbāna has been explained by the Buddha with all the necessary details and is laid open to all. The goal is now clouded, but the method of achievement is perfectly clear and when that achievement is realised the Goal is as clear as "the sun freed from clouds."

CHAPTER XXIX

THE WAY TO NIBBĀNA

THE way to Nibbāna is the Middle Path (Majjhima Paṭipadā) which avoids the extreme of self-mortification that weakens one's intellect and the extreme of self-indulgence that retards one's spiritual progress.

This Middle Path[1] consists of the following eight factors—namely; Right Understanding, Right Thoughts, Right Speech, Right Action, Right Livelihood, Right Effort, Right Mindfulness, and Right Concentration.

The first two are grouped in wisdom (*Paññā*), the second three in Morality (*Sīla*), and the last three in Concentration (*Samādhi*).

SĪLA —
1. Right Speech
2. „ Action
3. „ Livelihood

SAMĀDHI
1. Right Effort
2. „ Mindfulness
3. „ Concentration

PAÑÑĀ—
1. Right Understanding
2. „ Thoughts

Strictly speaking these factors that comprise the Noble Eightfold Path signify eight mental properties (Cetasikas) collectively found in the four classes of Supramundane Consciousness whose object is Nibbāna.

1. See pp. 106, 107.

According to the order of development Sīla, Samādhi, and Paññā are the three stages on the Grand Highway that leads to Nibbāna.

All these three stages are embodied in the following beautiful verse.

Sabba pāpassa akaraṇaṁ
Kusalassa upasampadā
Sacittapariyodapanaṁ
Etaṁ Buddhāna sāsanaṁ.

To cease from all evil,
To do what is good,
To cleanse one's mind;
This is the advice of all the Buddhas.

We reap what we sow. If we sow evil, we must reap pain; if we sow good, we must reap happiness. Both pain and happiness are the direct results of our own good and evil. This is a law in itself.

A right understanding person realises this just law of action and reaction and, of his own accord, refrains from evil and does good to the best of his ability. He does so for his own good and for the good of others. He considers his duty to be a blessing to himself and to all others, but not a curse to any, whether man or animal.

As life is precious to all and as there is neither any right nor power whatever to destroy the life of another, he extends his compassion and loving-kindness towards every living being, even to the tiniest creature that crawls at his feet, and refrains from killing or causing injury to any living creature.

There is no rule that one is to be preyed upon by another. The strong mercilessly kill the weak and feast on their flesh. This is the animal instinct. Such actions from ignorant animals are excusable, because they know not what they do, but when men, who are gifted with reason, and who should possess a high moral standard, perpetrate such crimes, they reveal their brutal tendencies and degrade themselves. Whether to satisfy our stomach or as a pastime it is not justifiable to kill or cause to kill another living being. When mother earth is so generous in giving us vegetables and other kinds of harmless and nutritious food, what necessity is there for us to kill our dumb brothers and sisters and feast on their flesh? If the killing of animals is wrong, it is needless to speak of the heinousness of killing human beings for the sake of peace or for the sake of religion.

Honesty, trustworthiness, and uprightness should also be the characteristics of a right understanding person. As such he tries to abstain from all forms of stealing "whether in its dissembled or obvious forms." Abstaining from sexual misconduct which debases the exalted nature of man he tries to be pure and chaste. He avoids false speech, harsh language, slander, and frivolous talk and speaks only that which is true, sweet, kind, and helpful. Pernicious drinks are also a hindrance to the progress of a right understanding person. They promote heedlessness and mental distraction. He, therefore, avoids intoxicating drinks, and cultivates heedfulness and clarity of vision.

These elementary principles of regulated behaviour are essential to one who treads the Path to

Nibbāna. Violation of them means the introduction of obstacles on the path which will obstruct his moral progress. Observance of them means smooth and steady progress along the path.

The spiritual pilgrim advances a step further and cultivates sense-restraint for over-indulgence in sensual pleasures is detrimental to moral progress.

It is an admitted fact that most dig their graves with their own teeth. Over-eating and carelessness in diet are responsible for more deaths than pestilences. To control this craving for food and to foster buoyancy of mind and body, abstemiousness or fasting at least once a month is advisable. Plain and simple living is preferable to a luxurious life which makes one a slave to passions. A life of celibacy is recommended as one's valuable energy thus conserved could then be utilised entirely for the intellectual and spiritual welfare of one-self and others. Besides one would be detached from additional worldly bonds that might impede one's progress. A glimpse into the history of all spiritual teachers will convince one that almost all of them nourished their bodies sparingly and led a life of strict celibacy, simplicity, voluntary poverty, and self-control.

Whilst he progresses slowly and steadily with regulated word and deed and sense-restraint, the Kammic force of this striving aspirant compels him to renounce worldly pleasures and adopt the ascetic life. To him then comes the idea that

"A den of strife is household life,
And filled with toil and need;
But free and high as the open sky
Is the life the homeless lead."

Realising thus the vanity of fleeting pleasures, he voluntarily forsakes his earthly possessions, and donning the ascetic garb, he tries to lead the Holy life in all its purity. Here he practises the Higher Morality to such a high degree that he practically becomes selfless in all his actions. Neither fame nor wealth nor honour nor worldly gain could induce him to do anything contrary to his lofty principles.

It is not, however, the external appearance that makes a man holy but the internal purification and his exemplary life. Transformation should come from within and not from without. It is not absolutely necessary to retire to solitude and lead the life of an ascetic to be a Saint. The life of a Bhikkhu expedites and facilitates spiritual progress, but even as a layman one could attain Sainthood.

He who attains Sainthood as a layman in the face of all temptations is certainly more praiseworthy than a Bhikkhu who fortunately lives amidst congenial surroundings.

Says the Buddha concerning a minister who attained Arahantship:—

"Even though a man be richly adorned, if he walk in peace,
If he be quite, subdued, certain, and pure,
And if he refrain from injuring any living being,
That man is a Brahman, that man is a hermit, that man is a monk."

There are several instances of laymen who realised Nibbāna without renouncing the world. The most devout lay-follower Anāthapindika was a Sotāpanna,[1] the Sākya Mahānāma was a Sakadāgāmi,[2] the potter Ghaṭīkāra was an Anāgāmi,[3] and King Suddnodana died as an Arahant.[4] An Anāgāmi must of course lead a celibate life, and a lay Arahant, according to the books, must either enter the Order or attain Pari-Nibbāna, for he cannot live amidst the uncongenial worldly surroundings.

If he chooses the homeless life, he is expected to lead a life of voluntary poverty and celibacy. He should also of his own accord observe the four kinds of Higher Morality—namely,

Patimokkha Sīla—the fundamental precepts,[5]

Indriya-saṅvara Sīla—Morality pertaining to sense-restraint,

Ājīva-parisuddha Sīla—Morality pertaining to the purity of livelihood,

Paccaya-sannissita Sīla—Morality pertaining to the use of the necessaries of life.

These four kinds of Morality are collectively termed *Sīla-Visuddhi*—"Purity of Virtue"—the first of the seven stages of Purity on the Way to Nibbāna.

When he enters the Order and receives his Higher (Upasampadā) Ordination he is called a Bhikkhu.

---

1. "Stream-Winner"—the first stage of Sainthood.
2. "Once-Returner"—the second stage of Sainthood.
3. "Never-Returner"—the third stage of Sainthood.
4. "The Worthy"—the final stage of Sainthood.
5. Various rules which a Bhikkhu is expected to observe.

A Bhikkhu is not a beggar as is often mistranslated. Neither is he a priest, since he does not act as a mediator between God and man. Nor is he strictly a monk, because he is not bound by any vows. There is no English equivalent that exactly conveys the meaning of the Pāli term. "Mendicant" may be suggested as the nearest translation, not in the sense of begging but in the sense of "living on alms."

The ascetics of other sects are invariably called Paribbājakas, Ājīvakas, Sannyāsins, etc. But Bhikkhu, or Sanskrt Bhikshu, has now become exclusively Buddhistic.

The Rules of a Bhikkhu do not permit him to beg anything from another. He may accept the four requisites[1] presented to him by others. If he is in need of any requisite, he is allowed to obtain it only from his parents and close relatives, such as brothers, sisters, uncles, aunts and from professed supporters who have requested him to do so.

There are no vows for a Bhikkhu. Of his own accord he becomes a Bhikkhu in order to lead the holy life as long as he likes. He is at liberty to leave the order at any time.[2]

A Bhikkhu has to observe 227 rules, apart from several other minor rules. The four major rules which deal with perfect celibacy, stealing, murder and false claims to higher spiritual powers, must strictly

---

1. The four requisites are :—robes, alms, beds and seats, and medicine.

2. In such Buddhist countries as Burma, Siam, Cambodia almost everyone enters the Order even for a day. In Ceylon, however, the custom is to remain in the Order for life.

be observed. If he violates even one of them, he suffers defeat (*pārājikā*), and automatically ceases to be a Bhikkhu. If he wishes, he can re-enter the Order and remain as a Sāmanera (Novice). In the case of other rules he has to make amends according to the gravity of the offence.

Purity, perfect celibacy, voluntary poverty, humility, simplicity, selfless service, self-control, patience, compassion, and harmlessness are some of the salient characteristics of a Bhikkhu.

He claims no property for he has renounced everything worldly. His needs are few, and contentment is his wealth. As he tries to eliminate his "I-notion" he grieves not for what he has not. He repents not for his past, nor is he worried about the future. Full of joy he always lives in the present, free from all responsibilities and trammels of the world. Like a bird he is ready to wander whithersoever he desires without clinging to any abode. Under all vicissitudes of life he maintains a balanced mind. He is cordial in his ways and refined in conduct. His free services are always at the disposal of others. The fund of energy at his command is not confined to satisfy personal ends, but is usefully directed to activities that tend to universal happiness. He practises harmlessness to such an extent that he does not even pluck a leaf or dig the ground.

A Bhikkhu who leads such a holy life is indeed a blessing to himself and to others. He teaches both by example and precept. Within he is pure, without he purifies.

CHAPTER XXX

THE WAY TO NIBBANA

(Contd)

MEDITATION

SECURING a firm footing on the ground of Sīla or morality, the progressing pilgrim then embarks upon the higher practice of Samādhi, the control and culture of the mind, the second stage of the Path of Purity.

Samādhi is the one-pointedness of the mind. It is the wilful concentration of the mind on one object to the entire exclusion of all irrelevant matter.

According to the Visuddhi Magga there are forty subjects of meditation.

They are:—

The ten *Kasinas* (devices)—namely; i. the earth Kasina, ii. the water Kasina, iii. the fire Kasina, iv. the air Kasina, v. the blue Kasina, vi. the yellow Kasina, vii. the red Kasina, viii. the white Kasina, ix. the light Kasina, x. and the space Kasina.

The ten impurities—namely; i. a bloated corpse (*Uddhumātaka*), ii. a discoloured corpse (*Vinīlaka*), iii. a festering corpse (*Vipubbaka*), iv. a dissected corpse (*Vicchiddika*), v. gnawed-to-pieces corpse, (*Vikkhāyitaka*), vi. a scattered-in-pieces corpse (*Vikkhittaka*), vii. a mutilated and scattered-in-pieces corpse

(*Hata-Vikkhittaka*), viii. a bloody corpse (*Lohitaka*), ix. a worm-infested corpse (*Pulavaka*), and x. skeleton corpse (*Aṭṭhika*).

The ten reflections (*Anussati*)—namely; i. Reflection on the Buddha (*Buddhānussati*), ii. Reflection on the Doctrine (*Dhammānussati*), iii. Reflection on the Sangha (*Saṅghānussati*), iv. Reflection on Virtue (*Silānussati*), v. Reflection on Liberality (*Cāgānussati*), vi. Reflection on Devas (*Devatānussati*), vii. Reflection on Peace (*Upasamānussati*), viii. Reflection on Death (*Maraṇānussati*), ix. Mindfulness regarding the body (*Kāyagatā-sati*), x. Mindfulness regarding respiration (*Ānapana-sati*).

The four illimitables or the four Modes of Sublime Conduct (Brahmavihāra) — namely, Loving-kindness (*Metta*), Compassion (*Karuṇa*), Sympathetic Joy (*Mudita*), and Equanimity (*Upekkha*).

The One Preception—i.e. the perception of the loathsomeness of material food. (*Āhāre Paṭikkūla Saññā*).

The One Analysis—i.e. the analysis of the Four Elements (*Catudhātu-vavatthāna*).

The Four Formless States—namely; the Realm of the Infinity of Space (*Ākāsanañcayatana*), the Realm of the Infinity of Consciousness (*Viññāṇañcayatana*), the Realm of Nothingness (*Ākiñcaññayatana*), and the Realm of Neither Perception nor Non-perception (*N'eva Saññā Nāsannayatana.*)[1]

---

1. For details see the Visuddhi Magga—Part ii, p. 118.

These subjects differ according to the temperaments and types of individuals. There are six kinds of temperaments (*Carita*)—namely.

i. Lustful temperament (*Raga Carita*)
ii. Irritable temperament (*Dosa Carita*)
iii. Illusive temperament (*Moha Carita*)
iv. Devotional temperament (*Saddhā Carita*)
v. Intellectual temperament (*Buddhi Carita*)
vi. Discursive temperament (*Vitakka Carita*)

Of the above subjects the ten Impurities and Mindfulness regarding the body are suitable for those of lustful temperament.

The Four illimitables and the four coloured Kasina circles are suitable for those of irritable temperament.

Mindfulness regarding respiration is suitable for those of illusive temperament and those of discursive temperament.

The first six Reflections are suitable for those of devotional temperament.

Reflections on Death and Peace, the Perception of the loathsomeness of material food, and the Analysis of the Four Elements are suitable for those of intellectual temperament.

The other subjects, chiefly the reflection on the Buddha, meditation on loving-kindness, mindfulness regarding the body, and reflection on death, are suitable for all.

* * * *

Before he really embarks upon the practice of Samādhi the qualified aspirant should give a careful consideration to the subject of contemplation. In the ancient days when Arahants were a common sight it was customary for the pupils to seek a competent teacher who choose a suitable subject for him. If such teachers are not easily available, he may use his judicious discrimination and choose the one most suited to his character.

This being satisfactorily settled, it is necessary for him to withdraw to a quiet place where he is least disturbed from outside sources. The forest or a cave is the most desirable, as it is not liable to interruption during his practice.

It should be understood that solitude is within us all. If our minds are not settled, even a forest would not be a solitary place. Even the heart of a busy town may be a congenial place if our minds are settled.

It must also not be forgotten that the atmosphere in which we live acts as an indirect aid to tranquillize our minds.

Having selected a place he should then choose a convenient time when everything is in the best possible condition for his practice.

Early in the morning when the mind is fresh and active or before bed-time, if not over-tired, is generally the most appropriate time. Whatever time we select it is advisable to adhere to it, for our minds then become more tuned to the practice when we commence our meditation at an identical time everyday.

The meditating posture is also another important point to consider. The posture, too, acts as a very powerful mechanical aid to concentration.

Easterners generally sit crosslegged with the body erect. They sit placing the right foot on the left thigh and the left foot on the right thigh and at right angles to each other. This is the full position. If they find this posture difficult, sometimes they adopt the half position, that is by simply placing the right foot on the left thigh or the left foot on the right thigh.

When this triangular position is assumed the whole body is well balanced.

The left hand should be placed on the right hand. The neck should be straightened so that the nose is in a perpendicular line with the navel. Before the practice, bad air from the lungs should be breathed out slowly through the mouth and then closing the mouth, fresh air should be inhaled through the nose. The tongue should rest against the upper palate.

The girdle should be loosened, and the garments should be neatly arranged.

Some prefer to have their eyes closed so as to shut out all unnecessary light and external sights.

Although there are a few advantages in closing the eyes, yet it is not always recommended as it tends to drowsiness. Consequently the mind goes out of control and wanders aimlessly, vagrant thoughts arise, the body loses its erectness, the mouth opens quite unconsciously, saliva drivels, and the head nods.

The Buddhas usually sit with half closed eyes looking through the tip of the nose not more than a distance of about two and half cubits.

Those who find the cross-legged posture too difficult may sit comfortably in a chair or any other support, sufficiently high to rest the legs on the ground.

It is of no importance which attitude one may adopt provided the position is easy and relaxed.

The aspirant who is keen on practising Samādhi should endeavour his best to control the passions he is obsessed with, even at their inception.

As mentioned in the Sutta Nipāta he may be beset with the ten armies of Māra, the Evil One, such as (1) sensual desires, (2) discouragement, (3) hunger and thirst, (4) attachment, (5) sloth and torpor, (6) fear, (7) doubt, (8) detraction and stubborn-ness, (9) gain, praise, honour, and fame wrongly obtained, (10) and self-praise and contempt of others.

On such occasions the following practical suggestions mentioned by the Buddha[1] will be beneficial to all.

(1) Attending to some good idea of an opposite nature *(aññaṁ nimittaṁ)*; e.g. love in case of hatred.

(2) Reflecting upon the danger of their evil consequences (*Ādīnava*); e.g. anger sometimes results in murder.

(3) Simple neglect or becoming wholly inattentive to them *(Asati-amanasikara)*.

(4) Reflecting upon the causes that led to the arising of the passions and thus forgetting them in the process (*Vitakka—Sankhara—Saṇṭhana*).

---

1. Vitakka—Saṇṭhāna Sutta (M.N. No. 20).

(5) Direct physical force. Just as a strong man would overpower a weaker man even so one should overcome evil thoughts by bodily strength. "With teeth clenched and tongue pressed to palate," advises the Buddha, "the monk by main force must constrain and coerce his mind; and thus with clenched teeth and taut tongue, constraining and coercing his mind, those evil, insalutary thoughts will disappear and go to decay; and with their disappearing, the mind of the monk within him will become settled, subdued, unified, concentrated."[1]

Having attended to all these necessary prerequisites, the qualified aspirant retires to a solitary place, and summoning up confidence (Saddhā) as to the certainty of achieving his goal, he makes a persistent effort to focus his mind and eye--in the case of a physical object, like Kasina—or mind alone—in the case of a mental object, such as loving-kindness, virtues of the Buddha etc., on the selected object (*Kammaṭṭhāna*) to the entire exclusion of all irrelevant matter.

Meditation on some virtue like compassion, it may be remarked, possesses the specific advantage of building up that particular virtue in the character of the individual.

Whilst meditating one may intelligently repeat the words—if there be a special formula—since they act constantly evoke the idea they represent.

---

1. Majjhima Nikāya—Sutta No. 20.
See Discourses of Gotama the Buddha—Vol. I., pp. 147—151.

However much he may be intent on the object, he will not be exempt from the initial difficulties that inevitably confront a beginner. Mind wanders, alien thoughts dance before him, impatience overcomes him owing to slowness of progress, and his efforts get slackened in consequence. The determined student only welcomes these hindrances; the difficulties he cuts through; the obstacles he surmounts; and looks straight to his goal, never for a moment turning his eyes from it.

Thus with renewed confidence and vigour he strives to concentrate his entire attention on the preliminary object (Parikamma Nimitta) until he becomes so wholly absorbed in it that all adventitious thoughts get *ipso facto* excluded from the mind. A stage is ultimately reached when he is able to visualise the object even with closed eyes. On this visualised image (Uggaha Nimitta) he now concentrates until it develops into a conceptualised image (Paṭibhāga Nimitta).

As an illustration let us take the case of Paṭhavi Kasina.

A circle of about one span and four fingers in diameter is made and the surface is covered with dawn-coloured clay and smoothed well. If there be not enough clay of the dawn colour, he may put in some other kind of clay beneath.

This hypnotic circle is known as the Parikamma Nimitta. Now he places this object about two and half cubits away from him and concentrates on it, saying—mentally or inaudibly—*Paṭhavi* or earth. The purpose is to gain the one-pointedness of the mind. When he does this for some time—perhaps weeks, or months or years—he would be able to close his eyes and visualise the object. This visualised object is called Uggaha Nimitta. Then he concentrates on this visualised image, which is an exact mental replica of the object, until it develops into a conceptualised image which is called Paṭibhāga Nimitta.

The difference between the first visualised image and the second conceptualised image is this:—

"In the former a fault of the device (Kasina) appears; the latter is like the disc of a mirror taken out of a bag, a well-burnished-conch-shell, the round moon issuing from the clouds, white cranes against a rain cloud, and makes its appearance as though bursting the grasped sign, than which it is a hundred times, a thousand times more purified. But it possesses neither colour nor form.

"For otherwise it would be cognizable by the eye, gross, a fit object for contemplation, and marked with the three characteristics. But it is not so. To the winner of concentration, it is just a mode of appearance, and is born of perception."[1]

As he continually concentrates on this abstract concept he is said to be in possession of "proximate concentration" (Upacāra Samādhi) and the innate five Hindrances to Progress (Nivarana), such as sensual desires, hatred, sloth and torpor, restlessness and brooding, and doubts, are temporarily inhibited.

---

1. The Path of Purity—Part ii, p. 146.

Eventually he gains "ecstatic concentration" (Appaṇā Samādhi) and, to his indescribable joy, becomes enwrapt in Jhāna, enjoying the calmness and serenity of a one-pointed mind.

This one-pointedness of the mind is termed "*Citta-Visuddhi*"—Purity of Mind—the second stage on the Path of Purity.

When once he succeeds in exercising perfect control over his discursive mind, he can, without the least difficulty, develop the five supernomal powers (*Abhiññā*)—Celestial Eye (*Dibbacakkhu*), Celestial Ear (*Dibbasota*) reminiscence of past births (*Pubbe-Nivāsanussati Ñana*), thought reading (*Paracittavijānana*), and various psychic powers (*Iddhividha*).

Samādhi and these supernormal powers, it may be mentioned, are not essential for the attainment of Arahantship, though they would undoubtedly be a valuable asset to the possessor. There are the dry-visioned Arahants (Sukkha Vipassakas) who, without the aid of Jhānas, attain Arahantship straightway by merely cultivating Insight.[1] For instance, Cakkupala Thera attained Arahantship without the Jhānas.

1. See Dhammapada Commentary—Buddhist Legends.

CHAPTER XXXI

THE WAY TO NIBBĀNA

(Contd.)

INSIGHT

WHEN the Jhānas are developed the mind of the aspirant is considerably purified, yet he is not wholly free from giving vent to his passions. For, by concentration, the evil tendencies are only temporarily inhibited. They may rise to the surface at quite unexpected moments.

Discipline regulates word and deed, concentration controls the mind, but it is Insight (Paññā), the third and the final stage, that enables him to annihilate completely the passions inhibited by Samādhi.

At the outset he cultivates "Purity of Vision" (Diṭṭhi-Visuddhi)[1] in order to see things as they really are. With his one-pointed mind he scrutinizes his self and on due examination discovers that his I-personality is nothing but a mere composition of mind and matter—the former consisting of volitional activities that arise as a result of the senses coming in contact with the sense-stimuli, and the latter of forces and qualities that manifest themselves in multifarious phenomena.

Having thus gained a correct view of the real nature of his self, freed from the false notion of an

1. The third Visuddhi.

identical substance of mind and matter, he attempts to investigate the cause of this "I" personality. He realises that everything worldly, himself not excluded, is conditioned by some cause or causes, past or present, and that his existence is due to past ignorance, craving, attachment, Kamma, and physical food of the present life. On account of these five causes this personality has arisen, and as the past activities have conditioned the present, so the present will condition the future. Meditating thus he transcends all doubts with regard to the past, present, and future (*Kankhavitarana Visuddhi*).[1] Thereupon he contemplates that all conditioned things are transient, (*Anicca*), subject to suffering (*Dukkha*), and devoid of an immortal soul (*Anatta*). Wherever he turns his eyes he sees nought but these three characteristics standing out in bold relief. He realises that life is a mere flowing, a continuous undivided movement. Neither in heaven nor on earth does he find any genuine happiness, for every form of pleasure is only a prelude to pain. What is transient is therefore painful, and where change and sorrow prevail there cannot be a permanent ego.

As he is thus absorbed in meditation a day comes when, to his surprise, he witnesses an aura emanating from his body (*obhāsa*). He experiences an unprecedented pleasure, happiness, and quietude. He becomes even-minded and strenuous. His religious fervour increases, and mindfulness becomes perfect and Insight extraordinarily keen. Labouring under the misconception that he has attained Sainthood, chiefly owing to the presence of the aura, he yearns for this state of mind.

---

1. The Fourth Visuddhi.

Soon he realises that these temptations are only defilements to Insight and that he has not really attained Sainthood. Accordingly he endeavours to distinguish between the right and the wrong path (*Maggāmagga Ñāṇadassana Visuddhi*).[1]

Perceiving the right path he resumes his meditation on the arising (Udaya Ñāna) and passing away (Vaya Ñāna) of conditioned things. Of these two characteristics the latter becomes more impressed in his mind, because change is more conspicuous than becoming. Therefore he turns his attention to the contemplation of the dissolution of things, (Bhanga Ñāna). He perceives that both mind and matter, which constitute this personality, are in a state of constant flux, not remaining for two consecutive moments the same. To him then comes the knowledge that all dissolving things are fearful (Bhaya Ñāna). The whole world appears to him like a pit of burning embers—a source of danger. Subsequently he reflects on the wretchedness and vanity (Adīnava Ñāna) of the fearful and wicked world, and feeling disgusted (Nibbidā Ñāna) with it, wishes to escape therefrom (Muñcitukamyatā Ñāna).

With this object in view, he meditates again on the three characteristics (Paṭisankhā Ñāna), and thereafter becomes completely indifferent to all conditioned things—having neither attachment nor aversion for any worldly object (Upekkhā Ñāna). Reaching this point of mental culture,[2] he takes for his object of special

---

1. The fifth Visuddhi.
2. These nine kinds of Insight, viz:—*Udaya, Vaya, Bhanga, Bhaya, Ādīnava, Nibbidā, Muñcitukamyatā, Paṭisankhā*, and *Upekkhā Ñānas* are collectively termed "*Paṭipada-Ñāṇadassana Visuddhi*"—Purity of Vision in Knowledge of Progress, the sixth Visuddhi.

endeavour one of the three characteristics that appeals to him most, and intently keeps on developing Insight in that particular direction until that glorious day comes to him when, to his indescribable joy, he realises Nibbāna, his ultimate goal, for the first time in his life.[1]

"As the traveller by night sees landscape around him by each flash of lightning and the picture so obtained long thereafter swims before his dazzled eyes, so the individual seeker by the flashing light of Insight catches a glimpse of Nibbāna with such clearness that the after-picture never more fades from his mind."[2]

When the spiritual pilgrim realises Nibbāna for the first time he is called a Sotāpanna—one who has entered the stream that leads to Nibbāna. He is no more a worldling (*Puthujjana)* but an Ariya. He eliminates also three fetters—namely, self-illusion (*sakkāya diṭṭhi*), doubts (*Vicikicchā*), and adherence to (wrongful) rites and ceremonies (*Silabbataparāmāsa*). As he has not eradicated the "will-to-live", he is reborn seven times at the most. In his subsequent birth he may or may not be aware of the fact that he is a Sotāpanna. Nevertheless he possesses the characteristics peculiar to such a Saint. He gains implicit confidence in the Buddha, Dhamma, and the Sangha, and can never be persuaded to violate any of the Five Precepts. He is moreover absolved from states of woe, for he is destined to Enlightenment.

Summoning up fresh courage, as a result of this distant glimpse of Nibbāna, the Aryan Pilgrim makes rapid progress, and perfecting his Insight, becomes a

---

1. Insight found in this Supramundane Path consciousness is known as Ñanadassana Visuddhi—Purity of Vision which is knowledge, the seventh Visuddhi.
2. Dr. Dhalke.

Sakadāgāmi, Once-Returner, by attenuating two other fetters—namely, sense-desires (*Kāmarāga*) and illwill (*Paṭigha*).

He is called a Sakadāgāmi because he is reborn on earth only once in case he does not attain Arahantship in that birth itself. It is interesting to note that the pilgrim who has attained the second stage of Sainthood can only weaken these two powerful fetters with which he is bound from a beginningless past. Occasionally he may be disturbed by thoughts of lust and anger to a slight extent.

It is by attaining the third stage of Sainthood, Anāgāmi (Never-Returner), that he completely discards the above two fetters. Thereafter he neither returns to this world nor does he seek birth in the celestial realms, since he has rooted out the desire for sensual pleasures. After death he is reborn in the Pure Abodes (Sudhāvāsa), a camping place exclusively reserved for Anāgāmins and Arahants. Even an Anāgāmi, it must be understood, has not completely got rid of his "will-to live."

Now the earnest pilgrim, encouraged by the unprecedented success of his endeavours, makes his final advance, and destroying the remaining five fetters—namely, lust after life in Realms of Form (*Rūparāga*) and in Formless Realms (*Arūparāga*), conceit (*Māna*), restlessness (*Uddhacca*), and ignorance (*Avijjā*), attains Arahantship, the last stage of Sainthood.

Instantly he realises that what was to be accomplished has been done, that a heavy burden of sorrow has been finally relinquished, and that all forms of the "will-to-live" have been totally annihilated. The happy pilgrim now stands on heights more than celestial, far removed from rebellious passions and defilements of the world, enjoying that unutterable eternal Bliss of Nibbāna.

Though an Arahant he is not wholly free from physical suffering, as he is not experiencing this Bliss of Deliverance uninterruptedly, and has not cast off the material body he bears. Nibbāna is assuredly attainable here and now, but a continuous realisation of Nibbānic bliss is to be experienced only after death.

An Arahant is called an Asekha, one who is not under training, as he has lived the Holy life and has accomplished his object. The other Saints from the Sotapatti stage to the Arahant Path Stage are called Sekhas because they are still under training.

It may be mentioned in this connection that Anāgāmins and Arahants who have adopted the Samatha path or, in other words, have developed concentration and acquired different kinds of ecstasies, could experience the Bliss of Nibbāna in this life itself. This, in Pali, is called the Nirodha Samāpatti. In this post-cataleptic state, the person is wholly free from pain, and his mental activities are all suspended.

With regard to the difference between one who has attained Nirodha-samāpatti and a dead man the Visuddhi Magga states:—"In the corpse not only are the plastic forces of the body (i.e. respiration) and speech and mind stilled and quiescent but also vitality is exhausted, heat is quenched, and the faculties of sense broken up;—whereas in the Bhikkhu in ecstasy vitality persists, heat abides, and the faculties are clear, although respiration, observation and perception are stilled and quiescent."[1]

According to Buddhism, this is the highest form of happiness that could be experienced in this life.

* * * *

Why does the Arahant continue to live when he has already intuited Nibbana, or when he has denied the will-to-live?

It is because the Kamma-force which gave him birth is not still spent. To quote Schopenhauer, it is like the potter's wheel from which the hand of the potter has been lifted, or to cite a better illustration from our own books,—an Arahant is like a branch that is severed from the tree. It puts forth no more fresh leaves, flowers, and fruits, as it is no longer supported by the sap of the tree; but those which already existed would last till life becomes extinct in that particular branch. The Arahant lives till his life-span is over, without adding any more fresh Kamma to his store, and utterly indifferent as to whether he dies or not.

Like venerable Sāriputta he would say:—

"*Not fain am I to die nor yet to live.*
I shall lay down this mortal frame anon
With mind alert, with consciousness controlled.
With thought of death I dally not, nor yet
Delight in living. I await the hour
Like any hireling who hath done his task."

(Psalms of the Brethren—p. 346.)

1. See The Path of Purity, Part ii, p 872.

What happens to the Arahant after his Pari-Nibbana? As a flame blown to and fro by the wind, goes out and cannot be registered, even so, says the Buddha, an Arahant, set free from mind and matter, has disappeared and cannot be registered.

One enquires:—**Has such an Arahant then merely disappeared, or does he indeed no longer exist?**

For him who has disappeared, states the Sutta Nipāta, there exists no form that by which they say "He is." When all conditions are cut off, all matter for discussion is also cut off.

The Udāna explains this intricate point thus:—

"*As the fiery sparks from a forge are one by one extinguished,*

And no one knows where they have gone—

So it is with those who have attained to complete emancipation,

Who have crossed the flood of desire,

Who have entered the calm delight, of those no trace remains."

The Majjhima Nikāya also relates an interesting discussion that took place between the Buddha and Vacchagotta concerning this very question.[1]

Vacchagotta, a wandering ascetic, approached the Buddha and questioned—"**But, Gotama, where is the Bhikkhu, who is delivered of mind, reborn?**"

He was of course referring to the Arahant.

---

1. Aggivacchagotta Sutta, No. 72.

The Buddha replies—"Vaccha, to say that he is reborn would not fit the case."

"Then, Gotama, he is not reborn."

"Vaccha, to say that he is not reborn would not fit the case."

"Then, Gotama, he is both reborn and not reborn."

"Vaccha, to say that he is both reborn and not reborn would not fit the case."

"Then, Gotama, he is neither reborn nor not reborn."

"Vaccha, to say that he is neither reborn nor not reborn would not fit the case."

Vaccha was baffled on hearing these seemingly preposterous answers, and, in his confusion, exclaimed—

"Gotama, I am at a loss what to think in this matter, and I have become greatly confused."

"Enough, O Vaccha! Be not at a loss what to think in this matter, and be not greatly confused. Profound, O Vaccha, is this doctrine, recondite and difficult of comprehension, good, excellent, and not to be reached by mere reasoning. Subtle, and intelligible only to the wise; and it is a hard doctrine for you to learn, who belong to another sect, to another faith, to another persuasion, to another discipline, and who sit at the feet of another teacher. Therefore, Vaccha, I shall now question you, and do you make answer as may seem to you good. What think you, Vaccha? Suppose a fire were to burn in front of you, would you be aware that a fire was burning in front of you?

"Gotama, if a fire were to burn in front of me, I should be aware that a fire was burning in front of me."

"But suppose, Vaccha, some one were to ask you, 'On what does this fire that is burning in front of you depend?' What would you answer, Vaccha?"

"I would answer, Gotama, 'It is on fuel of grass that this fire burning in front of me depends.'"

"But, Vaccha, if the fire in front of you were to become extinct, would you be aware that the fire in front of you has become extinct?"

"Gotama, if the fire in front of me were to become extinct, I should be aware that the fire in front of me has become extinct."

"But, Vaccha, if some one were to ask you 'In which direction has that fire gone, East or West, North or South?' What would you say, Vaccha?"

"The question would not fit the case, Gotama. For the fire depended on fuel, grass, and wood, and when that fuel has all gone, and it can get no other, being thus without nutriment, is said to be extinct."

"In exactly the same way, Vaccha, all forms, sensations, perceptions, mental activities, and consciousness have been abandoned, uprooted, made like a palmyra stump, became non-existent, and not liable to spring up in the future.

"The Saint, O Vaccha, who has been released from what are styled the Five Aggregates, is deep, immeasurable, like the mighty ocean. To say that he is reborn would not fit the case. To say that he is not reborn would not fit the case. To say that he is neither reborn nor not reborn would not fit the case."

One cannot say that the Arahant is reborn, as all passions that condition rebirth are eradicated ; nor can one say that the Arahant is annihilated, for there is nothing to annihilate.

Nibbāna, it may safely be concluded, is obtained by the complete cessation of passions (Kilesa), but the real nature of this Supreme State (Dhamma) cannot adequately be expressed by mere words.

In the words of Sir Edwin Arnold—

"If any teach NIRVĀNA is to cease,
Say unto such they lie.
If any teach NIRVĀNA is to live,
Say unto such they err."

(The Light of Asia)

CHAPTER XXXII

THE STATE OF AN ARAHANT

THE Tipitaka abounds with interesting and beautiful passages that describe the peaceful and happy state of an Arahant, who abides in the world like the lotus bloom, unsullied by mud, and enjoys the indescribable bliss of Nibbāna.

In the Dhammapada the Buddha states:—

For him who has completed the journey, for him who is sorrowless, for him who, from everything, is wholly free, for him who has destroyed all ties,—fever of passion exists not.

The mindful exert themselves;
To no abode are they attached.
Like swans that quit their pools,
Home after home they abandon (and go).

Those who do not accumulate, those who reflect well over their food, those whose object is the Void, the Signless, Deliverance,—their course, like that of birds in air, cannot be traced.

He whose corruptions are destroyed, who is not attached to food, whose object is the Void, the Signless, Deliverance,—his path, like that of birds in air, cannot be traced.

He whose senses are subdued, like steeds well trained by a charioteer; he whose pride is destroyed and is free from corruptions;[1]—such steadfast ones even Devas hold dear.

Like the earth, the steadfast and cultured person resents not; he is like an Indakhīla;[2] like a pool unsullied by mud, is he;—to such an unchangeable one, life's wanderings are no more.

Calm is his mind, calm is his speech, calm is his deed,—who, rightly knowing, is wholly freed, perfectly peaceful, and equipoised.

The man who is not credulous, who understands the Uncreate (Nibbāna), who has cut off the link, who has put an end to occasion (of good and evil), who has vomited all desires,—he, indeed, is the noblest of all men.

Whether in village or in forest, in vale or on hill, wherever Arahants dwell,—delightful, indeed, is that spot.

Delightful are forests, where worldlings find no joy. There the passionless will rejoice, (for) they seek no sensual pleasures.

Ah! happily do we live, benevolent amongst the hateful;
Amidst hateful men we dwell benevolent.

Ah! happily do we dwell, in good health amongst the ailing;
Amidst ailing men we dwell in goodhealth.

---

1. See *Āsava*—p. 37.
2. *Indakhīla*—a pillar, firmly set in earth, at a city gate. "Like the Indakhīla, set in earth, not moved by the four winds,—even so, I declare, is the righteous man who intuits the Noble Truths.' (Ratana Sutta).

Ah! happily do we dwell without yearning (for sensual pleasures) amongst those who yearn for them. Amidst those who yearn (for them) we dwell without yearning.

Ah! happily do we dwell,—we who have no
    impediments.
Feeders on joy shall we be, even as the Radiant
    Devas.

For him there exists neither a hither nor a farther shore, nor both a hither and a farther shore, he who is undistressed and unbound;—him I call a Brahmana.[1]

He that is meditative, stainless, and settled; he that has done his duty and is free from corruptions; he that has attained the Highest Goal;—him I call a Brahmana.

He that does no evil through body, speech or mind; he who is restrained in these three respects;—him I call a Brahmana.

He who has cut off all Fetters,[2] he who trembles not, he who has gone beyond Toils, he who is unbound;—him I call a Brahmana.

He who has cut the strap (of hatred), the thong (of craving)—and the rope (of heresies), together with the appendages (latent tendencies); he who has thrown off the yoke (of ignorance); he who is enlightened;—him I call a Brahmana.

He who is not hateful, but is dutiful, virtuous, not sullied with craving, controlled, and bears his final body,—him I call a Brahmana.

---

1. Here the term "Brahmana" is applied to an Arahant.
2. The ten *Saṅyojanas*—see pp. 290, 291.

Like water on a lotus leaf, like a mustard seed on the point of a needle, he who clings not to sensual pleasures;—him I call a Brahmana.

He who realises, here itself, the destruction of one's sorrow; he who has laid down the burden and is emancipated;—him I call a Brahmana.

He whose knowledge is deep, who is wise, who is skilled in the right and wrong way, who has reached the highest;—him I call a Brahmana.

He who is not intimate with either householders or homeless ones; he who wanders without an abode, who is without desires;—him I call a Brahmana.

He who has laid aside the cudgel towards beings, whether feeble or strong;—he who neither kills nor causes to kill;—him I call a Brahmana.

He who is friendly amongst the hostile, who is peaceful amongst the violent, who is unattached amongst the attached,—him I call a Brahmana.

From whom lust, hatred, pride, detraction are fallen, like a mustard seed from the point of a needle,—him I call a Brahmana.

He who utters gentle, instructive, true words;
He who gives offence to none;—
Him I call a Brahmana.

He who has no desires whether of this world or of the next;
He who is desireless and emancipated;—
Him I call a Brahmana.

Who here has transcended both good and bad, and the Toils as well; who is sorrowless, stainless and pure;—him I call a Brahmana.

He who is spotless as the moon, who is pure, serene and clear, who has destroyed craving for becoming,—him I call a Brahmana.

He who discarding human bonds and transcending celestial ties, is completely delivered of all fetters, —him I call a Brahmana.

He who has given up all likes and dislikes, who is cooled, and without substrata;[1] he who has conquered the world[2] and is strenuous;—him I call a Brahmana.

He who has no clinging to aggregates that are past, future or present; he who is without clinging and grasping;—him I call a Brahmana.

He who knows his former abodes, who sees heaven and hell, who has reached the end of births; he who, with superior wisdom, has perfected himself as a Holy Man, who has finished all finishings;[3]—him I call a Brahmana.

---

1. *Upādhi*—Aggregates *(Khandha)*, Passions *(Kilesa)*, Volitional Activities *(Abhisankhāra)*, Sense-desires *(Kāma)*.
2. I.e., he who has put an end to the arising of the Aggregates (world).
3. I.e., Arahantship.

CHAPTER XXXIII

THE BODHISATTA IDEAL

(I)

THERE are three kinds of Bodhi or Enlightenment by means of which one may intuit Nibbāna. They are the *Sāvaka-Bodhi*, *Pacceka-Bodhi*, and *Sammā-Sambodhi*.

Sāvaka-Bodhi is the Enlightenment of a disciple. This is known as the Arahant Ideal. He who aspires to become an Arahant must, despite his innate intelligence, hear the Dhamma from another superior enlightened instructor *(parato ghosa)*. After attaining Arahantship he devotes the remainder of his life to save other seekers of Peace by revealing the path to them. First he saves himself, and then he tries to save others. There is nothing selfish in this ideal as some hasty critics seem to think, for Arahantship is gained only by eradicating all forms of selfishness. Self-illusion is one of the fetters that one has to discard in order to attain Arahantship.

Pacceka-Bodhi is the Enlightenment gained by a highly evolved spiritual person as a result of his individual striving. His Enlightenment is independent. A person who attains this Bodhi is termed a Private *(Pacceka)* Buddha because he lacks the power to save others by teaching the Dhamma which he himself has realised by his own effort.

Sammā-Sam-bodhi is the Enlightenment of a most developed, most compassionate, most loving, all-knowing, perfect being. He who attains this Bodhi is called a *Sammā-Sambuddha* because he not only comprehends the Dhamma by his own will, wisdom, and love but also expounds that Doctrine to the seekers of Peace in order to save them from this ever-recurring cycle of birth and death.

It is indeed a high-minded person, who not only *comtemplates* but *feels* the sorrows of the world as his own, that aspires to become a *Sammā-Sambuddha.* So boundless is his love, so limitless is his compassion that he renounces his personal deliverance in order to perfect himself and serve humanity both by example and precept.

Such is the noble ideal of an ever-loving Bodhisatta. This is the most exalted and most laudable ideal that is ever presented to the ego-centric world, for what is nobler and higher than a life of selfless service and perfect purity.

The Bodhisatta Ideal, it should be remarked, is exclusively Buddhistic.

In parenthesis, it must be stated that it is the Bodhisatta of the Pali Tipitaka that the Catholic Church has canonised as St. Josaphat.

Prof. Rhys Davids says in his Buddhist Birth Stories:—

"There is a religious romance called Barlaam and Josaph giving the history of an Indian Prince who was converted by Barlaam and became a hermit. This history the reader will be surprised to hear is taken from the life of the Buddha; and Josaph is merely the Buddha under another name, the word Josaphat being simply a corruption of the word Bodhisat.

"Josaph is in Arabic written also Yudasatf; and this through a confusion between the Arabic letters Y and B, is Bodhisat."

The Pāli term Bodhisatta is composed of *Bodhi*, which means wisdom or Enlightenment, and *Satta*, which means devoted to or bent upon. Bodhisatta, therefore, means one who is devoted to, or bent upon, Enlightenment.

According to the commentaries he who aspires to attain Buddhahood makes at first a firm mental resolve *(Mano-Panidhi)* to become a Buddha in the presence of an Omniscient One. This he repeatedly affirms for a long period, but without intimating his desire to another. Later he gives verbal expression to his mental resolve *(Vacī-Panidhi)* in the presence of a Buddha, and repeats this for an equally long period.

Then with firm determination and strong will-power, he develops by degrees the self-sacrificing spirit latent in him, and cultivates wisdom until he reaches a high pitch of perfection, when unable to restrain himself any longer, he demonstrates his burning desire which has been so long held in abeyance. This outward demonstration is technically called *Kāya Panidhi*.

These three periods of a Bodhisatta are known as the period of Aspiration, of Expression, and of Nomination.

At this last stage of spiritual advancement he could attain Arahantship, if he is inclined to do so, but this golden opportunity he renounces to serve the world at large.

"Today, if such were my desire,
I my corruption might consume.
But why thus in an unknown guise
Should I the Doctrine's fruit secure?

Omniscience first will I achieve,
And be a Buddha in the world.
Or why should I a valorous man,
The ocean seek to cross alone?"

(Warren—*Buddhism in Translations*)

Such was the train of thought that passed through the mind of the Bodhisatta Sumedha, as he lay prostrate at the sacred feet of the Buddha Dipankara.

Generally it is on such a memorable occasion like this that a Bodhisatta receives the revelation or *Vivaraṇa* from a Buddha, who, perceiving with His Divine Eye, publicly proclaims that the person in question will definitely attain Buddhahood in the near future. Thereafter he becomes fully entitled to the honourable appellation of *Bodhisatta.*

The Sanskrtised form should be *Bodhishakta,* but the current term is *Bodhisatta* which means wisdom-being.

By Bodhisatta is generally meant a being who is destined to Enlightenment. In this general sense this term may be applied to any person who is trying to gain Enlightenment, but, strictly speaking, it is applied only to those who are destined to become a Sammā-Sambuddha, a fully Enlightened One.

In one sense we all are potential Buddhas, for the Bodhisatta or Bodhi-mind is latent in us all. It is within our power to develop it.

We Buddhists do not believe that there is within us a Divine spark which we should cultivate, for we do not believe in a God-creator, but we are aware of the innate possibilities and the creative power of man.

As a man Prince Siddhattha, by his own will, wisdom, and love, attained Buddhahood—that highest possible state of perfection any person could aspire to—and, without the closed fist of a teacher, He revealed to mankind the only straight path that leads thereto. A singular characteristic of Buddhism is that anybody may aspire even to the state of the Teacher himself if he possesses the necessary exertion. The Buddha does not claim the monopoly of Buddhahood. It is a sort of evolutionary process and is achieved by one's own effort without the help of another.

Any person who aspires to be a Buddha is called a Bodhisatta. Such a Bodhisatta, though unaware of his aspiration, may be found even amongst other religionists as awell. A Bodhisatta need not necessarily be a Buddhist. Just as we find ever-loving Bodhisattas amongst us Buddhists today, even so they may be found amongst Hindus, Christians, and others.

According to Buddhism there are three classes of Bodhisattas, viz:- Intellectual Bodhisattas (*Paññā-dhika*), Devotional Bodhisattas (*Saddhādhika*), and Energetic Bodhisattas (*Viriyādhika*). These three kinds of Bodhisattas correspond to Ñāṇa Yogi, Bhakti Yogi, and Karma Yogi of the Hindus.

The intellectual Bodhisattas are less devotional and more energetic; the devotional ones are less energetic and more intellectual; the energetic ones are less intellectual and more devotional. Seldom, if ever, are these three characteristics harmoniously combined in one person. The Buddha Gotama is cited as one belonging to the intellectual group.

The intellectual ones attain Buddhahood within a short period. Those belonging to the devotional group take a longer time, whilst energetic ones take a still longer time.

The intellectual Bodhisattas are more concerned with the development of wisdom and the practice of meditation than with the observance of external forms of homage. They are always guided by reason and accept nothing on blind belief. They make no self-surrender, and are not slaves either to a Book or an individual. They prefer meditation in solitary retreats from where they quietly radiate peaceful but powerful thoughts to alleviate the sufferings of humanity. Their knowledge is always at the disposal of others.

The element of piety—*Saddhā* or *Bhakti*—is predominant in the devotional Bodhisattas. With *saddhā* as their helpmate they achieve their goal.

These Bodhisattas would take great interest in all forms of homage etc. The image of the Buddha is a great inspiration to them. Even Count Kaiserling, the great philosopher, says: - "I know nothing more grand in this world than the figure of Buddha; it is an absolutely perfect embodiment of spirituality in the visible domain." (Travel Diary of a Philosopher.)

It should be understood that Buddhists do not worship an image. They pay homage to what it represents and reflect on the virtues of the Buddha. The more they think of the Buddha, the more they love

Him. This is the reason why Buddhism does not discountenance these external forms of homage-*Āmisa Pūjā*-though *Paṭipatti Pūjā*—the practice, is more commendable and indisputably superior. Dry intellect has to be flavoured sometimes with a pinch of Bhakti to obtain satisfactory results. As excessive Bhakti might also sometimes be detrimental, it has to be bridled by *Ñāna*—wisdom.

The energetic ones always seek opportunties to be of service to others. Nothing gives them greater delight than active service. "For them work is happiness, and happiness is work." They are not happy unless they are active. They bear this body of flesh and blood for the good and happiness of the world.

This spirit of selfless service is one of the chief characteristics of all Bodhisattas.

They work with relentless energy, not as slaves but as masters. They crave not for fame or name. They are interested only in the doing. It is immaterial to them whether others recognise their good services or not. They are utterly indifferent to praise or blame.

They forget their own selves in rendering service to others. They would even sacrifice their lives if such action would save another's life.

The Jātakamālā states that on one occasion when the Bodhisatta was passing through a forest, accompanied by his disciple, he saw a starving tigress and three cubs on the verge of death. Moved by this pitiable sight, he commanded his disciple to go in search of some food to be given to them. Making this a pretext to send him away the Bodhisatta thought:—

"Why should I search after meat from the body of another whilst the whole of my body is available? Not only is the getting of meat in itself a matter of chance, but I should also lose the opportunity of doing my duty.

"This body being foul and a source of suffering, he is not wise who would not rejoice at its being spent for the benefit of another. There are but two things that make one disregard the grief of another—attachment to one's own pleasure, and the absence of the power of helping. But I cannot have pleasure whilst another grieves, and I have the power to help. Why should I, therefore, be indifferent?

"I will, therefore, sacrifice my miserable body by casting myself down the precipice, and with my corpse I shall feed the tigress, thus preventing her from killing the young ones and the young ones from dying by the teeth of their mother.

"Furthermore, by so doing I set an example to those who long for the good of the world. I encourage the feeble; I gladden those who understand the meaning of charity; I stimulate the virtuous. And finally that opportunity I yearned for, when may I have the opportunity of benefiting others by offering them my own limbs, I shall obtain it now, and acquire before long Sammā-Sambuddhahood—Supreme Enlightenment."

Such is the self-sacrificing spirit of a noble-minded Bodhisatta.

A Bodhisatta who forgets himself in the service of others should practise *Karuṇā* and *Mettā* (compassion and loving-kindness) to an exceptionally high degree.

A Bodhisatta desires the good and welfare of the world. He loves all beings as a mother loves her only child. He identifies himself with all. To him nothing gives more delight than to think that all are his brothers and sisters. He is like a mother, a father, a friend, a teacher to all beings.

"The compassion of a Bodhisatta consists in realising the equality of oneself with others *(Para-ātma-samatā)* and also the substituition of others for oneself *(Para-ātma-parivartana)*." When he so regards he loses his I-notion and finds no difference between himself and others. He returns good for evil, and helps even unasked the very persons who have wronged him, for he knows that "the strength of a religious teacher is his patience."

"Being reviled, he reviles not; being beaten, he beats not; being annoyed, he annoys not. His forgiveness is unfailing even as the mother earth suffers in silence all that may be done to her."

CHAPTER XXXIV

THE BODHISATTA IDEAL

(ii)

PĀRAMĪS OR PERFECTIONS

Every Bodhisatta is expected to practise the ten Pāramis, the pre-requisites of Buddhahood. They are Generosity *(Dāna)*, Morality *(Sīla)*, Renunciation *(Nekkhamma)*, Wisdom *(Paññā)*, Energy *(Viriya)*, Patience *(Khanti)*, Truthfulness *(Sacca)*, Determination *(Adhiṭṭhāna)*, Loving-Kindness *(Mettā)*, and Equanimity *(Upekkhā)*.

According to the Commentary of the Cariyā Pitaka, *Pāramis* are those virtues which are cultivated with compassion, guided by reason, dominated by no worldly gain, and unsullied by misbelief and all feelings of self-conceit.

Dāna or Generosity is the first Pārami. It confers upon the giver the double blessing of inhibiting, on one hand, the immoral thoughts of selfishness, and developing, on the other hand, the pure thoughts of selflessness. It blesseth him that gives and him that takes.

A Bodhisatta is not worried by the question whether the recipient is truly in need or not. His object in giving is to eliminate craving that lies dormant within him. The joy of service, ensuing happiness and consolation, and the alleviation of suffering are the attendant blessings of generosity.

He makes no distinction in extending his love with supernormal generosity, not forgetting at the same time to use his judicious discrimination in doing so. If, for instance, a drunkard were to seek his help, and, if convinced that the drunkard would misuse his gift, the Bodhisatta would not hesitate to refuse him to his face, for such generosity would not constitute a Pārami.

Nevertheless, should someone expect his help for a worthy purpose, instead of assuming a forced air of dignity or making false pretexts, he would only express his deep obligation for the opportunity afforded, and willingly and humbly render him every possible aid. Yet, he would never set it down to his account as a favour conferred upon another, nor would he ever think in his mind of the man as his debtor for the service rendered. He is interested only in the good act, but nothing beyond. He does not expect any reward in return, nor does he crave for the empty reputation of having done some noble work.

A Bodhisatta is always ready to oblige, but seldom, if ever, does he stoop to beg for a favour. The Brahmadatta Jātaka (No. 323) relates that once the Bodhisatta was leading an ascetic life in the park of a certain king, who visited him daily and ministered to all his needs. Yet, for twelve long years he refrained from asking such a trifling boon as a pair of sandles and a leaf-parasol. When questioned as to his strange, but modest, attitude, he replied to the king :—

> " *Who begs, Pañcāla Lord, to weep are fain,*
> *They who refuse are apt to weep again.*"

In abundance he gives, irrespective of caste, creed or colour, but selfishly he seeks nothing. He is neither selfish nor self-possessive. Contentment is his wealth, and an Edward Dyer would sing with him :—

"Some have too much, yet still do crave;
I little have and seek no more.
They are but poor though much they have;
And I am rich with little store."

In the Kanha Jātaka (No. 440) it is mentioned that Sakka, attracted by his exemplary life of virtue, approached him and prayed to be given the privilege of granting him a boon. He acceded to Sakka's kind request, and expressed his desire to have the following four boons:—

1. May I harbour no malice or hatred against my neighbour!
2. May I not covet my neighbour's glory!
3. May I cherish no affection towards others!
4. May I possess equanimity!

Greatly disappointed, though more than pleased with the disinterested nature of his request, Sakka entreated him to make another. He replied:—

"Where in the woods I ever dwell,
where all alone dwell I,
Grant no disease may mar my peace,
or break my ecstasy."

Hearing this, the Sakka thought—"Wise Kanha, in choosing a boon, chooses nothing connected with food; all he chooses pertain to the ascetic life."

Delighted still more, he added thereto yet another. The Bodhisatta remarked:—

"O Sakka, Lord of the world, a choice
thou didst declare:
No creature be aught harmed for me,
O Sakka, anywhere.
Neither in body nor in mind;
this, Sakka, is my prayer."

A Bodhisatta exercises this virtue of Dāna to such an extent that he is prepared to give away not only wealth and other cherished possessions, but also his kingdom, his limbs, children, and wife. He is ever ready to sacrifice his own life wherever such sacrifice will benefit humanity.

The Vessantara Jātaka (No. 547) mentions how, when Prince Vessantara was a child of only eight years, he thought with all sincerity:— If one should ask my heart, I would cut open my breast and tear it out and give it; If one should ask my eyes, I would pluck them out and give them; if one should ask my flesh, I would cut off the flesh and give it."

The Sasa Jātaka (No. 316) and the Vyāghri Jātaka depict, in glowing terms, how willingly and joyfully he sacrificed his life for the good and happiness of others.

Dealing with the Bodhisatta's mode of practising Dāna, the Cariyā Pitaka commentary has the following interesting account.

In giving food the Bodhisatta thinks that he would thereby cause the people to acquire long life, beauty, happiness, strength, wisdom, and the Highest Fruit, Nibbāna. He gives water and other harmless beverages with the object of quenching the thirst of passion of beings; clothes for the acquisition of the golden complexion, modesty, and conscientiousness; conveyances to gain psychic powers; odours for the scent of *Sīla* (morality); garlands and unguents to acquire the glory pertaining to Buddha's virtues; seats to win the seat of Enlightenment; lodging with the hope of serving as a refuge to the world; lights to obtain the five kinds of eyes — namely, the physical eye, the eye of wisdom, the divine eye, the Buddha eye, and the eye of Omniscience; forms to possess the Buddha-aura; sounds to cultivate a voice as sweet as Brahma's; tastes so that he may be pleasing to all; contacts to gain the delicate organism of a Buddha; medicines for the sake of Deathlessness (Nibbāna); emancipates slaves in order to deliver men from the thraldom of passions; renounces children to develop the paternal feeling towards all; renounces wives to become the master of the world; renounces kingdoms to inherit the kingdom of Righteousness, etc.

This important text bears ample testimony to the altruistic attitude of a Bodhisatta. Furthermore, it indicates how he endeavours as best he can to direct all his disinterested efforts for the amelioration of mankind, not forgetting at the same time, his high aspiration,—the Buddhahood.

* * *

Combined with this supernatural generosity is the purity of his Conduct *(Sila)*. If he be living the life of a recluse, he would try his best to observe the Sila that pertains thereto. In case he leads the household life he would adhere, even if his interests are at stake, to the five elementary principles of regulated behaviour.

He would refrain from killing, stealing, unchastity, lying, slandering, harsh speech, frivolous talk, and intoxicants.

A Bodhisatta endeavours to observe these elementary principles as strictly as possible, for transgression of them means courting fresh troubles and obstacles almost impassable and insurmountable.

It must not be understood that a Bodhisatta is wholly infallible and totally free from evil. Some Jātakas, like the Kanavera Jātaka (No. 318), depict him as a highway robber of no mean order. This, however, is the exception rather than the rule.

The great importance an aspirant to Buddhahood attaches to Sila is evident from the Silavīmansa Jātaka (No. 362) where the Bodhisatta says:— "Apart from virtue, wisdom has no worth."

A Bodhisatta, it may be said, is truly a refined gentleman in the strictest sense of the term.

* *

Still keener is the enthusiasm he exhibits for *Nekkhamma* or Renunciation, for by nature he is a lover of solitude. *Nekkhamma* implies both renunciation of worldly pleasures by means of adopting the ascetic life, and the temporary inhibition of Hindrances *(Nīvarana)* * by means of cultivating Jhāna.

To him comes the idea, though he may sit in the lap of luxury, immersed in worldly pleasures, that household life is like a den of strife, but the homeless life is like the ever free open sky.

Realising thus the vanity and suffering of life, he voluntarily forsakes his earthly possessions, and donning the simple ascetic garb, tries to lead the Holy Life in all its purity. Here he practises the Higher Morality to such a degree that he practically becomes selfless in all his actions. Neither fame, nor wealth, nor honour, nor worldly gain, could induce him to do anything contrary to his lofty principles.

Sometimes the mere appearance of a grey hair, as in the case of the Makhādeva Jātaka (No. 9), is sufficient to compel a Bodhisatta to leave his uncongenial atmosphere in order to lead the independent, solitary life of a hermit. At times a tiny dew-drop acts as an incentive to him to adopt the ascetic life. The practice of renunciation is not, however, observed as

* See p. 285.

a rule by a Bodhisatta. In the Kusa Jātaka (No. 531), for instance, the Bodhisatta was subject to much humiliation owing to his unrestrained desire to win the hand of the beautiful princess Pabhāvati.

Again in the Darīmukha Jātaka (No. 378) it is mentioned that a Pacceka Buddha, a quondam friend of the Bodhisatta, approached him and said:—

"*Pleasures of sense are morass and mire,*
The triply-rooted terror them I call.
Vapour and dust I have proclaimed them, Sire,
Become a brother and forsake them all."

To which he promptly replied :—

"*Infatuate, bound and deeply stained am I*
Brahmin, with pleasures: fearful they may be,
But I love life, and cannot them deny:
Good works I undertake continually."

* * *

Nekkhamma is followed by *Paññā* or wisdom. It is the right understanding of the nature of the world in the light of transiency, sorrowfulness, and soullessness. A Bodhisatta meditates on these three Characteristics—*Anicca, Dukkha,* and *Anatta*—but not to such an extent as to attain Arahantship, for then he would be deviating from his goal.

He does not at the same time disparage worldly wisdom. He strives to acquire knowledge from every possible source. Never does he show any desire to display his knowledge, nor is he ashamed to plead his ignorance even in public; for under no circumstances does he prove to be a charlatan. He has no closed fist of a teacher. What he knows is always at the disposal of others, and that he imparts to them unreservedly.

Viriya or Energy goes hand in hand with the above. Here Viriya does not mean physical strength, as is ordinarily understood, but mental vigour or strength of character, which undoubtedly is far superior to the former. It is defined as the relentless effort to work for others both in thought and deed. Firmly establishing himself in this virtue, he develops self-reliance and makes it one of his prominent characteristics.

As Dr. Tagore has well expressed it, a Bodhisatta would stand on his own legs and say:—

"Let me not pray to be sheltered from dangers,
but to be fearless in facing them.
Let me not beg for the stilling of my pain,
but for the heart to conquer it.
Let me not crave in anxious fear to be saved,
but hope for the patience to win my freedom."

The Viriya a Bodhisatta exhibits is beautifully illustrated in the Mahā Janaka Jātaka (No. 539). Ship-wrecked in deep sea, he struggled strenuously for seven days until he was finally rescued.

All this pales into insignificance when one thinks of the indomitable energy displayed by him as a squirrel in the Kalandaka Jataka.

Failures he views as successes; opposition doubles his exertion; dangers increase his courage. Cutting his way through difficulties, which impair the enthusiasm of the feeble, surmounting obstacles, which dishearten the ordinary, he looks straight towards his goal.

To Māra who advised him to abandon his quest, the Bodhisatta said :— "Death in battle (with passions) is more honourable to me than a life of defeat."

Just as his wisdom is always at the disposal of others, even so is the fund of energy at his command. Instead of confining it to the realisation of private personal ends, he directs it into the open channels of activities that tend to universal happiness. Ceaselessly and untiringly he works for others, expecting no remuneration.

* * *

As important as Viriya is *Khanti*. It is the patient endurance of suffering inflicted upon oneself by others, and the forbearance of others' wrongs.

A Bodhisatta practises patience to such an extent as not to get provoked even when his hands and feet are severed. In the Khantivāda Jātaka (No. 313) it appears that the Bodhisatta not only cheerfully endured the tortures caused by the drunkard king, who mercilessly ordered his hands and feet, nose and ears to be cut off, but also wished him long life.

Lying on the ground, sunk in a deep pool of blood, with mutilated limbs, the Bodhisatta said:—

" Long live the king, whose cruel hand my body
thus has marred,
Pure souls like mine such deeds as these with
anger ne'er regard."

Of his forbearance it is said that whenever he is harmed he thinks:— This person is a fellow-being of mine. Intentionally or unintentionally I myself must have been the source of provocation, or it may be due to a past evil Kamma of mine. As it is the outcome of my own action, surely I must cherish no ill-will towards him.

It may be mentioned in this connection that a Bodhisatta is not irritated by any man's shameless conduct either. He tries to bear and forbear as well.

Advising his disciples to practise forbearance, the Buddha says:—

"Even if villainous robbers were to sever your limbs with a two-handled sword, and if you would thereby defile your mind, you would not be a follower of my teaching.

"Thus should you train yourselves:—Unsullied shall our hearts remain. No evil word shall escape our lips. Kind and compassionate shall we abide with loving-hearts, harbouring no ill-will. We shall abide, enfolding those very bandits with thoughts of loving-kindness. And forth from them proceeding, we shall abide, radiating the whole world with thoughts of loving-kindness, vast, grown great, measureless, benevolent, and whole." *(Kakacūpama Sutta)*

* * *

Sacca or Truthfulness comes next. By Sacca is here meant the keeping of one's promise. This is one of the salient characteristics of a Bodhisatta, for he is no breaker of his word.

According to the Hārita Jātaka (No. 431) a Bodhisatta, in the course of his life's wanderings, never speaks an untruth, although he may at times violate the other four precepts.

He makes Truth his guide, and holds it his bounden duty to keep his word. He considers well before he makes a promise, but, when once the promise is made, he fulfils it at any cost.

In the Hiri Jātaka (No. 363), the Bodhisatta advises:—

"*Be thou in need to every promise true,*
Refuse to promise what thou cans't not do,
Wise men on empty braggarts look askew."

Again, in the Mahasutasoma Jātaka (No. 537) it is stated that the Bodhisatta even went to the extent of sacrificing his life in order to fulfil a promise.

"*Just as the morning star on high*
Its balanced course doth ever keep,
And through all seasons, times and years,
Doth never from its pathway swerve;
So likewise he in all wise speech
Swerves never from the path of Truth."

A Bodhisatta is trustworthy, sincere, and honest. What he thinks, he speaks. As he speaks, he acts; as he acts, he speaks. There is perfect harmony in his thoughts, words, and deeds.

He is consistent and straightforward in all his dealings. There is no difference between his inner self and his external appearance. His private life exactly tallies with his public life.

He flatters not to win the hearts of others. Himself he exalts not to win the admiration of others. His defects he hides not; his virtues he exhibits not. The praiseworthy he praises without malice; the blameworthy he blames judiciously, not with contempt, but out of compassion.

Even the truth he does not always utter if it is not conducive to the good and happiness of others. Under such circumstances he remains silent. If any truth is beneficial to others, he utters it, however unpalatable it may be.

He honours the words of others as he honours his own word.

* * *

This is followed by *Adhiṭṭhāna*, which may be interpreted as resolute Determination. This will-power of his forces all obstructions out of his path, and no matter what may come to him—sickness, grief, or disaster—he never turns his eyes from his goal.

The Bodhisatta Gotama, for instance, made a firm determination to renounce his royal pleasures and gain Enlightenment. For six long years he struggled hard. He had to endure many a hardship, and face many a difficulty. At a time when help was badly needed, his five favourite disciples, who attended on him, deserted him. Yet he did not give up his noble effort. His enthusiasm was redoubled, and eventually he achieved his ultimate goal.

"*Just as a rocky mountain peak,*
Unmoved stands, firm established,
Unshaken by the boisterous gales,
And always in its place abides;
So likewise He must ever be
In Resolution firm intrenched."

A Bodhisatta is a man of principles. One could easily persuade him to do good, but none could so easily tempt him to do anything contrary to his lofty principles. As occasion demands, he will be as soft as a flower, and as firm as a rock.

Adhiṭṭhāna is the foundation of all his virtues.

* * *

The most important of all Pāramis, it may be said, is *Mettā* (Sanskrt-Maitri), which may be rendered as benevolence, goodwill, friendliness, or loving-kindness. It is this Mettā that prompts a Bodhisatta to renounce personal salvation for the sake of others. He is permeated with boundless goodwill towards all beings. He regards all as his fellow-beings—irrespective of caste, creed, or colour. Since he is the embodiment of universal love, he fears none; nor does he instil fear into any. Even the wild beasts in lonely jungles are his loving friends. His very presence amongst them fosters their mutual friendliness. He ever cherishes in his heart boundless goodwill to all that lives.

Mettā, in Buddhism, should be differentiated from affection *(Pema)* or ordinary carnal love. According to the Books the direct enemy of *Mettā* is hatred, whilst the indirect enemy is affection. Through affection arises fear and grief, but not so through *Mettā*.

In exercising this loving-kindness oneself should not be ignored. *Mettā* should be extended equally towards oneself as towards others. *Mettā* of a Buddhist embraces the whole world, including oneself. Self-sacrifice should not be confused with loving-kindness towards oneself.

In the Mahā-Dhammapāla Jātaka (No. 385), it appears that the Bodhisatta, though yet a boy of seven months, extended his loving-kindness, with equal measure, towards his cruel father, who ordered him to be tortured and killed, towards the wicked executioner, towards his loving, weeping mother, and towards himself.

* * *

Last, but not the least, of the Pāramis is *upekkhā* or Equanimity.

The Pali term *Upekkhā* is composed of "*Upa*", which means justly, impartially, or rightly (*yuttito*), and "*ikkha*", to see, discern, or view. The etymological meaning of the term is, therefore, discerning rightly, viewing justly, or looking impartially, that is, without attachment or detachment, without favour or disfavour.

Here the term is not used in the sense of indifference or neutral feeling.

The most difficult and the most essential of all the ten Pāramis is this equanimity, especially for a layman who has to move in an ill-balanced world with fluctuating fortunes.

Slights and insults are the common lot of humanity. So are praise and blame, loss and gain. Under all such vicissitudes of life, a Bodhisatta tries to stand unmoved like a firm rock, exercising perfect equanimity.

In times of happiness and in times of adversity, amidst praise and amidst blame, he is even-balanced.

> "*Just as the earth, whate'er is thrown*
> *Upon her, whether sweet or foul,*
> *Indifferent is to all alike,*
> *Nor hatred shows, nor amity;*
> *So likewise he in good or ill,*
> *Must even-balanced ever be.*"

Furthermore, a Bodhisatta who practises Upekkhā metes out justice to all, without being influenced by desire *(chanda)*, hatred (dosa), fear *(bhaya)*, and ignorance *(moha)*.

* * *

In addition to these Pāramis a Bodhisatta has to practise the following three modes of conduct (Cariyā) —namely, *Buddhi Cariyā*, doing good with wisdom, not overlooking self-development; *Ñātyattha Cariyā*, working for the betterment of relatives; and *Lokattha Cariyā*, working for the amelioration of the whole world.

By the second mode of conduct is not meant nepotism, but an endeavour to promote the well-being of one's kinsfolk, without in any way jeopardising the interests of those outside one's family circle.

Practising thus the ten Pāramis to the highest pitch of perfection, developing the three modes of conduct as circumstances permit, giving the five kinds of Dāna as occasion demands, he traverses this tempest-tossed sea of Sansāra, wafted hither and thither by the irresistible force of Kamma, manifesting himself at the same time in multifarious births.

Now he comes into being as a mighty Sakka or as a radiant Deva, anon as a human being, high or low, again as a helpless brute, and so on, until he finally seeks birth in the Tusita heaven, having consummated the Pāramis. There he abides, anxiously awaiting the opportune moment to appear on earth, and blossom as a Sammā-Sambuddha.

It is erroneous to think that a Bodhisatta purposely manifests himself in such various forms in order to acquire universal experience. No person whatsoever is exempt from the inexorable law of Kamma. It is a law in itself. It alone determines the future birth of every individual, except of course in the case of Arahants and Buddhas who have put an end to all life in a fresh existence.

Due to his intrinsic merit, a Bodhisatta, however, possesses some special powers. If, for instance, he is reborn in a Brahma realm, where the span of life extends for countless aeons, he exercises his will-power and ceases to live in that sphere, and comes to life in another congenial place so that he may serve the world and practise the Pāramis.

Apart from this *Adhimuttikālakiriyā* (voluntary death), as the Pali phrase runs, the Jātaka commentary states that a Bodhisatta enjoys the special privilege of not seeking birth in eighteen states, in the course of his wanderings in Sansara, as the result of the potential Kammic force accumulated by him. For instance, he is never born blind or deaf, nor does he become an absolute misbeliever (*Niyata Micchādiṭṭhi*) who denies Kamma and its effects. He is born in the animal kingdom, but never as a creature larger than an elephant or smaller than a snipe. He may atone in the ordinary states of misery (Apāyas), but is never destined to the nethermost state of woe (*Āvīci*). A Bodhisatta does not also seek birth in the "Pure Abodes (Suddhāvāsa)—the camping place of Anāgāmis and Arahants—nor in the formless realms, where one is deprived of the opportunity to be of service to others.

It might be asked: Is a Bodhisatta aware that he is aspiring to Buddhahood in the course of his rebirth?

Sometimes he is, at times he is not.

According to the Jātakas it appears that at times the Bodhisatta Gotama was fully cognisant of the fact that he was striving for Buddhahood. Visayha Setthi Jātaka (No. 340) may be cited as an example. In this particular story, Sakka questioned the Bodhisatta as to why he was exceptionally generous. He replied that it was not for the sake of any worldly power, but for the sole purpose of attaining Supreme Buddhahood.

In some births, as in the case of the Jotipala Mānavaka (Ghatikara Sutta No. 81, Majjhima Nikaya), he was not only unaware of his high aspiration, but also abused the Buddha at the mere utterance of the word.

* * *

Hence, who knows that we ourselves are not Bodhisattas, who have dedicated our lives for the noble purpose of serving the world? One need not think that the Bodhisatta Ideal is reserved only for supermen. What has been accomplished by one, could also be accomplished by another, with necessary effort and enthusiasm. Let us too endeavour to work disinterestedly for the good of ourselves and others, having for our object in life—the noble ideal of service and perfection.

Serve to be perfect; be perfect to serve.

May all be well and happy!

INDEX

n. refers to footnotes.

C

Q

R

S

T

ERRATA

Page	Line		
4	10	read	teacher,
6	24	,,	series of births
13	4	,,	Nanda's
14	6	,,	I was delicate,
17	14	,,	disgusted,
36	5	,,	Beings"
40	10	,,	Brāhmaṇa
47	9	,,	Uklā
60	23	,,	*Sammā-Samādhi*
61	14	,,	*Bhavatanhā*
,,	15	,,	*Vibhavatanhā*
,,	23	,,	*Viññāna*
,,	30	,,	suffering."
64	3	,,	*Bhāvetabba*
,,	9	,,	*Bhāvita*
65	10	,,	Dhammacakka
,,	21	,,	*Atappa*
67	14	,,	transitory:—
81	24	,,	the Tipitaka was, for the...... Buddhism, committed
85	11	,,	Vibhanga
88	8	,,	sorrow
92	11	,,	supposition.
94	9	,,	but they are useful
,,	26	,,	decease."
95	17	,,	God-creator
99	26	,,	forest.
,,	37	,,	turn,
104	13	,,	supreme.
107	24	,,	one-fathom
109	14	,,	Upāli,
111	6	,,	In conclusion

Page	Line		
112	26	read	Ingersol
116	1	,,	mother
131	29	,,	Sangaha
136	6	,,	*Khandhas*
139	15	,,	simile
143	21	,,	state,
144	14	,,	worldling
161	20	,,	now I
167	11	,,	properties
168	25	,,	is it
,,	30	,,	Him ?"
176	3	,,	God-creator
180	28	,,	Prof. Rhys Davids
181	30	,,	boldly
184	34	,,	Expositor,
186	6	,,	stupendous
193	4	,,	inevitable result
199	25	,,	*Sutta*
206	23	,,	physical
208	15	,,	arises
210	6	,,	state
211	11	,,	with,
216	21	,,	Russell
,,	29	,,	physicists
226	15	,,	he would be
229	9	,,	latter is
243	30	,,	parentage
246	1	delete	"The World as Will and Idea" and insert on p. 245 at the end of the quotation.
,,	26	read	sand
262	7	,,	ecstasy
269	11	,,	Wisdom

Page	Line		
274	13	read	*Pātimokkha*
278	18	„	Perception
283	19	„	Buddha
„	26	delete	act
286	10	read	supernormal
„	12	„	*(Dibbasota)*,
„	21	„	Cakkhupāla
289	20	„	Ādinava
„	1	„	defile-
„	20	„	Ādinava
„	25	„	Ñāṇa
„	28	„	Ñāṇa
291	18	„	Suddhāvāsa